MANHATTAN'S FIFTH WARD IN 1895

Chinatown was squeezed between Mott, Pell, Park Row and the Bowery, with Doyers [here spelled Doyer] winding from Pell to the southern tip of the Bowery [not indicated on this map]. Chinatown did not extend to Bayard until about 1890 and not to Canal Street until the 1930s. The Five Points, at the junction of Baxter, Worth, and Pearl, vanished when slums between Mulberry and Baxter were demolished to open Columbus Park as breathing space.

ALAS!
What Brought Thee Hither?
The Chinese in New York
1800–1950

ARTHUR BONNER

Doyers Street about 1935

Madison • Teaneck
Fairleigh Dickinson University Press
London: Associated University Presses

Associated University Presses
440 Forsgate Drive
Cranbury, NJ 08512

Associated University Presses
16 Barter Street
London WC1A 2AH, England

Associated University Presses
P.O. Box 338, Port Credit
Mississauga, Ontario
Canada L5G 4L8

Design and typesetting by
Terrence Nugent for Accutype Graphics

The paper used in this publication meets the requirements
of the American National Standard for Permanence of Paper
for Printed Library Materials Z39.48-1984.

Library of Congress Cataloging-in-Publication Data

Bonner, Arthur.
    Alas! what brought thee hither : the Chinese in New York,
1800-1950 / Arthur Bonner
        p. cm.
    Includes bibliographical references (p.   ) and index.
    ISBN 0-8386-3704-3 (alk. Paper)
    1. Chinese Americans – New York (State) – New York – History.
2. Chinese Americans – New York (State) – New York – Social conditions.
3. Chinatown (New York, N.Y.) – History. 4. New York (N.Y.) –
Emigration and immigration. I. Title.
F128.9.C5B66   1997
974.7'1004951—dc20
                                                        96-35536
                                                        CIP

Printed in the United States of America

To the memory of Wong Chin Foo
The first to proclaim himself Chinese American

And to the New York Public Library,
whose collection of New York newspapers,
dating from the earliest period of the
city's history, and its equally
extensive collection of magazines and books,
made this book possible,
and to the men and women whose
unfailing assistance eased the tedium of long research.

Contents

Maps

Frontispiece: Chinatown and vicinity in 1895
Page 179: Chinatown about 1965

Waifs and Strays

Chinese were in New York from the early days of the republic. Mortality was high on the voyage around the tip of South America, and captains sought replacements from among the experienced seamen on the junks crowding Hong Kong's harbor. However, the earliest identifiable Chinese in New York dates from 1808, when President Jefferson declared an embargo to prevent the capture of American vessels in a war with Britain he expected at any time. The embargo caused 120 failures among merchants and traders in New York, idled five hundred vessels, and left thousands of sailors destitute, except those who found work on British ships.[1]

In July, Samuel Latham Mitchell, a Democratic senator from New York, sent Jefferson a letter introducing Punqua Wingchong as a "mandarin" who had come to the city nine months earlier to collect debts owed to his father and now wanted to return home, "where the affairs of his family and particularly the funeral obsequies of his grandfather require his solemn attention."[2]

Treasury secretary Albert Gallatin suspected trickery, since the vessel that would carry the purported mandarin would be supplied by John Jacob Astor, but Jefferson told him to aid the stranded merchant and Gallatin issued the necessary documents. (Astor had endeared himself to Jefferson by establishing a colony on the Pacific coast to collect beaver skins for trade with China. The president also believed the vessel—named, appropriately, *Beaver*—could warn American ships along the way and in Canton to seek safety in port in view of impending war.) Newspapers learned of the preparations and charged Astor's mandarin was "a Chinaman picked up in the Park," "a common Chinese dock loafer," a Lascar (East Indian seaman), and even an American Indian "dressed in Astor's China silks and coached to play his not-too-difficult part." Jefferson dismissed the accusations as the work of his Federalist political enemies, but ordered a closer look into Punqua Wingchong's authenticity. By then, the *Beaver* had sailed with Punqua Wingchong, his attendants, baggage, and personal effects, plus a full cargo of trade goods. It returned the following June with a cargo netting Astor a two hundred thousand dollar profit. As for Punqua Wingchong, an American in the China trade later met him in Canton, where he owned a silk and fancy goods shop and talked of his voyage to America and his return on the Beaver.[3]

Since few of the early Chinese seamen in New York ventured far from the docks of lower Manhattan, the earliest opportunity for New Yorkers to see an authentic Chinese was on the stage or in variety houses. The first to achieve notoriety was Afong Moy who, in 1834, was displayed at 8 Park Place dressed in costume and seated in a room furnished with Chinese ornaments. In addition to her "monstrous small" feet—four inches long—that "would scarcely fill an infant's first slipper," she was described as "of a soft and sleepy cast, as all Chinese beauty should be."[4]

For more than ten years, Afong Moy was seen at the American Museum, the City Saloon, Niblo's Garden, and the Brooklyn Institute, becoming so familiar she was billed simply as "the Chinese lady." By 1847, when she shared a billing with Tom Thumb at the Temple of the Muses at 315 Broadway, variety had been added: She talked and counted in Chinese and ate with chopsticks, which, an advertisement said, "render the exhibition highly interesting to lovers of curiosities."[5]

1 AFONG MOY AMID FAUX CHINOISERIE.

2 THE PAINTER SAMUEL WAUGH CALLED THIS 1847 BATTERY SCENE "EMIGRANTS LANDING," BUT THE CENTERPIECE WAS THE *KEYING*.

"Curiosities" were the vogue. What the *Morning Courier and New York Enquirer* hailed as "one of the most remarkable curiosities ever witnessed in the United States" arrived in 1847.[6] Charles Kellet, a British captain, outfitted a Chinese junk, which he named *Keying*, as a floating museum to be shown at London's Crystal Palace exhibition. He sailed from Hong Kong in December 1846, rounded the Cape of Good Hope 114 days later, spent some time at St. Helena, and dropped anchor at Castle Garden on July 14, 1847, announcing his arrival by firing three guns as two crew members banged gongs.[7]

The *Keying*, made of teak, was 150 feet long, twenty-five feet at the beam, with a stern that rose about thirty feet above the deck, with three, lateen-rigged, teak masts. She carried a crew of twenty Europeans and forty Chinese. Kellet had painted the walls and ceilings of the main cabin with pictures of birds, monkeys, and landscapes and packed it with idols, elaborate "lanthorns," swords, spears, chairs, sofas, "opium lounges," and "specimens of almost everything produced or used in the Chinese empire." There were also dogs, with "black mouths and tongues"—the first time New Yorkers had seen Chows.[8]

Some crewmen were taken sightseeing, including a visit to the Chinese lady and a Bleecker Street dealer in Chinese tea. As time passed, the "queer looking, good natured Junkites" adapted themselves to the "mysteries of modern refinements" by pitching pennies with children in Battery Park and rolling tenpins with adults. They also "drunk themselves into oblivion," thereby demonstrating "abundant evidence of their capability for civilization. Ching Ching since his arrival in Gotham knows how to smoke segars, drink soda water, carry a cane and cultivate a moustache (along with a queue), ride in the omnibuses and eject, in tolerable good English, a dozen oaths in as many minutes."[9]

The *Keying* inspired a burlesque of P. T. Barnum's freaks and fakery. Under the title "Chinese Junk," W. K. Northall began a successful career playing various Barnum characters and exhibits, such as Tom Thumb.[10]

In September, seven of the crew were arrested for assaulting the mate, Edward Revett. Through an interpreter, they complained that Kellet had enticed them on board at Canton by saying the *Keying* was sailing to Java for a journey lasting no more than eight months. Instead, they said, he sailed west and, when they objected, they were whipped and threatened they would be shot unless they quietly continued the voyage. They said they assaulted the mate because they had not been paid their wages—eight dollars a month.[11]

2

The Chinese were acquitted and funds were raised to send some of them home on another vessel. The *Keying* resumed its voyage in October, making stops along the New England coast, where it was advertised as "The Wonder of the Western World." Another ten Chinese deserted before the junk sailed from Boston in February 1848. After a dangerous mid-winter Atlantic voyage, the *Keying* docked on the Thames on March 28, where it was declared "one of the most interesting sights of London."[12]

The *Keying* was followed by entire rooms of curiosities—a collection of artifacts assembled by John R. Peters, a New York merchant who spent several years in Canton. It was the second such collection brought to the United States. The first, assembled by a merchant named Nathan Dunn, opened in Philadelphia in 1837, where it attracted so little interest that it was sent on to London for a more welcome reception.

The new exhibit opened January 1849 at 539 Broadway, between Prince and Spring streets, in the "Chinese Museum," a building erected for the purpose. About sixty life-sized figures were ranged in rows of glass cases. One showed the "Emperor and his mandarins." Another contained a "Mandarin of the 4th rank, his secretary, interpreter, inferior ranking officer with whip, ditto with bamboo, culprit on his knees, culprit confined in a box." Others exhibited a retail shop complete with goods on the shelves, the house of a wealthy man, and, inevitably, a room for smoking opium. There were costumed figures of a beggar, barber, carpenter, blacksmith, farmer, fortune teller, soldier, and doctor; a small harbor boat with a modeled crew; models of other boats, a temple, a theater, a court of justice, plus pictures showing the manufacture or preparation of tea, silk, and cotton. One case had, among other things, twenty-eight pairs of shoes, slippers, and boots.[13]

In April 1850, Barnum closed his American Museum for alterations and moved to the Chinese Museum.[14] Not content with authenticity, he spiced the exhibit with fakery. A reporter noted: "The ship Ianthe…from Canton…has brought a group of the 'upper ten' of the Celestial Empire, consisting of a young woman and her maid servant, a professor of music, a little girl and a boy. Miss Pwan-ye-koo is seventeen years of age. Her feet are only about three inches in length—a choice mark of her *distingué* character."[15]

It was soon announced that "the great curiosity, the Chinese lady with her very small feet, as likewise her attendants, are being exhibited at the Chinese Museum." Afong Moy had left for Boston in the fall of 1847. Barnum assured curiosity lovers this was indeed a rarity: "Miss Pwan-ye-koo…is the first Chinese *lady* that has yet visited Christendom; the only other female ever known to have left the 'Central Flowery

3 CENTRAL HALL OF CHINESE MUSEUM.

4 BARNUM'S LITHOGRAPH OF PWAN-YE-KOO AND HER SUITE.

Miss PWAN-YE-KOO, aged 17 years
A young lady with feet 2½ inches long.

Miss LUM-AKUM, aged 23 years.
Her Maid Servant.

Miss AMOON. Master MUN-CHUNG.
Aged 7 years. Aged 5 years.
Son and Daughter of the Professor.

Mr. ALEET-MONG, aged 18 years.
An Interpreter.

Mr. SOO-CHUNE, aged
Professor of Music.

Nation' in order to visit the 'outside barbarians' has been one of apocryphal reputation and position in her own country." Crowds gaped at Pwan-ye-koo's lily feet as "master musician" Soo Chune entertained "with popular Chinese songs and extempore aires and accompaniments." The troupe went on to the Crystal Palace in London and was later seen in Toronto where, despite Barnum's claim she was a lady, Miss Pwan-ye-koo was heard speaking a "low Yankee slang."[16]

A little girl, Catherine Elizabeth Havens, recorded in her diary for May 10, 1851: "Sometimes on Saturday afternoons we go down to the American Art Union on Broadway to see the pictures, and now there is a Chinese Museum down on Broadway, and wax figures of Chinese people, and it shows how prisoners are punished. Some have a board around their necks and others around their feet."[18]

The next exotica arrived at the end of January 1853: Twenty men and women were imported from San Francisco for a variety show at the Broadway Theater, between Pearl and Anthony (now Worth). An advertisement promised: "Astonishing and unprecedented feats of Magic and Necromancy never performed but in the Celestial Empire. The Double Jointed Chinese

Dwarf, Chin Gan, 28 years of age, 30 inches high, joints of body and extremities all doubled." It was short-lived. A week later, their interpreter—John Antonio Periero from Macao—tried to strangle the juggler, Tong Ming, and later clubbed him with a heavy cane. Periero was arrested and the troupe left for parts unknown.[19]

New York's own Crystal Palace exhibition was due to open in the Spring of 1853, with hoped-for visitors from throughout the United States and points overseas. One of the most popular early American geography textbooks had a drawing of a vendor carrying a pole strung with dead rats and a

Chinese selling rats.

5 SAMUEL GRISWOLD GOODRICH'S *A CHILD'S SECOND BOOK OF HISTORY* REACHED ITS 35TH EDITION BY 1840. CHILDREN, LIKE MARIE ANTOINETTE PALMER, WHO INSCRIBED HER NAME IN THIS TEXT, WERE BORED BY THE CRAMPED TEXT AND LONG WORDS AND WERE TEMPTED TO PASS THE TIME BY INKING IN THE RATS.

6 New York's Crystal Palace explored emerging cast iron techniques, with wide windows to bathe the interior in natural light.

small dog, imprinting on the minds of generations of children that this was a customary part of Chinese diet. A cartoonist for *Yankee Notions* of June 1853 imagined visitors to a "Universal Restaurant," including a Chinese asking for his "national dish"—rat soup and roast pup. A month later, the paper had a cartoon of a Chinese with a knife behind his back tempting a cat with a piece of meat.

ORPHANED ACTORS

To perennially optimistic entrepreneurs, it must have seemed that a massive troupe of Chinese would be a sure success in conjunction with the Crystal Palace exhibition, and it just happened that such a troupe was available in California. The forty-member Tong Hook Tong Company had arrived in San Francisco from Canton in October 1852, complete with a portable theater, which it set up at Dupont and Union streets in "Little China." Later arrivals and local recruitment increased the company to 123. After about two months, the original entrance price, ranging from two to six dollars, was cut in half. Then it was lowered to one dollar and tumblers and American stock players were added to attract an English-speaking audience. At the end of March, the theater was closed and the building sold.[20]

George Beach, who claimed to be acting for a New York syndicate that included P. T. Barnum, signed about fifty members to a ten-month contract, promising them six thousand dollars a month plus travel expenses, with the first two thousand to be paid in New York within a month of the their arrival. Beach was bluffing. When the troupe arrived in May 1853, the steamship company presented a six thousand dollar bill for their passage. Barnum denied responsibility and Beach said he could not raise funds from other members of the syndicate. The steamship company placed a lien on the company's wardrobe for the passage money.[21]

Unfortunately, the Crystal Palace opening was delayed until summer, leaving a severely diminished potential audience. The troupe was booked into Niblo's Garden on May 20, with tickets at fifty cents. An advertisement promised, "Religious rites, peculiar ceremonies, extraordinary amusements, and wondrous feats of the inhabitants of China, Tartary, Siam, and Japan. Their wardrobe contains the exact dresses worn by the Emperors and Mandarins of every dynasty during four thousands years and is estimated to be worth one hundred thousand dollars."[22]

Opening night was a critical disaster. A *Tribune Semi Weekly* reviewer, after summarizing such things a "presentation to the Gods and

UNCLE SAM'S
CHRYSTAL PALACE
RESTAURAT !!

7 SCHOOL TEXTS LEFT AN INDELIBLE IMPRESSION.

Goddesses of the Beasts, Birds, and Fishes from the Throne of the Imperial Dragon," and a "Grand Marriage Ceremony and entrance of the emperor and train and unveiling of the bride," commented:

The whole reminded us of splendid gilded tea boxes galvanized into motion—the figures are so grotesque, pompous and that indescribable compound of cultivation and barbarism which distinguishes the great Empire. The dresses are gorgeous to the last degree. All that silk, crepe, gold-tissue—the cumulated splendors of Chinese taste—could conceive flaunted on the stage....The different characters came with glorious pomposity and ching-changed or cum-fee-hoed it in front of the platform and then ascended the platform. Sometimes one spoke alone, sometimes several the same words. Chinese music was rendered by sticks beaten together, cymbals, a bowed instrument played as a viola or violin sounding like a bagpipe, and using the Scotch scale identically or the black notes of the pianoforte, beating various discordances. The singing and playing were like a compound of distressed cats, an old pump handle, ungreased cart wheels, a poke on a tin kitchen, and the spiritual rappers in communion with the infernal regions. How a people who have designed a musical scale and even arrived at the *ne plus ultra* of a bowed instrument unknown to the classics, who have, besides, a musical notation, can grind, shriek, squeal, bawl, snort, snuffle, snivel, drivel, squall, howl, grunt, and groan in such a manner and call it music is as great a mystery as Chinese feminine feet, hallowed pig-tails, or blood relationships with the sun and planets. The tumblers were sufficiently active and the somersaults, doubtless revolving from the remotest antiquity, would do credit to modern performers....To see these evidences of

Chinese life, sets one to analyze the things of daily life at home and wonder if our ceremonials, civil, military, and religious, are not ridiculous too. These poor Chinese deserve a specially good reception at our hands....If they are any wise different they would cease to be genuine.[23]

The show closed within a week and George Beach disappeared with the receipts, leaving forty of the troupe stranded at the Shakespeare Hotel at 9 Duane Street, where the owner, Eugene Lievre, said they were running up a bill of $125 a week. He said some of Beach's shareholders had paid about $300 but he was still owed about $700.[24]

The performers depended entirely on their interpreter, Leong Mon Ahgeu, who had been educated at an English college in Canton and could speak and write English. Leong hoped to resume performances to raise money for their return passage to California, but the best that could be organized was a single performance at Castle Garden on July 4 to take advantage of the crowds celebrating Independence Day.[25]

The proceeds were slight. Then a committee "of wealthy and highly respectable gentlemen" organized "to aid the Chinese who were betrayed, defrauded, and then deserted and left to beg, steal, or starve" arranged a benefit at

The CHINAMAN, driven to despair for want of a national dish, attempts the destruction of the Landlady's favorite Tabby.

8 CAT EATING WAS NEVER CITED BUT FACTS DID NOT DETER SATIRISTS.

Castle Garden on July 21 to send the Chinese home "and thus save the city money for supporting them." Although two leading Europeans singers then in the city—Madame Sontag and Signora Steffanone—donated their services, receipts were only $680.50.[26]

In August, eight "Tumblers and Combatants" appeared at Burton's Theater. A critic wrote: "Their lofty somersets have not been equalled by any of the circus companies. To show the

9 As an artist imagined a Five Points scene.

strength of Chinese hair, two of the company stand upon chairs holding a stick across their shoulders, when another of the Chinese puts his pig tail over the sticks and raises himself from the stage by his hair a dozen times. This feat causes a roar of laughter."[27]

At the end of the month, when they were still at the Shakespeare Hotel, a shipping agent offered to carry them to Hong Kong for one hundred dollars each, but a donation drive raised only five hundred dollars. The patience of Eugene Lievre finally ran out. Some of the Chinese were taken to the workhouse on Blackwell's Island, where one attempted suicide.

The rest drifted away.[28]

But help was on the way. In April 1854, parishioners of Grace Church invited Edward Syle, a British missionary who had served in Shanghai, and who had a year earlier spoken in churches in New York and Brooklyn, to return to the city to help the orphaned performers.[29] Syle returned in June and began with a census of Chinese in the city, starting with "that place of unenviable notoriety," the Five Points.[30]

With a small, triangular park—known, cynically, as "Paradise Square"—at its center, the Five Points was the intersection of three streets. Its most notorious structure—the "Old

10 The Old Brewery

11 Mission that replaced the Old Brewery.

7

Brewery," dating from 1792—had become an infamous tenement. At its worst, more than a thousand men, women, and children were crammed into the rotting structure. In 1854, the Reverend Lewis Pease bought and demolished the building and erected a new mission house on the lot at 155 Worth Street.[31]

Pease told Syle there were about forty Chinese in the city, some on Ward's Island and others in boarding houses on Cherry Street, including some who "had been a long time in this country, and had married here; and others yet were to be found serving behind the counters in tea stores." One, known to Pease as "Okkeo," had been a servant for several months at the Five Points Mission, during which time "some twenty or thirty of his countrymen had come to see him…but they came no more; and he himself had wandered off somewhere." After his talk with Pease, Syle extended his search to the Fourth Ward:

> Made explorations in Cherry Street, among the sailors' boarding houses, a description of which does not fall within the range of my present record….I must remember that I am writing about the heathen, the Chinese heathen, I mean. And there I found some thirty or more of them stowed away, like steerage passengers in an immigrant ship, in two small rooms the wretched and filthy conditions of which I will not stop to describe. In the first I entered, I found eight Ningpo and Shanghai men sitting around a table gambling. On a sort of lounge were arranged the well known apparatus of smoking opium. One of the company was evidently under its influence. A sudden huddling away of cards and dice, etc, took place on my opening the door, and one of them, who had seen me in Brooklyn last year told the rest of them who I was.

Syle located members of the Tong Hook Tong Company in a separate house on Cherry Street:

> Their dialect was different from that which I spoke….Even the white cravat did me no service in their eyes, for they seemed not to know anything about Clergymen, or Missionaries, or Christians as such. I looked up in one corner of their little apartment and saw a shrine, with their little idols in it, before the ever burning lamp and the smoking incense. Need I say that I left that room with a heavy heart.

Syle visited another boarding house that had been operated for about twenty years by "an old Canton man" who spoke some English and who told Syle that thirty-three of the actors were still in New York. In three other houses he found three, twelve, and fifteen Chinese cooks and stewards from vessels docked a few blocks away. The largest number were in a house that had been operated for the past fifteen years by a man married to a non-Chinese woman. These thirty, plus the thirty-three from the dramatic company and the eight or ten Shanghai-Ningpo men, totaled more than seventy—a larger number than he expected to find. To complete his survey, he visited fourteen of the Chinese actors on Ward's Island.

Syle gathered about thirty men for a sermon at St. George's Episcopal Church, then on Beekman Street in lower Manhattan. He later held biweekly religious gatherings at St. George's for thirty to fifty men. The sight of the Chinese sitting in a church listening to the Bible had its effect on the congregation, which included some of the wealthiest men of the city. When Cornelius Vanderbilt offered to take them on his shipping line to California for sixty-five dollars a head, a committee of ten raised twenty-five hundred dollars. With this, twenty-two were sent to California and four to Canton. For those who remained, there was a promise of "decent lodging until jobs could be found." Syle rejected a suggestion that they be hired as servants: "Their personal character was so little to be relied on that to have introduced them into families as servants would have been at the risk of transplanting into our homes some of the worst vices of heathendom."[32]

In September, Syle reported that three had been helped to establish a tea store in the Gowanus section of Brooklyn, near Greenwood Cemetery, "where also may be seen exhibited some of those fantastic lanterns which the ingenuity of one of the partners has constructed." Thirteen others were hired as day laborers by a businessman near the store.

Syle's publicized money raising was an easy target for the humor of *Yankee Notions*. A cartoon captioned "Celestial Occupation in New York," showed a Chinese with a box of cigars and a tear in one eye and an outstretched palm. Another, in the same issue, captioned "Hibernian Celestial," showed an Irishman dressed as a Chinese asking a shopkeeper: "Misther Storekaper, would ye be afther imployin a pore craythur ov a Chaney man, as is fur away from home and counthry?" This technique—playing the Chinese minority off against the Irish—would become a cliché.[33]

Ten months after Syle completed his mission, *Ballou's Pictorial* printed sketches of "New York Street Figures," including a Chinese with a tray of cigars suspended from his neck and a beggar

12 In May 1855 *Ballou's Pictorial* included Chinese both as a cigar seller and as a beggar in a page of "street figures." The manner of wearing the queue can be seen on the seated man.

seated on a step, his chin resting on his knees, his queue coiled around his head and his hat upturned at his feet, with a small card, asking for alms.[34]

In the same month, the *United States Democratic Review* printed "On a Chinaman in Broadway:"

> Sits he by the dusty footway throughout the torrid day
> Alas! What brought thee hither, poor native of Cathay?
> And thine olive, moveless features, transfixed as in a dream,
> Mid the crowd of busy faces like wooden features seem.
> When our curious childhood marveled at figures quaintly wrought
> On the ancient heir-loom China—ah! me! we never thought
> E'er to see their breathing image beside us on the path;
> And what a strange discordant background the curious picture hath![35]

The doggerel continued for another seven verses.

The saga of the Tong Hook Tong Company ended in April 1856 when "the cumulated splendors of Chinese taste" was auctioned to pay the overdue passage money. Fifteen trunks contained "numerous costly and beautiful dresses and their appurtenances; blue satin dresses, scarlet aprons, blue crepe dresses, embroidered capes and caps, ladies white satin dresses, Queen's dresses, Emperor's caps, splendid necklaces, musical instruments, Chinese and military dresses, and a large quantity of articles valuable for theatrical use, together with many curiosities peculiar to the Chinese nation."

Another sixty lots included "vests, pantaloons, robes, jackets, aprons, banners, scarfs, boots, head dresses, ornaments, musical instruments, and trinkets. Some of them are exceedingly rich and characterized by every Chinese peculiarity." There were also "two hundred Chinese gongs, assorted sizes and of good tune." The Chinese valued everything at forty-eight thousand dollars. Some costumes may have been copies of ancient originals; others may have been handed down for generations within the troupe. Yet robes sold for as little as $3.50; the most expensive brought only $41. The entire auction garnered only $1,071.80.[36]

Although the actors moved off, their legend remained. For years afterward it was assumed all Chinese on the streets were former actors putting their "art of mimicry" to new use, as illustrated by a newspaper in December 1856:

> He peddled a few miserable segars, yet his politeness and attempt to his customers seemed to be quite a favorite among the street walkers of the vicinity, more particularly, the newsboys whose principal headquarters in the neighborhood....They seem to be a good natured, harmless set of people who can live wherever the ingenuity of a French cook would cease to find food....Upon our city face the Chinese are a necessary pimple, and if we should lose them a portion of our picturesque beauty would be gone.[37]

9

CELESTIAL OCCUPATION IN NEW YORK.

13 FOR MANY, THE CHINESE WERE FRAUDS.

Actually, only a few of the Chinese in New York were beggars. A year earlier New York State census takers—in tracking down thirty-four Chinese in the Third, Fourth, and Fifth wards—listed their occupations as peddlers, cigar makers, cooks and stewards, boarding-house operators, and two clerks in tea stores. Eleven seamen and boardinghouse operators were married to Irish women. Several had American names, such as John Lewis, John Huston, William Matlin, William Brown, and Lesing Newman, or had Anglicized their names as John Atchen and John Ahlong.[38]

Some were sufficiently American to resent the constant reference to beggars—and knowledgeable enough of American ways to complain in a letter to the *Tribune*:

> We, the undersigned, do earnestly protest against the system of begging pursued by a number of spurious Chinese, who are impostors, and who are utterly unworthy [of] the sympathy of the citizens of New York. They spend their money in drunkenness and among the vile dens of Water Street. We publish this to the world in order that these beggars may be arrested and stopped from pursuing such a life. They are from Shanghae, and are utterly unworthy of any help or aid from the citizens of New York.[39]

A PROMISING APPLICANT.

14 LIKE THE CHINESE, THE IRISH WERE STEREOTYPED, OFTEN, AS HERE, AS SLY TRICKSTERS.

15 THIS CRUDE SKETCH MAY BE THE EARLIEST REPRESENTATION OF A FAMILIAR SCENE: A CIGAR SELLER BEFORE THE FENCE AROUND CITY HALL PARK.

The letter bore thirty-seven otherwise unidentified names. A few days later *Tribune* publisher Horace Greeley used the letter as a text to urge men without jobs to seek work on farms where labor was needed.[40]

THE QUIMPO APPO SAGA

The letter apparently reflected rivalry between Chinese from Shanghai and Guangdong, since the name of the best known Chinese in the city—Quimpo Appo from Shanghai—was not on the list. Appo was so well known that Syle was advised to begin his search for Chinese by seeking Appo's help at the tea shop where he was a clerk:

> I saw a veritable Chinaman playing his part as a salesman with an alacrity of movement and flourish of manner that was quite exemplary. It was evident at a glance that he wanted nobody to take care of him but was abundantly able to be the guardian of his own interests. Indeed, that any one who should have to deal with him would require to keep a sharp lookout lest they found themselves on the worst side of the bargain. I observed him refuse, in the most authoritative manner, to give the change for a dollar note to a man who bought only a small quantity of coffee. Said he to the customer: "You want change this note, must buy half a pound, then can do." The man was so taken aback that he took the half pound with quite a subdued air.[41]

Appo was born in 1825 on the island of Chusan off the east coast of central China. He told Syle he was in Shanghai when it was bombarded by the British during the Opium War, which ended in 1842 with the treaty that opened five ports for foreign trade. He also told Syle he had traveled with Karl Friedrich Guztlaff, the missionary who translated the New Testament into English, and who defied Qing dynasty prohibitions by carrying his activities into closed areas. In 1844, Appo sailed to California, where he opened a tea store in San Francisco—well before Chinese joined the 1849 Gold Rush. Unluckily, he left a year too soon. In 1848, he sailed to Boston as cook and steward on the sloop-of-war *Vandalia*. He drifted to various cities along the east coast and, in New Haven, married Dublin-born Catherine Fitzpatrick. About a year later, they moved to 50 Spring Street and Appo became a clerk in the Catherine Street tea store, where Syle found him.[42]

In December 1856—always a slack news period—a *Times* reporter decided to investigate a recurrent rumor "that in this Christian city Chinese had a place in the Bowery where they worshipped idols." He went straight to Appo, the fountainhead of all things Chinese, and found him at home wearing a frock coat and white shirt and proudly displaying "a handsome boy, as white as his mother." Appo said the boy had been born on July 4, in honor of which he was christened George Washington Appo. Appo estimated there were 150 Chinese in the city and said some would, indeed, like to find work on farms, but since they did not speak English they could only earn a meager living by selling cigars. Four Chinese clerks from other shops were visiting: "One, dandyish, wearing a shawl, said he intended to learn to read and write English, become an American citizen, and marry an American girl."

Appo took the reporter to a boardinghouse for cigar sellers in the basement of a rear building at 391 Pearl Street, "down crazy steps" to a low apartment that "never saw sun," lighted by tallow candles and filled with tobacco smoke. The proprietor was John Akkomb, who spoke English, although his greeting was transliterated as "How do, Mosheer." He meant *monsieur*, a word he had acquired years earlier while serving as a cook on a packet boat between England, Germany, and France. Akkomb, twenty-four, had gone to sea at fourteen. Politely bowing and offering a chair, he said he had rented the room for eighteen dollars a month since 1851, and had fourteen boarders who paid three dollars a week. He did the cooking. "We saw no rats around, and they say they don't eat them," the reporter noted.

There were two-decker bunks on two sides, each of which slept three men. Four beds were occupied by men who appeared sick. Akkomb said they had been unable to work for a long time and were supported by the others. There is an alternate explanation: They were sleeping off the effects of opium. On the other hand, their sickness may have been genuine. Akkomb said four had died over the previous three years and that the men raised money among themselves to pay for the funerals.

Despite their poverty, the reporter was surprised to find a table in the middle of the room piled with boiled chickens, rice, tumblers of strong tea, and piles of empty plates and bowls. Akkomb explained this was one of two fast days that they observed on alternate Sundays:

> On these days they procured the best food their means afforded, placed it on a table, and each in turn stood before it and prayed. They asked God grant them a continuance of the blessings they had enjoyed and thanked

11

THE MUD LARK.

A GENUINE GARROTER.

ONE OF JUDGE RUSSELL'S CASES.

THE YOUNG CHIFFONIER.

THE WINDY-GLAZZ-MAN.

THE PERAMBULATING SHOE-BLACK.

16 "JOHN CHINAMAN," BEFORE THE SAME CITY HALL PARK FENCE, APPEARED IN SKETCHES FROM MAY 1855.

Him for those received. They religiously kept this fast, abstaining from food the entire day.

Again, Akkomb may have been putting things in the best light. Though described in Christian-like terms, it was a traditional Guangdong sacrifice, at the time of the new and full moons, to the invisible spirits of the neighborhood.[43] Akkomb denied there was idol worship in the Bowery or any other place. He conceded some Chinese "are still heathens," but said others attended various Methodist churches.[44]

Hard working or not, Christian or not, the Chinese had long since been established as the epitome of exotica, and reporters and cartoon-ists were determined to keep it that way: the search went on for beggars, miscegenation, opium smoking, and idol-worshippers. In July 1857, *Ballou's Pictorial* included "John Chinaman" among a gallery of street figures, saying this cigar seller had a place beside City Hall Park and that several others could be seen in prominent localities:

They are the remnants of a band of acrobats or jugglers which was organized under the management of speculators....They form a little community in the world of New York but not of it. They have their idol, which they worship in manner and form as at home, and in all respects conform to their original customs and habits, except perhaps in dress. This for a time was unchanged, but it was soon found that it served to make them butt for the overgrown boys and rowdies of the metropolis, and they have gradually adopted the 'latest style.' We have ourselves seen a scamp of the 'Mose' school walk up to one of their stands, coolly select a cigar, and walk off, and when poor John demanded payment for his wares draw back his fist and threaten to 'lam' him if he did not 'go away.' God grant them a speedy return to the Flowery Kingdom, for they are sadly out of place here.

In October 1857, *Yankee Notions* showed a Chinese standing at the familiar spot outside the gate around City Hall Park. One boy has tied his queue to the fence so that another can steal cigars. In the same month, *Harper's Weekly* reported twenty-eight Irish apple women had married Chinese cigar sellers "and most of them are happy mothers of a consequence." This

Smoking made Easy.

17 TAUNTING THE CHINESE WAS SEEN AS A MERE PRANK.

inspired a *Yankee Notions* cartoon showing an apple seller talking to her children, with her husband, a cigar peddler, in the background:

Mrs. Chang-Fee-Chow-chy (the better half of the Celestial over the way)—Now, then, Chang-Mike, run home and take Pat-Chow and Rooney-Sing wid ye, and bring the last of the puppy pie for yer daddy. And, do ye mind? bring some praties for yer mother, ye spalpeens.

(To her husband)—How be's ye, Chang-Honey?

Chang-Honey—Sky wi po kee bang too, mucho puck ti, rum foo, toodle skee sicks![45]

A month earlier, a reporter-artist team from *Leslie's Illustrated* had set out, with a policeman as guide, to explore the boardinghouses on Cherry Street. They mounted a flight of "narrow, dirty stairs" to the upper story at number 61, "one of the filthiest houses of the vicinity," where a man without a queue slammed a door in their faces. They were politely welcomed into another room, measuring nine feet square with a double row of bunks on two sides, a cook stove on the third and the door on the fourth side. The bunks, "about the size of a writing

THE RESULT OF THE IMMIGRATION FROM CHINA.

MRS. CHANG-FEE-CHOW-CHY (*the better half of the Celestial over the way*).—Now, then, Chang-Mike, run home and take Pat-Chow and Rooney-Sing wid ye, and bring the last of the puppy pie for yer daddy. And, do ye mind? bring some praties for yer mother, ye spalpeens.
(*To her husband*)—How be's ye, Chang-Honey?
CHANG-HONEY.—Sky wi po kee bang too, mucho puck ti, rum foo, toodle skee sicks!

Published by T. W. Strong, 98 Nassau St., New York.—Price 12½ Cents per Number, $1,25 per annum.

18 AN IRISH APPLE SELLER MARRIED TO A CHINESE CIGAR SELLER: THE EARLIEST OF WHAT WOULD BE REPEATED REFERENCES TO A VIOLATION OF THE MISCEGENATION TABOO.

13

desk," could sleep three men. The center of the room, measuring four by six feet, was half filled by a table covered with matting on which about a dozen "cocoa-nut heads" were gambling at dominos, using "coins with square holes" as stakes. Several of the men were dressed in European fashion, including one wearing a high, stiff collar and patent leather boots. The reporter asked about a Chinese woman who was said to live somewhere and were told she had been sent back to Canton.

19 "Piecee China—Piecee American." Another notice of miscegenation.

At 103 James Street, a boardinghouse keeper whose name they did not record showed them accommodations for sixty men. All of the bunks were full. In a number of them, they found men with the lamp and pipe for smoking opium. The main attraction was a child of about two, who sat on a table "surrounded by admiring Chinese."[46]

Later, a *Times* reporter found the same child—about five years old—at 78 James Street. His father's name was given simply as Pasching. His Irish mother was standing at his side. The reporter described the familiar communal arrangements: Rooms on two floors with bunks on two sides to sleep three men and a table in the center of the main room where men were playing cards. They were sailors, including some described as "dandies ashore," who "spoke English intelligibly, full half puffing at their cigars." Next: the obligatory discovery of miscegenation, manifested in a visit to the much-inspected house at 61 Cherry Street:

> In a little bedroom off the hall of the second story was the landlord's wife, a German girl

with protruding teeth, not pleasant to regard, and a whimpering face. She seemed rather proud of her position, but deferred to her companion, the Irish widow of a departed Chinaman, in the matter of permitting a visitor in the house. As they could not come to a conclusion we decided for ourselves and walked in. A narrow-faced fellow, the landlord, scowled at us from the end of his table...and to all our queries there came in answer only a growl.[47]

The Chinese colony was growing. At first glance, Quimpo Appo appeared the most successful. By 1859, when he was about thirty-four, he had a daughter as well as a son, and was a court interpreter should a Chinese have a brush with the law, but his wife was alcoholic, and they apparently were having a hard time making ends meet. They moved to smaller quarters at 47 Oliver street, where they rented a room from a Mrs. Fletcher.

Appo was under five feet tall and compensated for his lack of height with a fierce temper. In March 1859 he came home for his afternoon meal and found his wife drunk. Mrs. Fletcher gave him something to eat and he went back to work. When he returned that evening, he found that his wife had locked herself in their room after celebrating Mrs. Fletcher's birthday with the other women of the house. Appo smashed in the door and began to beat his wife. Mrs. Fletcher and two other women ran into the room to pull him away—one calling him a "China nigger" and hitting him with her fists. Another hit him with a flatiron. Appo struck back with a double-edged, silver-hilted dagger, about six inches long, wounding one of his attackers and killing Mrs. Fletcher. He fled to the James Street boardinghouse, where he was soon discovered and arrested.

20 The Criminal Courts Building, modeled on an Egyptian temple, was known as the Tombs.

Crowds of Irish gathered, calling for revenge. A week later, when the police took him to Oliver Street for an inquest at the scene, people tried to snatch him away for lynching. His trial lasted one day, and the jury, deliberating for only forty-five minutes, returned a verdict of guilty. Appo was sentenced to be hanged on July 2. *Leslie's Illustrated* welcomed the sentence with a reference to "miserable abortions of humanity called Chinese."[48]

But there were still a few drops from the "Alas! What Brought Thee" well of sympathy for the orphaned Chinese, plus a deep religious and class antipathy toward the Irish. A *Times* reporter visited Appo in the Tombs and described him as the most-to-be-pitied of the four men awaiting execution. In contrast, Appo's wife was described as a "low Irishwoman habitually drunk who would not cook his meals and neglected him in every particular." As evidence of her character, he wrote that she had recently been convicted of larceny and was currently in jail herself. Appo had made friends with the warden and surgeon and others at the Tombs. The reporter wrote that all were "anxious that the clemency of the Executive should be granted him," adding a final, inaccurate, tug at readers' heartstrings: "Only the English language, with which he is imperfectly acquainted, meets his ear. No syllable of his native tongue, no touching tone that would make his eyes overflow and his heart beat for you, even in the contemplation of his misery, can reach him."[49]

When Appo broke into his room to confront his wife, three-year-old George Washington Appo was sleeping in a cradle next to his mother. As the crowd howled for Appo's death, his wife and the boy were taken to a jail for safety. The baby girl was left with a neighbor. George was seen clinging "with wonder to his mother in the cell." After she was released from safe custody, only to be arrested for larceny, Mrs. Appo left for California, where her brother lived, taking her baby daughter. They both died when their ship was wrecked off the Pacific coast and all passengers and crew drowned.

George Washington Appo was left with a poor woman and raised in Donovan's Lane, which had succeeded Five Points as New York's hell's half acre.

Eventually, after several petitions for mercy signed by many leading merchants, Appo's execution was postponed and, in 1860, he was granted a new trial. He pleaded guilty to manslaughter and was sentenced to Sing Sing for ten years.[50]

A model of deportment, Appo was pardoned in 1863 after serving seven-and-a-half years, including time spent in jail during the appeals. He moved into the garret of a tenement in Donovan's Lane with a woman called Lizzie Williams. They quarreled, she attacked him, and he stabbed her. She died in a hospital a month later. He pleaded self defense and a jury returned a verdict of justifiable homicide. Appo served only a year in jail.

In September 1871 Appo—now identified as "the notorious Chinese ruffian"—got into a fight and killed a man, using a paving stone as a weapon. A jury found that paving stones, despite their potential lethal application, were not deadly weapons in the strict sense of the law and, in January 1872, found Appo guilty of simple assault and sentenced him to Sing Sing for five years. Again, within the protected environment of prison, he was a model of deportment and was pardoned in the summer of 1875, only to revert to the pathologic being he had become. He was soon sent to Blackwell's Island for six months for brutally kicking a German woman. After his release, he set up a cigar stand near Chatham Square and was soon arrested because his cigar box did not bear the required tax stamp. Out on bail, he committed his final slaying.

He was staying at a twenty-five-cents-a-night lodging house on Chatham Street (not yet renamed Park Row). He was proud of his skill at checkers and challenged all comers for a small wager. One night, in October 1876, a burly Irishman named Kelly accepted the challenge and lost several games. Appo went to bed and Kelly went off to brood over a few drinks. He returned to the lodging house, dragged Appo from his room on the second floor, blackened his eye, and kicked him down the entire flight of stairs. Appo sat on a bench to nurse his bruises. When Kelly came to resume the beating, Appo drew a penknife and stabbed him three times. Kelly fell dead, and Appo was arrested as he was running toward the sanctuary of what had become Chinatown's Mott Street.

A reporter commented: "Few of the thousands who passed the quiet, inoffensive man imagined that they were looking at such a fiend in human shape." He was locked in cell sixty-three, the same one he occupied after he killed Mrs. Fletcher eighteen years earlier. Since it was a case of self defense, Appo was only accused of manslaughter. He was found guilty, but now a way was found to keep him in prison: He was judged insane and was sent for permanent incarceration to the Hospital for the Criminally Insane at Matteawan on the Hudson River.[51]

As the night boat passed Matteawan on its trip

up the Hudson to Albany, it flashed its search-light and he would say: "That's my diamond. They bring it to me every night." He died at Matteawan at the age of ninety. There was another inmate in Matteawan at that time—George Washington Appo—but father and son were kept separate and never met.[52]

2 Hervey's Heathens

A Chinese in the United States was "John Chinaman" or simply "John," and sometimes "Charlie." He was also a "Celestial," a derisive epithet based on a Chinese term that can be translated as "Heavenly Dynasty." The most common slur, "Chink," was not confined to children, the unlearned, or the impolite. The patrician John Hay, who was secretary of state under presidents McKinley and Roosevelt, regularly called a treaty between Russia and China the "Russo-Chink Treaty" and, while expressing concern for the "poor devils of Chinks," he referred to the 1905 Open Door Treaty between the United States and China as "our Chink treaty."[1]

The slur became a child's skipping rhyme:

Chinkie, Chinkie, Chinaman,
Sitting on the fence;
Trying to make dollar
Out of fifteen cents.
Chink, Chink, Chinaman
Eats dead rats;
Eats them up
Like gingersnaps.

The Chinese were called "clannish," "dangerous," "criminal," "opium sodden," "cowardly," "callous," "debased and servile," "deceitful and vicious," "a persistently servile and alien population," and "inferior from a mental and moral point of view, immeasurably lower than the Indians." They were "a moral peril to our civilization," "filthy and loathsome in their habits," and their Chinatowns were "unsanitary quarters," "full of prostitution and gambling." America had to be protected from "Asiatic slavery" and the "degrading" labor of this "mass of yellow coolies" who "lowered the plane of living," "shut out white labor," and "carried back gold to their homes." Their yellow skin was "unpleasant." The angle of their eyes showed "slyness." Their conversation was "frightful jabbering." Their "treacherous mendacity," "Mongolian trickery," and "heathenish ways" were "a puzzle to the Western mind."[2]

Leslie's Illustrated summed it up: "Morally and ethically they are in a fourth dimension."[3]

The emphasis in early school texts on things like eating rats—such as Samuel Griswold Goodrich's *The Child's Second Book of History*, with its sketch of a rat catcher[4]—were mild compared to reports sent home by missionaries, which reeked of sexual metaphors like "orgies of idolatry" and "diabolical ecstasy." Chinese lust abounded: "Girls scarcely twelve years old were given up to the beastly passions of men; parents prostituted their daughters, husbands their wives, brothers their sisters—and this they did with diabolical joy." Another wrote that if young girls left the safety of their homes alone they could be lured by "pictures, songs, and aphrodisiacs" into the "gates of hell" to perform "abominable acts."[5]

One of the most severe critics was Samuel Wells Williams, who went to Canton in 1833, and whose *The Middle Kingdom* became the classic text on Chinese culture. Williams derided Chinese "ostentatious kindness" as a facade: "The politeness which they exhibit seldom has its motive in good will, and consequently when the varnish is off, the rudeness, brutality, and coarseness of the material is seen." He continued:

> Facts of daily occurrence…reveal the prevalence of the most fearful immorality and furnish a melancholy sight into the desolating horrors of paganism. Female infanticide, in some parts openly confessed, and divested of all disgrace and penalties everywhere …the alarming use of opium (furnished by British and American merchants) destroying the productions and natural resources of the people; the universal practice of lying and dishonest dealings; the unblushing lewdness of old and young; harsh cruelty towards prisoners by officers and tyranny over slaves by masters, all forming a full, unchecked torrent of human depravity, and proving the existence of a kind and degree of moral degradation, of which an excessive statement can scarcely be made, or an adequate conception hardly be formed.[6]

This is the reputation that preceded the increasing drift of Chinese to New York.

With fewer than a hundred Chinese in New York at the time of the Civil War, two, and pos-

21 THE 1863 RIOTS TO PROTEST THE CIVIL WAR DRAFT BECAME ATTACKS ON BLACKS. THE BURNING OF THE COLORED ORPHAN ASYLUM ON FIFTH AVENUE LIVED LONG IN THE CITY'S MEMORY.

sibly three, joined the battle. John Akkomb, who in 1856 welcomed a reporter to his Pearl Street boarding house with a polite "How do, Mosheer," was a steward on the gunboat *Massachusetts* in river engagements in Texas and Louisiana. He was twice wounded, once severely in the chest. He returned to the city and lived with his wife, Kitty, and three children on Cherry Street.[7]

Hong Kee Kang, a former sailor who lived on Cherry Street, enlisted in the Navy in July 1863 and served as a steward on the gunboat *Albatross*, handing out powder for the guns when Admiral Farragut blockaded Mobile. He received an honorable discharge in September 1864 and settled down in New York. He operated a grocery store on Staten Island and, for many years, owned a cigar business at 500 Pearl Street under the name of William A. Hong.[8]

The third recruit may have been John Ah Woh. At an 1878 meeting of Chinese claiming American citizenship, Ah Woh—a cigar maker living on Baxter Street—showed a document dated 1863. Since immigrants were readily granted citizenship as an inducement to enlist, he may have volunteered for service then.[9]

In the early years, the racism faced by the Chinese in New York was a mild reflection of the greater antipathy toward black slaves. In July 1863, New York was swept by five days of rioting touched off by what were seen as unfair laws regulating the drafting of men for the army. At least 105 people were killed and tens of thou-

22 OTHER RIOTERS LYNCHED A BLACK.

sands of dollars worth of property was destroyed. The mobs lynched a black man, burned the Colored Orphan Asylum, and threatened or attacked brothels and homes of racially mixed couples. When someone persuaded a mob that the Chinese were but a "modification" of blacks, the Chinese in the Fourth Ward were also attacked:

> Someone disputed this theory, and quite a family quarrel occurred at once. Several blows were struck, the anti-Chinaman in the end getting the worst of it. Afterwards there

17

was a general attack upon all "American citizens of Chinese origin" and John in a state of terror has thrown himself upon the police for his protection. The representatives of this race in New York are a peculiar people. They seem to have a thorough dislike of white men but a very great regard for white women. Most of them are married to females who are only for a husband not particular about his nativity or appearance. The wives "wear the breeches" and John is as obedient to their orders as a child. He is a harmless creature, anyhow, and only the idea that he is a "modification of the Negro" as the orator expressed it, brought down the blows upon his head in the Fourth Ward. In a few days they will be about as usual.[10]

In these years, racism was still softened by exoticism. Aside from seamen, newcomers were escaped or freed "coolies" from Cuba, where they had worked in cigar factories and learned the skills needed to get started in New York. Cuba (where long-term "coolies" lost their queues) was probably the origin of the Candy Man:

This brown-faced Asiatic discards his national peculiarities and appears upon the street in ordinary American attire, with his thick black hair cut Christianly short instead of dangling in a long braided cue. His stand is a low frame supporting a wooden tray with a ragged zinc lining. On it rests two huge round cakes of candy, one white as snow, one yellow as cream, and both smeared over the top with a hard scarlet coating. A stout black-handled, broken-bladed carving knife, and a short heavy hammer serve for breaking these cakes into small angular fragments, about the size of a cubic inch. These pieces fill two tins and a half a dozen small cone-shaped bags of brown paper. One cent a piece, or five cents a bag, is the tariff of prices.

"What do you call this?" we inquire.

"Pineapple candy," is the prompt reply, for our Chinese friend has been here nearly five years and has learned to speak very fair English….We taste and find the flavor very pleasant, which seems to be the opinion of others, for the purchasers are many. The smiling vender keeps his stand scrupulously clean with a wet cloth, which he politely offers to us to wipe our sticky fingers on, and we come away with an improved opinion of John Chinaman's courtesy and neatness.[11]

Chinese seamen lived near the docks in the Fourth Ward, east of the Bowery. Later arrivals congregated in the Five Points slums of the Sixth Ward, west of the Bowery.[12]

Interest in the Chinese was spurred by the

23 THE CHINESE WERE SEEN AS "BUT A MODIFICATION OF THE NEGRO." AN 1868 *HARPER'S WEEKLY* SKETCH OF A CANDY SELLER CONTRASTS HIM WITH THE PALE-FACED CHILDREN.

arrival of a Chinese diplomatic delegation led by former Senator Anson Burlingame. They negotiated what became known as the Burlingame Treaty, which ostensibly afforded equal protection to foreign nationals in each other's country. Actually, the aim was to assure protection for American missionaries in China. Reacting to fears of furthering the flood of Chinese to the United States, the treaty specifically restricted such immigration.

But few wanted to know about well-dressed diplomats. The Chinese were heathens, and that's what newspaper reporters wanted to find out about. A *Herald* reporter, guided by an obliging policeman, set out to find the grail of a heathen temple, this one said to be complete with two "priests." He picked his way along Baxter Street, "with eating rookeries and gin mills wide open and wretched women in tattered garments, spotted with chronic sores," and on to the second floor of a three-story frame house, where he entered a room, stale with the smoke of opium and tobacco, in which clothes were drying

24 Anson Burlingame, in top hat, leading Chinese delegates on their departure from New York for Europe.

before a red-hot stove. James Baptiste, an English-speaking former house servant, said eight cigar makers rented the room and shared the rent of $14 a month, helping to keep their costs, including food, to $3 or $4 a month per man. Baptiste said they made from 150 to 180 cigars a night and sold them by day for from one to three cents, depending on the quality of the tobacco. Far from needing the services of heathen priests, Baptiste said, some Chinese in New York were Catholics and others were "Jews, Episcopalians, and Methodists," who were "mostly married to Irish women" and "had a good many children who attend the Five Points Mission School."[13]

THE HOUSE OF INDUSTRY

After Louis Pease retired, there was a division in the work at the Five Points. Methodist women who organized the original Five Points Mission concentrated on traditional missionary work of preaching and seeking conversions, while the building constructed by Pease became the Five Points House of Industry, stressing education, job training, English lessons and similar social programs. Among the challenges: the growing number of Chinese in the area. A "City Missionary," Lycurgus Railsback, described as "one of the most faithful and successful chaplains of colored regiments during the Civil War," was added to the staff, and in the fall of 1868 he persuaded six cigar makers to come for English lessons, and soon as many as forty came for classes from seven to nine every evening except Sunday.[14]

The superintendent of the House of Industry was Samuel Halliday, for thirty years one of the most active of city missionaries. To counter charges of Chinese "cheap labor," Halliday wrote

19

25 THE POST-CIVIL WAR HOUSE OF INDUSTRY.

a letter to the *Times* saying some seamen earned as much as twenty-five dollars a week. Although he conceded most earned less than eight dollars a week, that was still a decent wage for the times. He lavished praise on the Chinese who came to the mission to study English, describing them as "docile, industrious, and frugal" and "eminently polite, kindly, and generous." He also revealed that there were three Chinese women in New York, including one who came to the classes: "She is quite intelligent—reads Chinese and English. She was for some time in one of the American mission schools at home. Their whole family came to one of the West India islands as coolies, where her friends that are living still remain. She said they were treated very badly by their masters."[15]

Her name was Mary Chang, the wife of Chang Tsing Chow, who kept a boardinghouse on or near Baxter Street. She was described as "very well looking for an oriental, and possessing a mass of jet-black hair at the back of her head sufficient to make half a dozen chignons."[16]

When students and friends of the House of Industry Chinese school gathered for Christmas celebrations, a sketch in *Leslie's Illustrated* showed a woman with two children who may have been Mary Chang.[17]

Halliday saw himself as a pioneer welcoming a new stream of immigrants to America. In one of his final reports before retiring in 1870, he wrote:

26 THE CHRISTMAS RECEPTION FOR THE CHINESE AT THE HOUSE OF INDUSTRY.

20

27 ANTI-CHINESE HYSTERIA WAS FED BY RUSSELL CONWELL'S 1870 BEST SELLING *WHY AND HOW*, WITH ITS PREDICTION THAT A MILLION CHINESE MIGHT EMIGRATE EVERY YEAR.

28 CONWELL CLAIMED TO PRESENT A BALANCED ACCOUNT. HE DESCRIBED THE CHINESE AS STRONG AND HEALTHY AND SAID RATS AND DOGS WERE FAMINE FOOD, NOT THE COMMON DIET. BUT, CITING MISSIONARY REPORTS, HE WROTE "PARENTS DO NOT HESITATE TO STRANGLE OR DROWN THE HELPLESS HUMAN BEING WHO WAS SO UNLUCKY TO BE BORN A FEMALE."

It can hardly be a question that we are not long hence to have their people with us in great numbers and to have made so pleasant a beginning with them, to find them so appreciative, so teachable, patient, persevering, so courteous and polite, it is to me most significant as to the result. They are, I think, to occupy no unimportant position in and to exert a great influence upon the national welfare; and we may regard it as a great privilege to have been allowed to take the initiatory step with the representatives of people constituting one-third of the population of the globe.[18]

He was curiously blind to racial realities. A year earlier, on May 1, 1869, Tribune publisher Horace Greeley printed a letter from Henry George, who later gained fame as America's foremost Utopian. He is remembered for his theory that most of society's problems could be solved by making land the basis of taxation. George was then the editor of a San Francisco newspaper and a leading anti-Chinese racist.

29 THE GIANT GENIE WAS CONWELL'S MILLIONS WAITING TO EMIGRATE.

George's letter restated the arguments against Chinese immigration that were developed by

30 SINCE LITTLE WAS KNOWN OF THE FEARED "ORIENTAL HEATHENISM," CARTOONISTS DEPENDED ON THEIR IMAGINATION.

San Francisco's "anticoolie clubs," trade unions and the renascent Democratic Party of California. Unless checked, he wrote, an inexhaustible Chinese torrent would inundate the United States:

> The Chinaman can live where stronger than he would starve. Give him fair play and this quality enables him to drive out stronger races....Here plain to the eye of him who chooses to see are the dragon's teeth [which will]...spring up armed men marshalled for civil war. Shall we prohibit their sowing while there is still time or shall we wait until they are firmly embedded, and then try to pluck them up?"

Mixed with the invective was economic theory. George's other hobbyhorse was an end to monopolies. In this, he felt himself to be a follower of John Stuart Mill. He argued that the Chinese "clannish social structure" made them ready instruments for monopolists "to make the rich richer and the poor poorer, to make nabobs and princes of our capitalists and crush our working classes into the dust; to substitute (if it goes far enough) a population of serfs and their masters for that population of intelligent freemen who are our glory and strength."

George was pleased with the acceptance of his ideas, implied by the display in three full columns in the *Tribune* and sent a copy of his letter to Mill in England. Mill replied politely on the subject of opposition to monopolies. But he thought of himself as a moralist as well as an economist and added:

22

WHAT SHALL WE DO WITH JOHN CHINAMAN?
WHAT PAT WOULD DO WITH HIM   WHAT WILL BE DONE WITH HIM

31 In this September 1869 sketch the Chinese are again shown with dark skin.

One of the most difficult and embarrassing questions of political morality [is] the extent and limits of the right of those who have first taken possession of the unoccupied portion of the earth's surface to exclude the remainder of mankind from inhabiting it....The institutions of the United States are the most potent means that have yet existed of spreading the most important elements of civilization down to the poorest and most ignorant of the laboring masses. If every Chinese child were compulsorily brought under your school system, or under a still more effective one if possible, and kept under it for a sufficient number of years, would not the Chinese population be in time raised to the level of the Americans?[19]

Racist Americans were deaf to the reasoning of the author of *On Liberty*.

In October, the Protestant Episcopal Board of Missions warned: "The most inveterate, oriental heathenism transplanted to our soil...may yet strive for political ascendancy on this continent." The proposed solution was for Christians to gird their loins and "convert them as soon as possible, in addition to educating them."[20]

THE INFLUX BEGINS

In June 1870, the "influx" (the *Times* commented in a July 3, 1876 editorial that the Chinese never arrived like ordinary human beings, they always "influxed") reached New England. Calvin Sampson had closed his shoe factory in North Adams, Massachusetts after a long dispute with the secret order of St. Crispins, the largest (although ephemeral) trade union of the time. The Crispins had gone on strike and were demanding the right to examine Sampson's books to fix wages in proportion to his profits. Sampson saw this as arrant socialism. He read of Chinese employed in San Francisco shoe factories and sent his foreman, who signed a three-year contract for seventy-five Chinese at a starting salary of $23 a month, with the Chinese to supply their own food and clothing. Sampson had to pay a railroad fare of $125 per man, amounting to an outlay of almost $10,000 before the first man set to work. Word spread of their impending arrival. They were met at the station by an angry crowd and a policeman guarded their flanks as they walked in a line—Sampson leading the way—to the factory. There were

23

32 CHINESE RAILROAD WORKERS, IDENTIFIED AS "COOLIES," CROSSING THE MISSOURI IN JANUARY 1870 EN ROUTE TO TEXAS. THEY APPEARED TO SIGNAL THE "INFLUX" FROM THE WEST.

scuffles at the end of the line.[21]

Amid a heat wave, a protest meeting was held in Tompkins Square on June 30, with two platforms for English speakers and one for Germans. Mayor A. Oakey Hall, who prided himself on his wit, began with a remark that the "coolie question was a good one to talk about." Oakey Hall's appearance represented what Iver Bernstein, writing on the political significance of the Draft Riots, described as Tammany's response "to the changing racial outlook of the labor movement." There is evidence Tammany paid the head of the Workingmen's Union to help stage the rally. Speakers, amounting to "a directory of the city's most militant and class-conscious trade unions," took the stand one by one to denounce the importation of "cheap" Chinese labor.[22]

One resolution warned that the Chinese would "debase our manhood, destroy our morals and prostitute our virtues." An acerbic *Times* editorial called the morals argument "an insult to American women, who would have as much to say on that particular question involved as the Mongolians." After three other rallies in New York and Brooklyn in early July, the protests wilted in the

33 THE WORK ROOM IN NORTH ADAMS.

24

34 THE DORMITORY.

summer heat.[23]

Reporters, seeking ways to keep the story alive, pounced on Ling Wau as he debarked from the Pacific Mail's steamship *Alaska*, along with his wife, several assistants, and huge boxes of three hundred varieties of roots, leaves, powders, and extracts. Ling, dressed in a loose, black silk, sleeveless jacket and white linen trousers, had enjoyed success in treating the ailments of non-Chinese citizens of San Francisco. He later opened a clinic at 40 East 14th Street and announced he could cure partial paralysis, diseased liver, kidney infection, listlessness, general debility, inflation of the lung, and any number of aches, pains, agues—and even, as a reporter noted, "knock spots out of the most vicious Jersey fever." He was aware of the American squeamishness. He could not speak English but, through an interpreter, he assured future patients his pharmacopoeia did not

include a single toad or lizard.[24]

The Five Points House of Industry had its own antidote for anti-Chinese fever: It invited guests to its chapel to demonstrate that the Chinese could be good neighbors. The gathering was arranged by a new missionary—Arthur Folsom—who had recently returned after eight years with the Presbyterians in Canton. The main attraction was a Chinese magician and juggler named Hang Chow, but whose poster proclaimed him as "Dr. Ah Foon, the renowned Chinese prophet of Toulum." He was from California, visiting his brother in New York. He strummed on what he called a Chinese banjo and joked about the Chinese stereotype: "American laugh at Chinaman because he eat rat," making a rat out of a handkerchief. He made the handkerchief produce a live snake and two pigeons, poured lemonade from an empty tea cup and caused a cup and saucer to spin in

25

the air and remain suspended in space.[25]

The fever returned in September when the influx finally lapped the shores of New York. Captain James Hervey, who left the sea seventeen years earlier, had for the past four years operated the Passaic Steam Laundry in the village of Belleville (now enveloped by Newark). Weekly, the laundry cleaned and dried six thousand shirts manufactured in the sweat shops of New York, but Hervey found it difficult to recruit and keep women to hand-iron the shirts after they had been mechanically cleaned and dried. He recruited German and Irish women directly from the immigrant ships at Castle Garden. When the groups clashed, he limited himself to Irish women. He built a dormitory complete with a maid, cleaning women, and a Roman Catholic chapel. Still, many women remained only long enough to earn a stake and left to find other work or husbands—or both. Hervey heard about North Adams, wrote to Sampson for advice, and sent his foreman to San Francisco to obtain workers from the same Chinese contractor. Wages had gone up. Hervey had to pay thirty dollars a month in gold and employ two men as cooks. He also had to pay their interpreter, Charley Ming, sixty dollars a month in gold.

On the morning of September 20, 1870, a railroad engine shunted two cars containing sixty-eight Chinese onto a siding at Port Jervis in the northernmost corner of New Jersey. The cars were later moved to a rural station called Santiago Park, arriving at ten o'clock at night. The Chinese got down, removed piles of boxes and bamboo baskets from a freight car, and loaded all this and themselves onto a dozen horse-drawn wagons and were driven through the sleeping countryside of Belleville, six miles away. The carts passed through a heavy oak gate in a newly constructed fence around the Passaic Steam Laundry, and the Chinese settled down in a storeroom converted into a dormitory. The secrecy did not last. By mid-morning, their presence was discovered, and reporters from New York and Newark newspapers converged on Belleville to examine "the influx of haythen Chinee into this country."[26]

They found some sitting in the yard having the front of their heads shaved and their hair washed and plaited into queues. Others were cooking something in a large boiler. One man was cutting up strings of dried pork. Others were seated at a table and were being served a dish of stew made of dried fish from China. All this was repeatedly examined for the presence of cats and puppy dogs. The Chinese were young: One was only twelve. Some wore American trousers, others loose Chinese pantaloons. All wore coarse blue or white muslin blouses that fell below the waist, dark blue trousers, dark American felt hats, and shoes with wood soles and plain or embroidered uppers.

Asked if they would marry American girls, Charley Ming said no, because American girls laughed at the Chinese. Scotching at the start any thought of Chinese lusts let loose in New Jersey, Captain Hervey assured a reporter from the *World* that the Chinese work area was separated from the women's: "Neither can see the other while at work and the Captain has given strict orders that the Celestials shall not encroach on the women in the slightest degree and has begged the latter to notify him of any impropriety."[27]

Hervey had furnished their sleeping quarters with iron beds with cotton mattresses, but the men removed them and used sleeping platforms about two feet above the floor, with a board at the head and at one side and with a thin straw mat. During the day, they hung their mats and blankets over a wire to air and keep them free of vermin and, when relaxing, sat cross-legged on the beds.[28]

After the Belleville story was milked for many column inches, a *Tribune* reporter explored the Chinese on New York's side of the Hudson:

> Many people accept it as a matter of course that if there is any general immigration to this country, a large portion of it must come to this never-exhausted receiver, New York. Such people...having pictured...a large colony of painted and pig-tailed Mongolians residing here, will be surprised to learn how few the number really is and how largely they have conformed themselves to the manners and customs of those about them.

He estimated that there were only two hundred Chinese in the city, "all of them from Havana," including "two or three women, all of whom are mothers of families." As for cheap labor, he wrote that cigar makers earned twenty to twenty-five dollars a week and that one, who had arrived a year earlier, had saved five hundred to six hundred dollars during the winter and "is now the proprietor of a large tobacco store in an Iowa city."

He got his information in an interview with Arthur Folsom at the House of Industry, who told him most Chinese in the city had given up opium, thanks to treatment by "a method...borrowed from the hospital of Hang Chow, China, where it has had a considerable success." Folsom also told of "throngs of thrifty housewives" who had rushed to the House of Industry

26

"with ideas of getting tidier and more good-natured and attentive servants and of saving something by the transaction, but they found the Mongolians thoroughly informed as to their market value." Many had earned twenty to forty dollars a month as cooks and stewards on ocean vessels and would accept nothing less than fifteen dollars a month, plus board, for work ashore. Folsom said if the Chinese would work for ten dollars a month and board, as Irish women did, he could find jobs for ten thousand men.

Folsom also reported on his school, saying there were about forty students, using the Bible as their text. Two had been sent to Howard University in Washington D.C. Folsom also showed a letter from "John Ah Ting," who had studied only two months, and was then at Gibraltar and "sent his regards to Miss [Sara] Goodrich," the school's principal.[29]

In early 1871, when the men at Belleville were given a three-day holiday for the Chinese New Year, reporters flocked to the "somniferous" village of Belleville to be shown through twenty "scrupulously clean" rooms and offered tea, oranges, and sweets. A picture of what Charlie Ming called "Big Joss" was displayed in the dining hall, with an altar in front piled high with food and wreathed by incense. Another picture showed the goddess of plenty seated on a lion. The holiday climaxed with a rising crescendo of banging on two huge kettle drums and a large gong and the clashing of a pair of massive cymbals—plus firecrackers, roman candles, rockets, some old guns, and a small cannon.[30]

However quaint their customs, the arrival of the Chinese in Belleville coincided with the murder of French nuns and priests in Tianjin, with front-page reports telling how the nuns were allegedly stripped, raped, and mutilated.[31]

Hervey received a letter threatening to kill him unless he got rid of the Chinese within a week. Handbills were posted for an "indignation meeting" near his home.[32] Some two hundred people came to cheer Dr. M. H. C. Vail of Newark:

35 RECEPTION AT BELLEVILLE. WHILE HOSTILITY GREETED THE CHINESE IN MASSACHUSETTS, THEY WERE RECEIVED IN NEW JERSEY AS EXOTIC OBJECTS OF MISSIONARY ZEAL.

These idolaters come here under task-masters and as slaves. They come not like the Irish, the Frenchman and the German. We have no trouble with the people of Europe. They came here and mingled with us. They went out and in with us. They brought muscle. They brought bone. Some of them brought gold. They helped to increase the wealth and prosperity of this country. They are of the same race with us. But these Chinese, can we ever mingle with these people? (Voices: No, no, never.) Can they go out and in with us? (No, no.) You answer well, for these people who believe not in our God and Savior can never mingle with us, for they bow down and worship the works of their own hands. They are idolaters. Now, in the name of common sense, is not the world wide enough for us to hire those who accept the law of Christ as their guide? The Chinese race are the only people who lift the dagger to plunge it into Christian missionaries. (Cheers, shouts of good, good.)[33]

THE CHINESE FIND DEFENDERS

But others welcomed the Chinese. Two long-term missionaries on home leave—the Reverend and Mrs. Stephen Livingston Baldwin—were lecturing in churches in Newark. In November 1870, some Chinese from the laundry appeared at one of the churches. Soon a Sunday School was started at Passaic Hall on Main Street in Belleville. In June 1872, students presented their pastor with a silk banner embroidered, in Chinese characters, "Boys of the Province of Canton Go For Jesus," less formally translated as "China Boys Accept Jesus." In September the school's first annual report said it had started with fifteen students, at times drew as many as sixty, and had an average attendance of thirty-five each Sunday. Two students had learned to read and write English. At a Christmas eve entertainment they gave their superintendent "a handsome gold ring."[34]

When one of the men died of pneumonia in November 1871 (after refusing "American" medicine and insisting a Chinese doctor be brought from New York), the coffin was put on a wagon and the men walked behind, two by two, followed by many of the women workers and, finally, Captain Hervey and his family. A Methodist minister performed the obsequies and the coffin was lowered into the grave and covered with earth. Then there were Chinese ceremonies. A small ditch had been dug nearby. Into this were placed a teapot, a rice bowl, a cooking pan, chopsticks, and new clothing—all to be used by the spirit in the afterlife. A large pottery vessel with rice, cooked chicken, and salted fish was placed inside, and the pile was covered with dirt. The dead man's clothing was put on top of the mound and burned as fire-crackers exploded to drive away hungry spirits. Each man approached, interlaced his fingers, and placed his hands on his forehead, palms outward. He extended his palms three times and bowed three times. When all had said this last farewell, more firecrackers were exploded and each mourner was given a small bunch of flowers and five cents. A Newark *Daily Advertiser* reporter who witnessed the ceremony noted: "On the face of the Chinaman an expression was noticed indicating genuine sadness, proving that death raises the same feelings in the breast of the heathen as in the Christian."[35]

The Chinese also found defenders in two of New York's most influential publications: *Harper's Weekly* and the *Times*. When Tammany boss William Marcy Tweed introduced a bill in the state legislature to prohibit the employment of Chinese under contract to "build railroads, grade streets, make boots and shoes, or perform other labor," a *Harper's Weekly* editorial commented: "The Chinese invasion, of which he seems to be so much afraid, is altogether mythical....Mr. Tweed presumes too much on the ignorance or the prejudices of the workingmen if he expects to delude them with such a flimsy cheat....A majority of this country still adheres to the old Revolutionary doctrine that all men are free and equal before the law, and possess certain inalienable rights which even Mr. Tweed is bound to respect."[36]

THROWING DOWN THE LADDER BY WHICH THEY ROSE.

36 THOMAS NAST OF *HARPER'S WEEKLY*, AS EARLY AS JULY 1870, DEFENDED THE CHINESE WITH A SIMPLE CALL FOR EQUAL TREATMENT.

THE CHINESE QUESTION.

COLUMBIA.—"HANDS OFF, GENTLEMEN! AMERICA MEANS FAIR PLAY FOR ALL MEN."

37 IN FEBRUARY 1871 NAST POSED COLUMBIA BEFORE A WALL OF THE SLURS HEAPED ON THE CHINESE IN CALIFORNIA. HE SAW THE ISSUE AS RACISM, LINKING ATTACKS ON THE CHINESE WITH THE DESTRUCTION OF THE COLORED ORPHAN ASYLUM DURING NEW YORK'S 1863 DRAFT RIOTS.

Harper's Weekly artist Thomas Nast had long defended the powerless. In July 1870, when calls for exclusion of the Chinese gained strength in California, he sketched a wall around the United States, with Americans kicking a ladder down on the Chinese below. In February 1871, he pictured Columbia standing before a litany of anti-Chinese slurs, defending a Chinese from a mob.

The *Times* favored satire. On December 20, 1872, the Newark *Daily Advertiser* had a report from Belleville about a feast that it called "Monks," saying a few of the men played cards, but most romped about pulling each other's queues—dancing and jumping to the tune of an "odd-looking fiddle" and the "kicking up of capacious trousers...that caused the ironing apartment to resemble a room full of insane women." In the evening there was a meal—supplied by Captain Hervey—of rice, fruits, preserves, and sweets followed by fireworks. The celebration, a *Times* editorial said, demonstrated

<blockquote>
the depraved and ignorant nature of the Chinese pagan....They began to celebrate their festival, not by drinking whisky, but by a temperate indulgence in tea. Having begun the day in a manner so preposterous and contemptible, these wretched heathen naturally went on to prove their infinite inferiority to civilized people. They indulged in the effeminate folly of dance, the means for which was furnished by an absurd Chinese violin. They played a few games—doubtless of an extremely ridiculous nature—with cards, and not one of the players had the spirit to engage in the least approach to a quarrel with any of his companions. They occasionally twitched each other's pig-tails in a way so obviously good-tempered as to excite disgust of every civilized spectator who saw such admirable opportunities for an enlivening riot so utterly thrown away. Toward the end of the day they sat down to a dinner, of which we may assume that the toothsome puppy, the "gamey" rat, and the indigestible bird's nest—upon which viands the entire population of China notoriously subsists—formed the principal part. Incredible as it may appear, these barbarians drank nothing at dinner stronger than tea, and even during the evening, when the blazing of fireworks excited their childish natures, they still refrained from whisky, with a stupid indifference to rational enjoyment, which conclusively proved the depths of ignorance and degradation in which they are sunk. Finally they all went to bed soon after dark, and not a single Chinaman thought of doing honor to the mysterious "monks" by stabbing a fellow heathen.
</blockquote>

38 KWAN KUNG AND ATTENDANTS.

<blockquote>
Perhaps after a few years...we shall enjoy the inspiriting spectacle of the drunken Chinaman celebrating his holiday by perpetual libations of whisky, varied with free fights of a really creditable character, and when we read in the newspapers of the following day of Chinese wives knocked down and trampled upon, and perhaps of two or three vigorous Chinese stabbing matches, we can feel that the example of civilization has not been wholly in vain.[37]
</blockquote>

The elaborate New Year celebrations at Belleville became an interethnic social event, with two hundred and fifty to three hundred men and women visitors from New York, Newark, and small towns in New Jersey. Visitors eagerly sought what newspaper reporters invariably described as the "chapel" or "church," with its image of Kwan Kung with his scribe (male, though with his soft face he seemed female) sitting at one side and his sword bearer on the other. The table with offerings became an "altar" and elderly men became "priests."[38]

In 1877 what visitors took to be an image of a deity (called "Joss," derived from the Portuguese Dios), was described as a being with "a light blue beard and a body like a king of clubs...attended by a smiling-faced woman and a furiously

39 Divination instruments: throwing blocks and container of numbered sticks.

bearded man holding a two bladed sword." The "priest" knelt on a bit of matting, holding two pieces of wood in the air. An assistant gave him little bowls and filled them from a teapot. The "priest" poured a libation and threw up the blocks and the Chinese "peered to see how they fell. This was repeated several times. Another man stood nearby, bowing again and again, with his two hands together and lifting them from his chest to his forehead. All the while a three-man orchestra played furiously."[39]

It was divination, not worship. The man standing nearby had posed a question that could be answered with a simple yes or no. The blocks were elliptical pieces of hard wood, rounded on one side and flat on the other. They were thrown into the air and if they fell with their flat sides down the omen was neutral. If they fell with one flat side and one curved side down, the omen was favorable. If they fell with both curved sides down the omen was unfavorable. The blocks were dropped repeatedly until three signs—neu-

THE CHINESE EXPLODING FIREWORKS IN FRONT OF THE DORMITORY.

THE CHINESE RECEIVING NEW YEAR'S CALLS IN THEIR PRIVATE APARTMENTS.

THE CHINESE ORCHESTRA.

OFFERING FOOD AND TEA TO JOSS IN THE TEMPLE.

40 Chinese New Year celebrations at Belleville in 1877.

tral, good, or bad—were received in succession.[40]

BELLEVILLE AS A CENTER OF CHINESE LIFE

Until as late as the 1890s, racial animosities and ever-present hoodlumism forced the Chinese in New York to keep their festivals indoors. The isolation of Belleville, and the fact that the laundry was surrounded by a high fence, allowed the Chinese to feel free to indulge themselves. The New Year celebrations became more elaborate, attracting friends and relatives from New York and the surrounding towns of New Jersey. Their contributions paid for the import of finely carved shrines and mounds of lanterns, incense, and candles from China. A visitor in 1882 wrote:

> The table is covered with a multitude of burning joss sticks and lighted candles, all stuck up in boxes of sand; tall red tapers directly in front of the image; huge pyramids of gilt and red tinsel and bunches of artificial and natural flowers. All these form a study in red and gold, with the image at the back scowling through a veil of incense rising from the burning joss sticks. In different parts of the room great globes of gaudy paper hang from the ceiling and the walls are covered with quaint Chinese pictures. ...Each worshipper, after praying for a time on his knees, took a small round box filled with splints, each having a number on one end, and shook the box till one fell out. The number of his splint referred to a passage in the Chinese sacred writings, which they believe foretells their fortune for the coming year.[41]

This was a more sophisticated method of fortune telling. There were one hundred sticks, each about seven inches long. The number on the stick corresponded to a page in a book called the *Kwan Kung Divining Lots*. The page contained a verse of poetry about a well-known personage of Chinese history with a short passage of explanation. As such, it took someone with a knowledge of the Chinese annals to understand the full meaning of the text and correlate this with the questions asked by the person who shook out the stick. The advantage of the divining sticks was that they could give more than a simple yes or no answer. The Belleville shrine attracted laundrymen from throughout the New York-New Jersey metropolitan area. The New Year was the time to peer into the future. A man could ask a series of questions: Should I start my own laundry? Which location should I choose? Should I take a partner? Will we be successful? The divining sticks, shaken one after another, could be interpreted as a pattern of replies, giving a guide for the months ahead.[42]

By the early 1880s, the "civilizing" influence of American culture the *Times* editorial had satirized ten years earlier was well in evidence. Several "from the fashionable clubs of Mott and Park street rode...in Chatham Square coaches, carrying a liberal supply of liquor and cigars, which they shared with drivers." Some were "accompanied by their Irish wives, many of them young, buxom, and attractive." Others, "less aristocratic," went by the New York, Lake Erie, and Western Railroad and took coaches from Belleville "up the hill to the laundry grounds in high glee."

In the center of the yard stood fifty-foot-high poles with crosstrees at the top. The inevitable musicians took up positions near the entrance of the living quarters, where bunches of firecrackers, tied in a string about ten feet long, were "deposited in trays zealously guarded by committeemen." At the top of each string was a box made of fancy paper. Ropes, strung through pulleys at the ends of the crosstrees, were pulled to lift the strings of firecrackers to the crossbar, with guy ropes holding the strings from the side of the pole. Then the lower ends of the strings of firecrackers were lighted "by grave and serious Chinamen" and "an awful din began." The band played furiously. Great bombs placed on the ground were also touched off. When the firecrackers at the upper end of the strings banged their last, they exploded the contents of the paper boxes and "gave vent to a howl that might have aroused the dead." The air was thick with smoke and flying paper as fresh strings were pulled to the top and touched off, resulting in the final explosion of the paper boxes. This went on for two hours "as the band played and the firecrackers and boxes snapped and shrieked and no one except the Chinamen attempted to speak" pausing only for "ecstasies of delight" every time the paper boxes exploded.[43]

By then the romance was ending. The number of Chinese had dropped to about seventy-five. Hervey had retired, to be succeeded by his assistant, George Casebolt. In 1884, Casebolt tried to fire one of the workers, and that led to the first and only strike. The quarrel was patched up, but a year later all contracts were canceled and the Chinese drifted away, most of them to open their own laundries. Casebolt closed the laundry about a dozen years later and the building remained vacant until World War I, when it became an ammunition factory. Casebolt died in 1932 at the age of ninety.[44]

Stereotyping

41 "Chang the Chinese Giant" on his arrival in New York. He stood eight feet four inches tall, and could reach to twelve feet. Chang Yu Sing became familiar across the United States. In 1883, he was reported with the Barnum, Bailey and Hutchinson circus.

To a greater extent than other immigrants, the Chinese were stereotyped as living exotica, like the two versions of "the Chinese lady" or "Chang the Chinese Giant," who was twenty-three when he was first shown in New York in 1869 following a European tour, and was subsequently seen at sideshows in the United States, Canada, and Europe for about twenty years. But they were more than exotics. They were the Other: both a challenge to the Christian injunction to save souls and, as "dragon's teeth," a threat to white, European dominance.

The prefix "Ah" to a male name was a Guangdong diminutive, like Johnny or Charley. The usual name for a first-born boy was Sing, or Sin, meaning "one" or "first"—in diminutive, Ah Sin.

Bret Harte called the Chinese loyal, patient, and persecuted, and described their detractors as bigots, drunkards, and hypocrites. He meant no harm when he wrote "Plain Language from Truthful James," and was being whimsical when he chose "Ah Sin" as the name of his mock-hero

but, from then on, five lilting lines would be quoted as revealed truth:

> Which I wish to remark
> And my language is plain
> That for ways that are dark
> And tricks that are vain
> The heathen Chinee is peculiar.

Ah Sin, "with a smile child-like and bland," pretends he can't play poker and sits down against Bill Nye, who stuffs his sleeves with "aces and bowers." Ah Sin stuffs his more ample sleeves with twenty-four packs of cards and wins. Nye is incensed at being "ruined by Chinese cheap labor" and beats him up.

(This was not poetic license. In 1871 a *Harper's Weekly* artist captured a New York waterfront scene of a huge docker pulling a Chinese by his queue.)

When the poem—usually called "The Heathen Chinee"—was published in *Overland* magazine in September 1870, it was hawked through the streets of San Francisco and telegraphed to newspapers across the country. By January 1871 the New York *Globe* had printed it twice, saying there was not a secular newspaper in the country that had not reproduced it at least once. It went through four editions in England in its first year. Illustrated versions in *Leslie's Illustrated* and *Every Saturday* were made into pamphlets for sale on news stands. The *Globe* on January 7 reported hundreds gathered to see an illustrated version displayed in a shop window: "In all our knowledge of New York nothing like this has ever been seen on Broadway." It was the most popular piece of poetry of the 1870s and was set to music for singing.[1]

An imitation Chinese appeared on stage in New York as early as early as 1856, when the minstrel Eph Horne ("Brudder Bones") "acted the Chinese Wash Man and sang a Chinese song." He later took the role to California.[2]

In 1870 James McCloskey added a Chinese character to his topical *Across the Continent: or, Scenes from New York Life and the Pacific R. R.* Someone says: "Watch me telephone to China." He takes up the end of the queue of an imitation Chinese named Very Tart and says, "Hello, Tart." The Chinese takes back his queue and replies, "Hello." A version of Bret Harte's Ah Sin reached the stage in May 1872 when *California: or, The*

33

42–44 Illustrations for *The Heathen Chinee*.

Heathen Chinee opened at the Bowery Theater, with Charles Warwick "especially engaged for the great character part of Ah Sin...a Chinaman who can't play poker." Harte's *Two Men of Sandy Bar* was adapted for the stage in August 1876 with Charles Parsloe as a laundryman named Hop Sing. When called to testify at a trial, Hop Sing says: "Me washee shirt. He no pay washee. He say, Go to hellee. Alle time Melican man say, 'Chalkee up, John. No smallee change, John.' Plenty foolee me."[3]

In 1877 Bret Harte and Mark Twain collaborated on *Ah Sin*, which Augustin Daly brought to the Fifth Avenue Theater. The title role was a showcase for Charles Parsloe, "the great impersonator of Chinese character." Despite the fame of its authors, Ah Sin failed in a Washington try-out and again, after terrible reviews, in New York. A *Times* critic wrote:

> Ah Sin...presents a variety of phases of Chinese humor, cleverness, and amusing rascality. His comical naiveté, his propensity to beg and steal, his far-seeing policy thanks to which a happy *denouement* of this particular story is brought out, are happily illustrated. ...The second act, concluding with an attempt to arrest Ah Sin on a charge of mur-

der, and the flight of the vigilantes who are routed by Ah Sin expectorating water upon them as though he were dampening linen in the Chinese fashion is tedious.[4]

Joaquin Miller's long-lasting *The Danites: or, The Heart of the Sierras* opened the same month. In court, when the judge pulls a laundryman named Washee Washee around by his queue, the Chinese draws a pistol and a parson shouts: "A Chinaman draws a pistol on a white

Drama of the Gold Mines—opened in New York in the fall of 1880. It featured "Wun Lung, the heathen Chinee." Here the comedy, if such it was, involved a play of dialects between Wun Lung and an Irishman.[8]

For journalists seeking copy in "ways that are dark," the grail was still a heathen temple. In 1856 a *Times* reporter had sniffed at the rumor of a temple somewhere in lower Manhattan. In 1869 a *Herald* reporter tracked a similar rumor

45 THE FACTUAL BASIS OF BILL NYE'S FICTIONAL VIOLENCE: A PANEL FROM SKETCHES OF NEW YORK WATERFRONT EATING PLACES.

man in California. Bring that rope." Just in time, a widow, who is missionary at the mines, enters and throws off the rope.[5]

The *Times* critic now commented: "Mr. Pratt portraying Washee Washee is the fourth Chinaman now before the public, and, we sincerely hope, the last."[6]

No such luck. In 1879 Bartley Campbell's *My Partner* opened at the Union Square Theater with Parsloe giving a "very striking imitation of the imported Chinaman." His character, Wing Lee, was the stock Chinese bragging about being brave, having his queue pulled, and identifying the culprit by a laundry mark.[7]

The last major melodrama involving a comic Chinese—T. W. Hanshew's *The Forty-Niners, A*

without success. Finally, a *Times* reporter claimed victory:

> Here, where the Methodists can say no good word for Episcopalians, and where Baptists hold their hands in holy horror at the doings of Congregationalists, where the Catholics are continually seeking for supremacy and German Lutherans are gradually but securely growing in strength, calmly in the darkest and most loathsome portion of the city does the Chinese worshipper pray to his heathen gods....Perhaps no other foreign emigrant to the shores of America clings so tenaciously to his national habits as does the Chinese. ...Even the Italians, who have more recently begun to seek a home in the New World, are

35

rapidly developing traits which give evidence of their speedy transformation into good, industrious American citizens. The Chinese, on the other hand, always remain the same …and no contact with American life can alienate them from the peculiar vices, habits, and customs of the Celestial Empire.

With blinkered vision, the reporter peered into a corner of the Chinatown slowly taking root a few blocks from City Hall in lower Manhattan. At 34 Mott Street he found the "Poolon Kun Cee," which he called a club, or mutual benefit association, with about fifty members. The room was divided by a partition into two areas. There was a "gaming room" in the rear, where some twenty men were playing mah jong, described as "a game of dominoes. …The pieces, however, were of different colored wood, curiously marked and numbered, and were much more numerous than in the ordinary game." The front portion was used for "the business meetings of the association." More probably, it was a lounge and mess room, where two men were preparing a meal on a stove in the corner:

> The man who seemed to be the head cook first put about a half a pound of lard in a monster frying pan, his assistant in the meantime chopped up a large head of white cabbage, and as soon as the lard was melted threw it, and about half a dozen scraped carrots, into the pan. Salt and pepper were shaken profusely over this, and then came a layer of chopped meat. Cold boiled potatoes followed, the whole mess being supplemented by what look liked a pulled codfish. The fumes...can be better imagined than described...but the Chinese seemed very much offended when it was intimated that the smell of their kitchen was not very pleasant.

The reporter described the "heathen temple" he discovered at 12 Baxter Street as a club "to aid members in distress, and to extend a helping hand to young Chinese who might come as strangers to the city":

> On the first floor of the house [in] a badly lighted, musty room, some twenty feet long by twelve wide...placed against the wall, is fixed a large stand, which serves as the altar; above this, and suspended from the ceiling, are two large Chinese lanterns. On the altar is placed one large kerosene lamp, which is kept continually burning; on either side of this are brass censers filled with earth. In these are stuck incense tapers, which are constantly smoldering, giving forth a not unpleasant odor. In the front of the censers are two stuffed birds....Most conspicuous is

a large picture of Buddha, his son, and the evil one, which is hung high over the altar, and to which the attendant bowed his head on entering. Idolatrous worship is held in the temple three times a month by the Chinese as a congregation, and on these occasions a priest officiates; as individuals they visit the place for prayer at any and all times.

Later, he referred to the image as "the great god Fo." Continuing his tour, he said the doctor who had set up shop on 14th Street had left, "on account of the refusal of the Customhouse authorities to admit the serpents, poisonous drugs and revolting salves which he attempted to import," but another had arrived from New Orleans and was living on the third floor of a rooming house at 66 Cherry Street, which "every evening is visited by numerous young white girls of the neighborhood. Three of them were found there last evening, none of the three could have been more than 18 years of age, two of them quite well-looking, but all of them sat side by side with a greasy, loathsome, wrinkled, old Chinaman, and brazenly looking the visitor in the face."

At 13 Mott he found a boardinghouse operated by John Assing, the former student at the Chinese School of the Five Point House of Industry who, three years earlier, had written a letter to Sara Goodrich from Gibraltar. Assing had partitioned a large basement into six rooms. One, in the rear for cooking and eating, had a stove, two long wooden tables, two benches, and a cupboard "all doors of which are of broken glass and which contains a large variety of cracked cups, plates, saucers, and a rare assortment of chopsticks." Assing said he served roast beef and boiled chicken and, when it could be procured, roast hare. The charge was four dollars a week for board and lodging or three dollars for board without sleeping accommodation. The front room, used as a lounge, had "a dilapidated sofa" and "some half-dozen cane-bottom chairs in bad condition." In the other rooms, instead of the usual bunks, there were "ten wooden bedsteads, over which a few coarse bed clothes are thrown." One small room was "devoted to the uses of opium smokers and is fitted up with all the appliances necessary for the practice of that baleful vice."

The great cliché of opium smoking could not be passed over lightly. The reporter ended with a return to Baxter Street for the lurid details:

> In Donovan's Lane, a miserable little alley opening from Baxter Street, a room is kept...by a withered old wreck....A slanting board shelf is fixed lengthwise to one of the

walls; this is long enough to allow a man of small stature to lie at full length, but not more than four persons could lie on it at a time....The Chinese...admit that the effects of the drug...are ruinous in the extreme. They argue, however, that all nations indulge in some dissipation. The Americans, they say, drink whisky until they are drunk, and they ask if this is so, why is it wrong for a Chinaman to become senseless with opium....What is far more terrible, a large number of young white girls residing in their neighborhood are rapidly becoming addicted to the same vice. They live with the Chinese when they can find no other home, for although people of their own race close their doors against them, they are always welcome at the firesides of those to whom they sell their souls for the sustenance of their bodies.[9]

Stripped of sensationalism, the ground covered was the future Chinatown. Literally, *kongsi* means "company," or "business house." The Poolon Kongsi at 34 Mott would become the prototype of the commercial operation that would dominate the enclave's social and economic life: a combination food, clothing, and hardware store where men from a single clan and territory could shop, receive mail, and get information about work or commercial opportunities. Such shops might have as many as ten partners from the same clan and territory—hence the term kongsi. With prosperity—and as more parts of the building became available—some of the original partners, or additional clan recruits, would branch out to a gambling room in the basement or a restaurant upstairs for employees and clan members in the area. Above that might be a communal dormitory for employees or workers in the area. The fact that there seemed to be more men in the building than could be accounted for by a mere store or restaurant gave Americans the impression of some sort of club.

What Americans knew as a Joss House was a different organization. Oddly, a *Daily Graphic* reporter had written about the much sought-after heathen temple on Baxter Street nine months earlier. He described "a tinted picture representing Confucius with considerable adiposity, supported by two fierce executioners," and lists of members on a wall, written in red and yellow in Chinese characters and English, and a sign reading "Chinese Society." A man he identified as "President Ye Sing," showed him several "stamping dies" (known as "chops"—a block with incised characters). Ye Sing demonstrated their use by stamping "on coarse brown paper the name of the society, giving however a

caution not to allow any Chinaman to have the impress, as the document bearing it was a sort of free pass and claim on every branch of the society throughout the world."[10]

Apparently, this was a branch of the Triads, the only organization among immigrant Chinese claiming international ties. Further evidence of the Triads—and their links with gambling and other illegal activities—would not come for several more years.

The following February, when preparations were made for the Chinese New Year ceremonies, reporters flocked to 12 Baxter Street, "conveniently located only five minutes walk away from City Hall." *Harper's Weekly* sent Winslow Homer. The result—a static drawing of the shrine with and a separate sketch of the inevitable opium smoker—is unrepresentative of his talents.

The newsmen trooped to the second floor and passed through a dilapidated hallway to an outer room and were then shown into a "worship hall" by two English-speaking young Chinese, "neatly dressed with their hair cut like others." A demijohn was uncorked to serve visitors a glass of wine. Reporters were told dues were ten cents a week. Below the "idol Fo," a four-foot-high "altar" had two candles and dishes of fruits, nuts, and vegetables and stuffed birds. Balloons hung from the ceiling and bits of colored paper were pasted on the walls. Their inscriptions were translated as "Majestic King of Darkness," "Shades of Ancestors and Evil Spirits Do Us No Harm," "Heaven King Grasp all the Empire," and "Pure Running Brook." The reporters were told that one-hundred members had gathered the previous evening for a feast "two or three days in preparation" at a cost of seventy-five dollars. There had been a suggestion that the New Year be celebrated with a parade, bonfire, and fireworks but "recollection of previous attempts of that kind induced them to abandon the notion....The religious rites of the Chinese in Baxter Street are always very quiet and the people themselves are inoffensive and always welcome visitors. They give the police no trouble and are therefore unmolested by the law officers."[11]

In addition to a community store, such as the Poolon Kongsi, and a community hall, such as the room on Baxter Street, overseas Chinese needed a burial society or, more accurately, a society to arrange the temporary internment and eventual return of the bones of deceased members to their villages. Such a society was formed in the earliest days of the New York settlement. In 1854 John Akkomb told a reporter who visited his rooming house on Pearl Street that the Chinese raised money among themselves to pay for funerals. Then during the first Belleville excitement, when a *Tribune* reporter sought another angle on the story, he went to the House of Industry where, among other things, Arthur Folsom told of a man he called Een E Jong, who came in with a document that he could not read and that he wished to have examined so that he might be sure that it was all that it should be. It proved to be a receipt for $280, which Een had just paid for a burial lot of his family. Een is a man of mark. He is married to an excellent Irish woman and has three children. He rents a brick house in Cherry Street and keeps a Chinese boarding house. He also keeps a sort of intelligence office, finding places for Chinese cooks, waiters, etc. on outward-bound ships in need of such servants, receiving a fee for his service from both employer and employee. He was one of the first Chinamen to come to New York. By strict attention to business he has become a prosperous citizen.[12]

It was a garbled report. This became clear in 1877, when the murder of Chinese in a tenement at 17 Forsyth Street gave reporters an excuse to barge into Chinese homes searching for "ways that are dark."

Three cigar makers shared the rent of the Forsyth Street room. During the night of January 28, someone mortally wounded Ah Fung with the blow of an axe. The murder was never solved. Ah Fung was taken to Bellevue Hospital, where he was visited by "a good looking Irish woman who claimed to be…his lawful wife.…He recognized her by her voice and cried out, "Katie, Katie, come here. Katie, why don't you come Katie? I'm going to die." Katie, wearing a diamond ring and earrings, was described as "bright and intelligent and not the least crushed by affliction."[13]

At 38 Baxter, "after climbing two flights of a dangerously-dark and pungently perfumed stairway," a *World* reporter was invited into the apartments of the Irish wives of Ah Muk and Ching Si:

> The rooms were scrupulously clean and handsomely furnished. An immense high-topped black walnut bedstead with really elegant fitting was the most conspicuous object in the rooms but there was no appliance of comfort lacking and everything was kept in perfect order.
>
> "How did you come to marry Chinamen?" Mrs. Ah Muk laughed immoderately, but Mrs. Ching Si was indignant. "Because we liked 'em, of course, why shouldn't we?"

It was suggested that it was more in accordance with the nature of things that they should marry white men, whereupon Mrs. Ching Si said that they were as white as anybody and a good deal whiter than many of their neighbors, and Mrs. Ah Muk showed her little baby as proof that she was more than content with her lot. It was sleeping in a tidy crib and was certainly a beautiful child, being chubby and healthy in appearance.

"Joe is his name," said the proud mother. "He don't look like a Chinaboy, does he, when he's asleep? His eyes show it, though, when he's awake.[14]

When Ah Fung died, it was clarified that Ene E Jong (as it was now spelled) was a burial organization, not a person. The president was identified as "John A. Cong, of 66 Cherry Street, a Chinese boardinghouse keeper [who]…is one of the most influential Chinamen in the New York colony." When interviewed, Acomb (as his name was now generally spelled) said Ah Tung was not a member of the society and would be buried in a separate plot.[15]

The Chinese had a fear of death and left their funerals to a man named Kennedy, on Pearl Street, near Chatham. Seated on the foot of one coffin with his feet propped on the head of another, Kennedy was a fount of exotica:

> Chinamen don't go in for ostentatious funerals, but they have a cheap, respectable affair. Now the society Ene E Jong has raised $200 to bury this man. His funeral won't cost more than $60 or $70—a hearse and four or five carriages—and I'm blessed if I know what they mean to do with the rest of the money. The Chinamen always have plenty of money and in flush times they are good for any amount they say they will pay. They are honest too. I've trusted them for as much as $150 and they never failed to pay what they agreed to. Twice a couple of Chinamen tried to cheat me a little, but that's the only time I ever had any trouble with 'em. They haven't any priest here that I know of, but the burial service has been said three or four times over dead Chinamen at the Five Points Mission.[16]

The funeral was on February 4, with the streets crowded with idlers anxious to get a glimpse of the procession. Instead of Acong, the president of Ene E Jong was now identified as Ah Sing. It was he who went with the coffin to New York Bay cemetery, two miles south of Jersey City.

Ah Sing was the John Assing who had studied at the House of Industry Chinese School in 1870

46 Winslow Homer pandered to the cliché of opium smoking as central to Chinese life.

and later operated the boardinghouse at 13 Mott mentioned by the *Times* reporter in his 1873 tour of the colony. Assing, now about 50, was married to an Irish woman and the father of a son. He was now also the landlord of the boardinghouse at 66 Cherry Street once operated by Acong. (His name was also spelled as Acomb. To avoid confusion, Acong is used here throughout.)

Acong's once-promising career had been destroyed by opium. His three children had died and he was almost blind—just able to distinguish light from dark. In August 1878, still only forty-four, Acong and three men were arrested in Chatham Square for selling cigars without the revenue stamp. They were put in a cell in the Tombs and began to suffer withdrawal pains. Several reporters who knew Acong's history visited him there. He begged them to go to an address on Baxter Street to buy opium, giving them a thimble and saying the dealer would recognize it and furnish the drug. (Addicts had individual cups, about the size of a thimble, crafted to measure a quantity of opium paste.) Apparently it was the same establishment visited by the *Times* reporter in 1873. Now it was described as "a squalid little room," where the dealer lay "on a bunk covered with China grass matting and smoking opium from a magnificent-looking pipe made of curious wood." The dealer's name was Ah Que, "lean, saturnine with yellow jaundiced eye and skin like parchment." At first, he denied knowledge of Acong, but he recognized the thimble and filled it from a small earthen jar. He also filled a small wooden box with opium for the other two men, charging thirty cents for the lot. A "stout, almost comely Irish woman, about twenty-five," stood in the doorway between the inner and outer apartments:

> She spoke familiarly, at times in a mandatory way, to the opium seller and was evidently Mrs. Ah Que....Two other Chinese lay with their legs crooked up on a bunk. One was aged, the other young. The older, when asked by the reporter to send word of Acong's arrest to his wife, said he didn't know him nor the wife. But Mrs. Ah Que promptly replied, "Yes, you do; you know Kitty, Acong's Kitty." "Yeh," he grunted, "Chelly Street."

The reporters took the opium to the prisoners, who dipped match sticks into it and greedily licked them off. Acong was never heard of again.[17]

 # Hysteria and Exclusion

Before the Civil War, Mott Street was "the Irish Broadway" and Transfiguration church at Mott and Park was the nucleus of "the most flourishing Irish parish on the American continent." The low stone church was built by Episcopalians. When they moved uptown, it was bought by the Irish, who opened it for worship in May 1853. A school was added in 1856 and then a belfry tower with a clock. In 1867 the church was redecorated and an altar of Italian marble was installed. In 1871 Tammany boss "Honest John" Kelly donated a bell for the tower. As successor to the flagrantly corrupt Boss Tweed, "Honest John" was also corrupt but more discreet.[1]

When the rich Irish followed the Episcopalians uptown, their homes were divided into stores and apartments and rented out to Chinese. However, there was no marked increase of Chinese in the city until 1879, when a *Sun* reporter noted that the number of Chinese laundries in Manhattan had increased within six months from fewer than twenty to at least two hundred.[2]

A report earlier that year on Chinese laundries in New York served as the text for a poisonous Congressional diatribe against Chinese immigration. Senator Lafayette Grover of Oregon quoted a newspaper report that Chinese washermen in New York had "organized a large system of washhouses and there are indications that they all belong to one company. The style of their signboards in the various streets and avenues is as uniform as those of tea stores." Grover waxed eloquent:

> The Chinaman has a very mole-like fashion of creeping into business and capturing it after creeping in....This means that before long twenty thousand washerwomen are to be without employment and that fifty thousand children are to cry for bread in the streets of our great metropolis. They will next attack a New England village. I think I see that village now—a little city, with its two thousand happy homes, and its ten thousand happy people. It sits peacefully upon its irregular hillsides, with its shaded lawns and streets, fronted by a clear river furnishing

47 Chinese laundrymen were in the East in about 1875, the date of this imagined scene in Philadelphia.

motive power for its many factories....Go there and find busy men, women, and children, all engaged in those manufactures which are even now rivaling the best skills of Europe in the struggle for the mastery of the world's commerce....The Mongolian comes. The capitalist can have his services for less money than before paid, and he is installed in full possession of all the mills. The thousands of American operatives are discharged. They struggle for a while against hope to establish some other employment with indifferent success. Property depreciates, mortgages carry away titles to homes for little or nothing, and the owner is homeless. The paint fades from the once bright walls and fences of the doomed city; glass is broken from tenantless houses; Christian churches are turned into heathen temples and homes for idols. The men of sciences are gone, the men of the professions are gone, the happy families are gone. The music and song that once swelled out upon the evening air are hushed and in their place comes the harsh chatter of the Asiatic and the discord of his gong and strings. This is the deserted village, once living, now dead![3]

The new arrivals in New York were fleeing oppression in California. In 1877, when San Francisco's City Hall was being built, the unemployed and disaffected gathered on the nearby sandlots to hear stump speakers call for such things as an eight-hour day and nationalization of the railroads. No one paid much attention until a hot afternoon in July, when members of a new "Anti-Coolie Club" enticed part of the crowd away with demands for immediate action. The resulting riot spread over two nights, with Chinese-occupied buildings burned, several Chinese murdered, and many more beaten. A month later, a sailor-turned-drayman named Denis Kearney emerged as mob leader with the slogan, "The Chinese Must Go." The Chinese took him at his word and moved east for their safety. When a group of Chinese wearing loose, flowing trousers, blouses, and wooden-soled slippers were seen at the Erie Railroad station in Jersey City, a *Herald* headline proclaimed:

MONGOLIAN REFUGEES
THOUSANDS COMING

Breathlessly, a reporter told of a mysterious "Mrs. Timothy Sergeant, daughter of Don Juan D'Alvardo, one of the first Mexican governors of California," who was said to be directing the traffic from her home on 25th Street.[4] Closer

41

48 Demonstrations at San Francisco's sand lots.

examination disclosed that the newcomers were twenty or thirty men taking advantage of a fare war between the Central Pacific Railroad and the Pacific Mail Steamship Company. The railroad had reduced its fare to thirty-five dollars for the period when the steamer was taking on passengers, making it a good time for the Chinese to "turn their backs on the city of Kearney and shake the dust of sandlots from their pigtails." James Baptiste, now living at 11 Mott, assured a reporter there was no threat of cheap labor, explaining that Chinese cigar workers at factories on Maiden Lane and John Street demanded fifteen to sixteen dollars per thousand, where Germans would take eight or nine dollars. "Our people live well and dress as well as the foreign immigrants of the same class from Europe," he said.[5]

One of Kearney's malignant expressions was "moon-eyed lepers." When a report spread of a Chinese with leprosy at 45 Mott, a Board of Health doctor was summoned and found Wong Gan, the owner of a Maiden Lane cigar factory, with swelling on his face and hands. More doctors were called and diagnosed the swelling as some other ailment. Sam Weeks, who had lived

on Mott Street all of his seventy-nine years, and who owned several houses on Mott and Pell streets, including number 45, told a reporter that Wong Gan had been under treatment for several months and blamed the rumor on "some malicious persons." (Still, the rumors did not deter a half dozen men and women "including several ladies from Madison Avenue and other fashionable uptown quarters" from descending on Mott Street looking for Chinese servants. They could not find an employment service and left disappointed.")[6]

TOM LEE AND GAMBLING

Immigration and other movements of Chinese were never haphazard. After the first pioneers, others followed from the same district, speaking the same dialect. This ensured some form of reception organization would be in place. In New York this took the form of Tom Lee, who would symbolize New York's Chinatown for the next forty years. In August 1878 Lee signaled his authority with what a reporter called "One of the most unique dinners ever given in New York." Lee, dressed in a black broadcloth suit and wear-

49 THE MEDIA-MANUFACTURED "INVASION" OF CHINESE FLEEING KEARNEY'S DEMAGOGUERY.

ing a high silk hat, met attorney Edmund Price and others at the top of his stoop at 2 Mott Street and showed them into a room with "Home Sweet Home" and "Remember Me" on the walls. The table was set with silver, snowy napkins, and fresh roses. Servants included two American girls as well as Chinese men.

The cook, Domingo "Mingo" DeLuce, was a Macao Chinese who normally cooked at a boardinghouse for sailors on Baxter street. It was run by another Macao Chinese named Cruz, who claimed to speak Chinese, Japanese, Javanese, Filipino, Cochinese, Korean, Hindustani, English, French, Spanish, Portuguese, and

50 TOM LEE'S COMBINED HOME AND HEADQUARTERS OF THE LUNG GEE TONG AT 4 MOTT. A FORMER PRIVATE RESIDENCE HAS BEEN JERRY-RIGGED AS A HOME, STORE, RESTAURANT, AND POLITICAL HEADQUARTERS. THE KITCHEN HAS A BRICK BAFFLE AGAINST THE HEAT OF THE COAL-FIRED STOVE.

Dutch. DeLuce, befitting a chef at this Berlitz of boarding houses, bragged that he cooked in all languages, demonstrating his skill with a menu of suckling pig with bird's-nest sauce, roast chicken with sweet stuffing, dried oysters, fish, imported mushroom, plums, fricasseed chicken, duck, and potted pigeon. The guests drank champagne and rice brandy and Lee entertained by playing two Chinese musical instruments.[7]

Tom Lee was born Wong Ah Ling in either 1837 or 1841. He had been a labor contractor—a lucrative occupation—in California and then moved to St. Louis, where he was in the cooperage business, and where he was naturalized in 1876, using the name Thomas Ling Lee. After a visit to China using an American passport, he became a

merchant in Philadelphia. He settled in New York in 1878, returning to Philadelphia briefly in 1879 to marry a German woman, Elsie Kaylor.[8]

In early accounts of the Chinese in New York, there are frequent references to mah jong and card games, but never organized gambling. This changed with the advent of Tom Lee. In March 1879 Captain Brogan of the Sixth Precinct noticed heavy traffic at "Ah Wong's" grocery and apothecary at 13 Mott. He massed forty-five patrolmen and two detectives and led them into a back room, where a number of Chinese were discovered seated or standing around a fan-tan table, the most popular form of organized gambling among Chinese at home or abroad. The arrested men spent the night at the Tombs.

44

Lawyer Price—wearing his trademark ten-carat diamond ring—arrived the next morning and explained that Ah Wang was a doctor and not the proprietor of the room. As for gambling, Price said it was only a social gathering. The police showed little, round brass objects with square holes and a number of buttons and other implements, but admitted they had not seen any money on the table. A complacent judge dismissed the charges and the Chinese shook Price's hand and they all left smiling.[9]

In February 1879 Tom Lee, now identified as "the President of the Chinese Society of this city," gave another dinner with an "enormous menu, almost entirely American in style." Guests included lawyer Price and four others prominent in Democratic Party politics. A year later, the New York State Supreme Court accepted articles of incorporation for an organization whose name was given as the "Long We Tong Eng Wi," interpreted as "The Order and Brotherhood of Masons." In a separate action in the local Court of Common Pleas, Thomas Ling Lee changed his name to Tom Lee and was simultaneously appointed as a deputy sheriff. Thereafter he flaunted his rank among Tammany's ethnic faithful by displaying a large gold badge. When the articles of incorporation were later filed in Albany, the trustees were given as Wang A. Ling, James A. Baptiste, Domingo DeLuce, Wang Gee, and Tom Gee.[10]

The Lun Gee Tong—as it was more generally known—opened headquarters at 4 Mott, where it flew a red flag with a device described as a "white rising sun with large rays streaming upward."[11]

It was a lodge of the Triads, who took their name from a Buddhist term expressing the unity of Heaven, Earth, and Man and traced themselves to five Buddhist monks who scattered after the defeat of the Ming dynasty in the seventeenth century and vowed to wait for a time

51 Popular magazines legitimated newspaper scare stories of Chinese using opium to seduce young women. Pell Street, lower left, shows the elevated train on the Bowery. The Mott Street steeple, right, is Transfiguration church.

45

to revolt against the successor Manchu (Qing) dynasty. The Triads had many names, including Freemasons, a misidentification of European Freemasonry that originated in the early 1800s in Southeast Asia, when Europeans saw a similarity between their own society of Masons—with its sworn brotherhood, ritual humiliation of new members, and threats if secrets were disclosed—and groups the Chinese called Triads. The Triads happily accepted this new disguise.[12]

Stewart Culin, the early ethnologist of Chinese communities in New York and Philadelphia, used the name *I Hing* or "Patriotic Rising" for the Triads and estimated that nearly two-thirds of the Chinese in the United States were members. He said the I Hing was known in New York as the *Lun I Tong*, or "Hall of United Patriotism." ("Patriotism" refers to their claim to represent nationalist, anti-Manchu sentiments.)[13]

With a gold-shield-toting "mayor," and American lawyers to buy the favors of a corrupt political and police establishment, Chinatown was ready to welcome refugees from Kearney's mobs.

In 1880 following the headlines proclaiming an invasion of "Mongolians," a *Times* reporter set out to discover what the fuss was about. Walking south from (the original) St. Patrick's Cathedral on Prince Street, he passed "bucket shops," and "big brick boxes" of tenements "divided inside into smaller brick boxes." One, "with filth hanging out of windows like icicles," was "filled with Germans, Jews, and Italians" working as shoemakers, tailors, cigar makers, and at other trades. Finally, he reached "what has come to be known as Chinatown: The lower two or three hundred yards of Mott Street emptying into Chatham Square. A visitor expecting to see much of the Oriental business—pagodas and temples, walking merchants with strings of rats—will be disappointed. [There are] no dragon wings on the floor or serpents tails disappearing beneath beds."

No reporter worth space rates would walk away with a statement that there was no story. A helpful detective from the Sixth Precinct led him to Baxter Street, through a narrow alley to a little court, to a low, brick building "swarming with people [and] shutters hanging crooked," down three wooden steps, and into a room for the now-cliché description of preparation and smoking of opium.[14]

A *Sun* reporter looked beyond gambling and opium rooms to describe the evolving fragment of a Chinese market town and entertainment center. He visited the Poolon Kongsi at 34 Mott:

There are an infinity of diminutive paste-board boxes filled with Chinese medicines—gigantic pills, roots, herbs, barks, seeds, and such like. There are incense sticks, jade bracelets, strange evolutions of Celestial fancy in the way of ornamentation, like glorified valentines; quaint and pretty tea services; dried sharks fins, looking like mangled strips of amber-tinted glue; ducks split, baked in peanut oil and flattened out dry so as to look like strange caricatures of dragons; sweetmeats in infinite variety; nuts that nobody but a Chinaman knows the names of; dried mushrooms; opium and pipes to smoke it; tobacco; teas of many kinds, some of them exquisite and much more expensive than any American store sells; silks; fungus-looking lumps of which it is guaranteed that a small bit will make the drunkest man immediately sober; sandals and Chinese clothing.

All this was crammed into the front and back parlor of an old private house. A little open space in the center of the store was just enough for three or four customers. For their convenience, a pot of tea and a number of small cups rested on a little table near the window. The Chinese never drank unboiled water. The proprietor, Wong Acton, popularly known as Wo Kee—round-faced with a slight moustache, always courteous, adding sums on his abacus, making entries in his account books with a camel's hair brush, and weighing purchases on various scales, including an ivory-and-thread balance for the minute quantities of opium in constant demand—sat behind a little desk.

The reporter had been told of an organization "down the street" called the Sam Hop Hui (another Triad name). Wo Kee said it was the same as the Freemasons. When the reporter demurred, he and his clerk, Quong Lee, insisted it was the same: "Both blood brotherhood, both secular, both mechanic, not real mechanic but ideal mechanic."

The reporter found "the apparent influx of Chinamen" exaggerated:

The great obstacle...is the difficulty they have of procuring buildings for habitations and business purposes in any desirable part of town....The lower end of Mott Street is an unsavory locality, disagreeably close to the associations of vice, crime, and poverty by reason of which the Chinese are unjustly but naturally compelled by mere proximity to bear a worse reputation than they deserve. Yet even here landlords, especially Irish property owners, are becoming more and more unwilling to rent houses to them.

Quong Lee, "who gets along splendidly with English," was indignant about proposals then being mooted to exclude the Chinese and deny citizenship to those already here: "There are nearly two thousand Chinamen now in New York and as many more in Jersey City and Brooklyn; but how seldom do you hear of one committing even the smallest offense against society. When they come before your courts it is as victims, not as aggressors."[15]

Just as the Chinese were settling on Mott Street, it appeared they would be swept away. Sam Weeks said the Rutgers Fire Company had refused a Chinese offer to rent a vacant house at 3 Mott for a thousand dollars a year. He quoted an official as saying the company would "sooner tear the house down than allow a single Chinese in." Weeks said the owner of a house further north on Mott—beyond Pell—had refused sixty dollars a month for two small, cramped houses.[16]

At first the Irish were blamed. They were said to complain "they had to cut their way through an army of heathen" on their way to Sunday mass at Transfiguration church. As it turned out, the source was the United Christian Brethren of the Moravian Church. They owned the buildings from 24 to 38 Mott and another around the corner on Pell. They wanted to sell them and thought they would get a better price if they first cleared them of Chinese tenants. They ordered the eviction of those Chinese whose leases had expired and specified that new leases must include a clause forbidding subleasing to Chinese and blacks. Wo Kee moved his shop a few steps away to 105 Park, by the side of Transfiguration church, and awaited better times.[17]

There was another scare a few years later. James Barry, a new assistant pastor of the church, organized the Young Catholics Association to fight—he claimed—the surrounding sin. In May 1883, after one member had his sister arrested for consorting with Chinese gamblers, Barry stationed his troops on rooftops and in the streets to gather evidence and summoned reporters to investigate for themselves. A *Herald* reporter did—or at least pretended he did. The headline over his story shouted:

HORRORS OF
THE OPIUM DENS

…In one den in Pell Street, which is conducted by a hag of the most depraved type, there have been girls of from ten to twenty years of age ruined. In a murky backroom, up a still murkier flight of stairs, is the den where the front room serves as a sort of parlor. Here it is that little girls are induced to first taste of the fell drug which is introduced to pave the way to worse sin. The victim is coaxed upstairs by one who knows her and once in among the haggard, slatternly young creatures who have already been wrecked, they are induced to try a pipe.[18]

The balloon was soon punctured. The arrested girl proved to be eighteen, not fifteen, and agreed to accept help and counseling.[19] An official of the Society for the Prevention of Cruelty to Children called it "newspaper buncombe," adding: "If these little girls smoke opium and do other things that are imputed to them, they do what their companions do elsewhere. I believe that they tempt the Chinamen to immorality as often as they are tempted."[20]

Thomas Lynch, the church's pastor, said he had been there eighteen months and "not a single instance of the ruin of a young girl by a Chinese had come to his note." He objected to "the stirring up of a race prejudice," and, while conceding there was prostitution among the Chinese, said they they were no more immoral than Christians.[21]

THE EXCLUSION ACT

All the while, Congress debated barring Chinese immigration. The Constitution originally limited citizenship to "white" persons. It was amended after the Civil War to include "persons of African nativity or African descent." Left undecided was the meaning of "white." Was it meant to exclude persons of all hues or only former slaves and other blacks?

And who had the right to decide on citizenship? Could the states enroll citizens or was this the exclusive right of the federal government? California and other western states denied citizenship to the Chinese but they continued to be enrolled in New York and other eastern states. The Democratic Party in New York was built on the wholesale distribution of citizenship to immigrants on the eve of elections.

Federal courts tended to diminish state's rights. In July 1878 Justice William Choate of the United States Circuit Court in New York ruled on an application for naturalization by a Chinese who called himself Charles Miller. He was forty-six, married to a woman of Irish descent, and had been a resident of New York for twenty-eight years, during which time he had amassed considerable property. Along with citizenship, there was the parallel question of who could own land. Miller said he wanted to be a citizen because, according to law, when a foreigner died in New York, his property escheated to the state. Nominally, the law was a dead letter. Every year, the legislature relinquished without debate the state's rights to such property. Nevertheless, the law was on the books and a non-citizen could never be sure his children would inherit his property. Justice Choate denied the application, saying he was guided by a decision of Justice Lorenzo Sawyer of the Circuit Court in California, who had denied citizenship to an applicant named Ah Yup on the grounds he was not white and not of African descent.[22]

Local courts tended to defend state's rights. In November Judge Peter Larremore of the state Court of Common Pleas granted citizenship to Wong Ah Yee, a Baxter Street cigar maker who had lived in New York for six years, during which he married an Irish woman in a ceremony at Transfiguration church and filed his declaration of intention to become a citizen. Larremore explained he granted citizenship to Wong Ah Yee because he wanted the law clarified: "If Negroes are admitted, and all other foreigners, I don't know upon what ground we could put a refusal to Chinamen. The constitution provides for no other classes of color than white or black and I hold that Chinamen must come within one or the other."

To celebrate his victory, Wong Ah Yee and other citizens met for a Thanksgiving Day turkey dinner at Thomas Ah Yee's restaurant at 20 Mott. (The turkey was cut into bits to be eaten with chopsticks.) Among those present was John Ah Woh (the assumed Civil War veteran), who showed a citizenship certificate from 1863 and said he had voted every year since, and Tom Lee, here identified as "Ah Ling." Another guest was William Assing, the eldest son of John Assing, who had succeeded Acong as head of the Ene E Jong burial society.[23]

(In 1884 William Assing would become the first Chinese American policeman. He was assigned to the Fourth Precinct and made his first arrest in September, taking John Haley of 25 Cherry street to the Tombs on a charge of public intoxication. Reporters would find this amusing: A half-Chinese officer arresting an Irishman on a drunk charge. Apparently, Assing did not remain a policeman. It was recalled many years later that the first Chinese policeman had retired in the 1890s to "engage in the trucking business.")[24]

A few months later, Larremore naturalized Charles Wing, a cigar maker who lived in a rear tenement at 49 Bayard Street. Wing said he left China when he was sixteen, lived in Havana for a year, and then came to New York, where he studied English at night and became Christian, attending Seaman's Church on Madison Street.[25]

The exclusionists lost the first round. In March 1879 President Hayes vetoed a bill to restrict Chinese immigration, saying it contra-

vened the Burlingame Treaty of 1868 that stipulated free travel between the United States and China. (The clause was designed to allow free entry of missionaries into China.)

The debate went on. As noted earlier, when the Chinese were brought to Belleville in 1871, Mr. and Mrs. Stephen Baldwin were on home leave from their mission in China. Their preaching inspired the first Sunday Schools for the

A WORD OF CAUTION TO OUR FRIENDS, THE CIGAR-MAKERS.
Through the smoke it is easy to see the approach of Chinese cheap labor.

52 A CARTOONIST IN *LESLIE'S ILLUSTRATED* PRESENTED THE ISSUE AS ONE OF PROTECTING "WHITE" (MEANING ETHNIC EUROPEANS) FROM CHEAP "COOLIE" LABOR.

HARD TO PLEASE THE "WHITE TRASH."
U. S. "I hate the 'Nigger' because he is a citizen, and I hate the 'Yellow Dog' because he will not become one."

53 THOMAS NAST REPLIED IN 1878.

48

JUST SO.

Hoodlum. "'Tain't their color I mind s'much— (hic) it's their (hic) habits I 'bject to."

54 In March 1879, as debate in Congress grew louder, Frank Bellow, another *Harper's* artist, used satire to counter the charges of cheap "coolie" labor and degraded Chinese.

Chinese in New Jersey. The Baldwins returned to China and, after a total of eighteen years as missionaries, settled in New York. In an 1881 pamphlet, "Must the Chinese Go," Esther Baldwin argued that the Chinese were from farming families, the same class as immigrants from other lands, and that there was no danger of an inpouring of millions of Chinese because this was a local emmigration from a small part of China, and what Canton Chinese did had no influence on Chinese elsewhere in China. She asked:

> Did you ever see a drunken Chinaman, did you ever see a noisy, boisterous one on the streets, did you ever see one disturbing others or lounging at saloons or gossiping, did you ever see one on the street who did not seem to have some object in view and to be going right toward it? Has a Chinese tramp ever come to your door? Do you hear of them committing murder, burglaries, or other crimes against our laws?[26]

Protestants were whispering in a storm. A New York City Democrat, Representative Rosewell Pettibone Flower, was a typical speaker during the 1882 Congressional debate: "Shall we protect our labor, or shall we allow it to be degraded to the coolie standard?.. His rice, rats, and clothes ...are his items of expenditure and cost him almost nothing....Not like the European immigrant, who brings us wealth and love of liberty, he comes to take wealth away, and to stamp upon labor the servile characteristics of his race."[27]

Flower, a wealthy banker, was later elected Governor of New York. With the support of such elite eastern Democrats, restricting Chinese immigration was inevitable.

A new treaty was negotiated giving the United States the right to regulate the flow of Chinese laborers but "not absolutely prohibit it." Congress ratified it in 1881 and passed a bill to suspend immigration for twenty years. President Arthur, who succeeded after Garfield's assassination, vetoed the bill on the grounds that a twenty-year period was the equivalent of prohibition. Congress then approved a revised Exclusion Act, limiting it to a period of ten years, which President Arthur signed in 1882. Immigrants were specifically denied the right of citizenship, and hence the right to vote, and Chinese already in the country were forced to obtain residence certificates—in effect, internal passports.[28]

HOW THE CHINAMAN MIGHT GAIN FAVOR.

55 In April 1879, a third *Harper's* artist presented a Chinese pretending to be Irish, complete with a whiskey bottle and shillelagh. This reversed the 1854 *Yankee Notions* drawing of an Irishman imitating a Chinese, reflecting a persistent linkage of Chinese and Irish stereotypes.

"EVERY DOG" (NO DISTINCTION OF COLOR) "HAS HIS DAY."

RED GENTLEMAN TO YELLOW GENTLEMAN. "Pale face 'fraid you crowd him out, as he did me."

56 THE ISSUE OF EQUALITY BECAME A PERSONAL CRUSADE FOR THOMAS NAST. IN FEBRUARY 1879, HE SKETCHED A CHINESE AND AN INDIAN BEFORE A WALL OF SLOGANS FROM THE ANTI-CHINESE CAMPAIGN IN CALIFORNIA.

Which Color Is To Be Tabooed Next?

FRITZ (to Pat). "If the Yankee Congress can keep the *yellow* man out, what is to hinder them from calling us *green* and keeping us out too?"

57 IN MARCH 1882, NAST CALLED ATTENTION TO A BROADER PRINCIPLE: WHERE WOULD RESTRICTIONS END? ALTHOUGH THE IRISH AND GERMANS WERE NOT THREATENED, HIS FEAR WAS CORRECT. EXCLUSION WAS SOON EXTENDED TO ALL ASIANS. THEN THE VOCABULARY OF DISCRIMINATION THAT HAD BEEN PERFECTED AGAINST THE CHINESE WAS EMPLOYED TO OBTAIN PASSAGE OF THE IMMIGRATION ACT OF 1924: VIRTUAL EXCLUSIONARY QUOTAS WERE APPLIED AGAINST ITALIANS, GREEKS, AND OTHER SOUTH EUROPEAN "LESSER BREEDS."

E Pluribus Unum (Except the Chinese).

58 A MONTH LATER, HE REPEATED WHAT HE HAD BEEN SAYING FOR MORE THAN TEN YEARS: AMERICA MEANT EQUALITY FOR ALL.

(Dis-) "Honors Are Easy."
Now both parties have something to hang on.

59 THROUGHOUT, NAST HAD PICTURED THE REPUBLICAN PARTY AS A DEFENDER OF EQUAL RIGHTS. WHEN REPUBLICANS JOINED DEMOCRATS IN APPROVING THE FINAL TEN-YEAR EXCLUSION BILL, HE EXPRESSED HIS BITTER SENSE OF BETRAYAL.

51

Wong Chin Foo

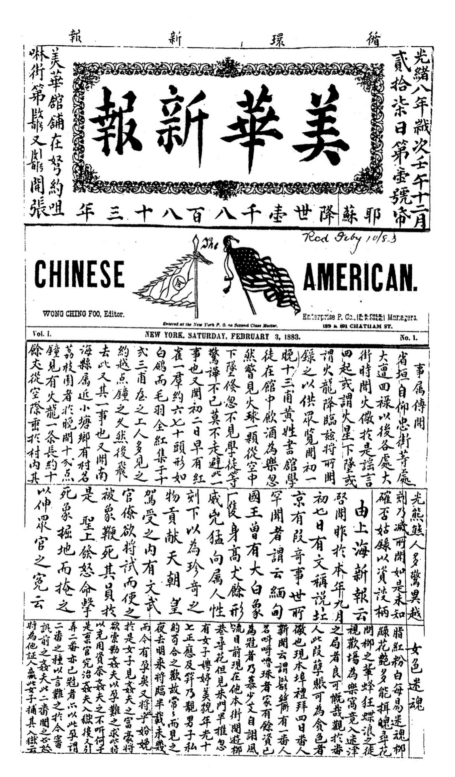

60 Wong Chin Foo was the first to use the phrase "Chinese American." His name, in this first page of the first addition of his newspaper, is spelled Wong Ching Foo, which is the correct transliteration of his name in Chinese. However, he was always known as Wong Chin Foo and signed his name that way.

The first Chinese-language newspaper published in New York was a weekly, the *Chinese American*. Its appearance in February 1883 was a novelty sufficient to rate a brief notice in the far-off *Times* of London, which said it would be photolithographed with an initial circulation of eight thousand copies.[1] The paper survived only nine months.

Its editor and publisher was Wong Chin Foo, who first came to public notice in San Francisco in about 1873, when he was involved in a disturbance at a shoe factory. He had tried to get a promotion for a Chinese worker. Somehow the editorial writer of the *New York Times* learned of Wong's earlier history:

> Some eight years ago, his bright, handsome face and engaging manners won the admiration of an American lady philanthropist who, having procured leave for him to go abroad to be educated at her expense, sent him to the United States. Here he entered upon his studies with a zeal that pleased and astonished his teachers. He went through a preliminary course of instruction at Washington and subsequently graduated with honors at a Pennsylvania college....In four years he declared that he accomplished all he desired and set out for San Francisco, homeward bound....He traveled about from place to place, delivering addresses, full of information on subjects so entirely new to his hearers, and so much at variance with their notions of life, as to speedily cause him to become an object of concern and distrust to government officials.

Wong, the editorial continued, formed a secret society, the *Tung Shang Whey*, which had as its object the "abolition of opium orgies, the propagation of the better social customs of America, and the elevation of the masses." When the government ordered it suppressed, "Mr. Foo's co-laborers were all captured and tortured to death, and he himself would have shared the same fate, had it not been for the extraordinary swiftness of foot he displayed in getting beyond the reach of his would-be executioners." Then, with the aid of "foreign Consuls at one of the sea-ports," he sailed back to San Francisco.[2]

A year later the *Times* published a letter from Wong concerning the ill-treatment of a "coolie" who had escaped to Boston from a Cuban sugar plantation. Wong said he did not like "to lower my country in the estimation of other nations" but felt compelled to tell the truth: "The whole government is in the hands of shrewd and unscrupulous speculators who plunder the people without a shadow of law or justice, and

crush them with the iron heel of a relentless despotism."[3]

By then he had become a lecturer on Chinese culture and religion, attempting to correct—as he saw it—errors propagated by Christian missionaries. In April 1877 a reporter in Chicago covered his lecture and sent a story to the *World* in New York:

> He is of very small stature, smaller even than the average Chinese, and as slender and graceful as a woman. His face is somewhat angular in outline, after the national characteristic, but his eyes are large and level and sparkling with intelligence. His mouth is rather large and mobile, displaying teeth of dazzling whiteness. His hair is short, excepting at the back, where it is brushed in the customary queue. He wore a black skull cap of lusterless silk, a black velvet coat and waistcoat, black silk petticoat, white socks, ,and gaily colored embroidered shoes and soles an inch thick.

61 WONG CHIN FOO, FROM A PHOTOGRAPH IN 1877.

The story he told the *World* varied from the one that formed the basis of the *Times* editorial in 1873. Wong said his father was a commoner who, through merit, had raised himself to a "fair position" in the army and was able to educate his son in a private school in Shanghai. He said he was sent to the United States in 1868, then returned to China in 1869 and was "appointed by the Emperor as interpreter in the imperial court." He claimed his anti-opium society had no political opinions but nevertheless was suppressed in 1874. He escaped, wandered for weeks in swamps, and made his way to an English missionary station in Hong Kong. When he told the missionaries who he was, he was locked up and the authorities were notified. He escaped and found passage on a ship "where slave dealers had two hundred women in steerage." He claimed to have obtained their freedom, when the vessel arrived in San Francisco, with the help of Otis Gibson, then the best-known Christian missionary among the Chinese. Together they raised money to send the women back to China, for which, said Wong, a price of fifteen-hundred dollars was put on his head and he had to flee the city.[4]

Wong's next lecture was in New York, where he met Madame H. P. Blavatsky, the founder of the Theosophy movement, whose book—*Isis*—had just been published. It was a case of like meeting like: both needed whatever publicity they could garner. Madame Blavatsky invited reporters to her apartment on West 47th Street to meet "the native missionary who has been announced as being on the errand of converting the forty million Christians of this country to Buddhism."[5]

She called her living room "The Lamasery." In addition to the usual potpourri of palms, bearskin rugs, and statues on pedestals, a tiger's head was mounted over one door, a stuffed crocodile swung from the ceiling, and a stuffed bat with outstretched wings was displayed over another door. There was also a stuffed owl, a stuffed baboon, stuffed lizards and snakes, and a suit of armor. One wall was decorated as a jungle, with a cardboard elephant and tiger staring out from dried leaves. Scattered about were strange symbols and mystic triangles. Madame Blavatsky, smoking a cigarette at the end of a long holder, was seated on a large armchair in the center of the room. Wong Chin Foo blended nicely, with his dark silk and velvet clothing, embroidered boots, and with a large gold chain around his neck.

Interviewed by a *Times* reporter, he denied he had come as a Buddhist missionary, saying he merely wanted to disabuse Americans of gross errors regarding China. He took the opportunity to embellish his adventurous past. The fifteen-hundred dollars price on his head, he now said, was imposed not by disgruntled slave dealers in San Francisco but by the Chinese government. When he fled to Hong Kong, he went to English missionaries for shelter:

> Those pious men told him at first that they were his friends and would protect him, but on finding out who he was announced that they must give him up to the Emperor, although they knew he would be tortured in the most horrible manner and be cut into eighteen pieces. They said, however, that they would get his sentence reduced to simple decapitation and then left him in a room of the mission after locking the doors and windows and telling him to "put his trust in Jesus."[6]

A week later, calling him "the enthusiastic young Chinese who was educated at Harvard College some years ago," the *Herald* reported his lecture before an audience of six hundred at Steinway Hall:

> He spoke with great earnestness, and at times had to pause from sheer breathlessness. He had occasionally to stop a moment to recall a word, but as a rule his speech was remarkably fluent. The only gestures he made were with his left arm, and they were simple and graceful. "I never knew," he said, "that puppies were good to eat until I was told by American people" (laughter). If mistakes were entertained here about such simple matters as the diet of the Chinese, he argued, that much greater errors of belief would prevail in respect to their religion and other abstruse matters....God, he claimed, had given to every race of men a system of revelation according to their peculiar wants and their peculiar nature, and the practice of sending out missionaries to other nations only ended to confound matters in religion....He contended that Buddhism did not teach that the soul is annihilated and quoted from the Bible in support of his declaration that Christ wanted men not to believe in his name merely, but to do good deeds. Confucianism and Buddhism taught the same doctrine; so that a man who lived up to the doctrines of either of these would lead just such a life as would a good Christian.[7]

Harper's Weekly commented: "If Mr. Wong Chin Foo had taken the pains to inquire into the real condition of American ideas respecting China and the Chinese, he would have discovered that he has no occasion to be quite so

THE IDES OF MARCH.
DON'T—PUT HIM OUT OF HIS MISERY.

62 DENIS KEARNEY WAS SOON DISCREDITED. WHEN HE COMPLAINED THAT, LIKE CAESAR, HE WAS BEING STABBED IN THE BACK, THIS WAS THOMAS NAST'S COMMENT.

smart and flippant in his criticisms. But some of his points were well made and deserving of consideration."[8]

Wong returned to Chicago. In a few years the novelty of a quaintly dressed Chinese lecturing—and hectoring—Americans on matters religious ran its course. Wong came back to New York, where, "persuaded that I was the coming journalist of the Occident and Orient alike," he began publication of the *Chinese American*.[9]

As an English-speaking Chinese in an office a few blocks from newspaper row, Wong was a ready source for comment—often flippant—on Chinese affairs in New York. Anti-Chinese would-be labor organizer Denis Kearney came to the city in 1883, by which time he had long been dismissed as a mere publicity-seeker. Kearney's request to speak to the Central Labor Union was refused on the ground that he did not represent any union. When the city administration refused him permission to speak in Union Square, Kearney had to pay seventy-five dollars of his own money to hire Cooper Institute Hall on Astor Place.

Wong challenged Kearney to a duel to the death. When a reporter, who found him smoking a cigar in the office of the *Chinese American*, asked what weapons he would suggest, Wong replied: "I give him his choice of chopsticks, Irish potatoes, or Krupp guns." Kearney dismissed the challenge, telling reporters he had weightier matters to discuss, such as the evils of capitalists, railroad trusts, and assorted newspaper publishers: "I'm not to be deterred from this work by the low blackguard vaporings of Chin Foo, Ah Coon, Kee Yah, Hung Fat, Fi Fong, or any other representative of Asia's almond-eyed lepers."

Nevertheless, in his speech that night, Kearney included Wong Chin Foo in his denunciation of publishers.[10]

Wong enjoyed such fencing. He next took on the rat-eating shibboleth. A *Times* story in August 1883 began:

> Do the Chinese eat rats? This has always been a mooted question. Geographies contain the assertion that they do, and an old woodcut of a Chinaman peddling rodents strung up by their tails to a rack which he carried on his shoulders, is a standard illustration of the common school atlases of ten years ago. A large portion of the community believe implicitly that Chinamen love rats as Western people love poultry, and the small boy from time to time gives expression to the faith that is in him by occasionally shying one of the small deer into the shop of a patient laundryman.

A complaint had been filed by François Cepirio, who had just installed a restaurant and saloon in a new building at 155 Worth Street (replacing the Five Points House of Industry). To the rear was the backyard of a building at 5 Mott Street that served as a combination store, restaurant, and dormitory for the Quong clan. Cepirio objected to cooking smells coming through his rear windows and summoned Charles Kaemmerer, a former city sanitary inspector, to prepare a legal complaint. Kaemmerer said he looked into the other yard and "saw some Chinamen handling some things that looked like very small cats or very large rats."

For his part, Cepirio said his little son had seen two dead cats lying on a board in the kitchen near the window and had watched as a cook skinned the animals, cut off their heads, chopped their bodies into small pieces, and put them into a pot.

An official sanitary inspector visited the scene and found no cat or rat skins but only a cook preparing a dish of Chinese turnips, soft-shelled crabs, and pigs' ears. In his office in Chatham Square, Wong offered a five-hundred dollars reward for anyone who could prove the Chinese ate rats or cats. He admitted they might eat dogs and—in times of great famine—they ate anything to keep from starving, but there was no need to eat such things in New York since laundry hands received three dollars a day and board, and exceptionally good workmen got as much as five dollars and could afford to buy the best the market afforded.[11]

Wong—always alert to defend his identity and individuality—was once walking along Baxter Street when a merchant took his arm to pull him into a store. When Wong resisted, the shopkeeper struck him with a newspaper. Wong filed a complaint and the shopkeeper was sentenced to three months in jail.[12]

Wong Chin Foo's adventure as a publisher was a disaster. He said in an editorial note in the first edition that he hoped the paper would circulate among all Chinese living east of the Rockies, whose number he estimated at one-hundred thousand. There were fewer than ten thousand Chinese east of the Rockies, for whom he had printed an extravagant eight thousand copies of his first edition. He said his cashier ran off with what little money the edition returned. When he wrote about gambling and opium smoking in New York, some Chinese toughs invaded his office and beat up the staff. He also wrote incautious words about a local gambler and endured—and eventually lost—a long suit for libel.[13]

The paper failed, but Wong gained a powerful friend in Tom Lee. They were frequently seen together and Wong may have handled the Lun Gee Tong's English correspondence. He also made his living by writing detailed, factual articles on Chinese life in the city of New York in the 1880s and early 1890s, for which historians of New York in general and of the Chinese in particular may be grateful.

In August 1887 Wong Chin Foo—who had spent his life defending lost causes—reworked his lecture notes from the 1870s into a mock-serious article in the *North American Review* titled "Why I Am A Heathen."

"Love your neighbor as yourself," he summed up, "is the great divine law which Christians and

THE WAIL OF WONG CHIN FOO.

It is not necessary for me to remark that I was born in the Middle Empire, and that I am now an American citizen; for ever since my advent in this land of the free I have been systematically styled a "pig-tailed renegade," a "moon-eyed leper," a "demon of the Orient," a "gangrened laundryman," a "rat-eating Mongol," etc.

I started life as a lecturer, and, through my connection with a Literary Bureau, was very successful in purveying to the intellectual pleasures of Western Sunday-schools and Southern clubs. That they seldom asked me to come back and lecture again does not invalidate my statement; neither is it inconsistent with popularity when an enthusiastic audience welcomes a speaker with revolvers and shot-guns, and otherwise induces him to depart via a second-story window rather than the stairs. These are incidents in the life of every lecturer.

In an unguarded moment I listened to the voice of the tempter, and fell from my high estate. Persuaded that I was the coming journalist of the Occident and Orient alike, I came to New York City and started the *Chinese American*. I knew nothing of journalism save in a vague way, and went to work accordingly. I took an American partner and a Chinese one, engaged a city editor, a staff, and an artist.

The first issue, after many sleepless nights, appeared. I shall never forget it. It circulated fifty thousand copies, and brought in one thousand five hundred dollars.

That is, it brought in three hundred dollars cash, and one thousand two hundred dollars in notes, bills receivable, and promises. I have a hundred of the latter assorted, which I will sell at one cent on the dollar. I was proud of the issue until I had read the criticisms upon it in my E. C.s. The American E. C.s were contradictory in substance, but unanimous in their drift. The English articles were badly written, poorly thought and wretchedly printed; they were also splendidly written and composed, but displaying signs of some trained journalist, who was posing in my name. The editor, they said, was

a Chinese gentleman with more money than brains. He was also a myth and a joke. He was also a Jesuit, a Buddhist missionary, and an Imperial emissary in disguise. Then came the Chinese E. C.s. My native tongue, as I wrote it, was uncouth, illiterate, unintelligent, vapid, hollow, fantastic, bombastic and idiotic. I was a wretch who was endeavoring to ruin the Flowery Kingdom in the eyes of Christendom; I was a renegade, an apostle, and the victim of American gold.

I had written a moral screed against gambling and opium-smoking. The gamblers and joint-keepers invaded my office a week after, and proceeded to flog the associate editor, cashier, and city reporter. The trio did not wait for the end of the performance, but departed for the Empire the same day.

I heard from them at—Panama. They were intact; but the nine hundred and fifty dollars, my entire assets they had carried with them, were not.

I did not come out altogether unscathed. I was "knocked out" twice, arrested four times for criminal libel, once for civil libel, under twenty-five thousand dollars bail, locked up in Ludlow Street jail, and twice poisoned.

I think the paper would have succeeded, if I had had more experience—say a hundred years. But my artist, Jung Fan Tai, became a Bohemian and used too much beer in his designs. Chinese art does not present many differences to the civilized eye; but it does to the Mongolian connaisseur.

Jung's second sacred dragon contained a superfluous cocktail, and was denounced in Chinatown as blasphemy. The luckless draughtsman was thereupon put under the ban of ostracism, and in a fortnight had shaken the dust of Go-

—*I then came to New York and started the "Chinese American."*

tham from off his feet. My second cashier was a reporter in bad luck. I do not think he was dishonest; but when you miss your treasurer and treasury, and find the first paralyzed in a neighboring bar-room the next day, and don't find the second at all, it's high time for a head editor to kick. I kicked; but the reporter, with an indescribable oath, swore that no "almond-eyed double blank" could kick him with impunity, and in less time than it takes to tell it had converted me into a ghastly ruin.

My journalistic career culminated recently in the Supreme Court. I had, with the best intentions in the world, allowed an article to appear in my sheet which "showed up" a certain individual in a moderately sensational way.

The style was patented after that employed in many E. C.s, and contained such pleasing epithets as "assassins, cut-throats, viper, scorpion, thief, embezzler, robber, liar, and a member of the Young Men's Christian Association." In short, it was a thoroughly American article. Yet, an imbecile jury gave a verdict for the fellow against me in one thousand dollars. At present there is an order of arrest out for me, and a deputy-sheriff is watching my regular haunts.

It's the old story. I had the capital; now I haven't; but I have the experience. Any paper wishing the services of an experienced editor, who can write in every vein and on every subject, and create libel-suits, can obtain a gem by applying to

WONG CHIN FOO,
Care of PUCK.

—*When you find the treasurer paralyzed in a neighboring bar-room.*—

63 WONG JOKED OF HIS NEWSPAPER'S FAILURE FOR *PUCK* IN APRIL 1885. HE COULD FIGHT THE RAT-EATING SHIBBOLETH BUT, TO EARN A LIVING, HE HAD TO ACCEPT RIDICULE. THE WASH TUB, UPPER LEFT, IS PARTICULARLY CRUEL, IMPLYING CHINESE WRITERS ARE SIMPLY LAUNDRYMEN WITH INK.

THE DRAGON.

[*Contributed to* PUCK *by* WONG CHIN FOO, *the Eminent Chinese Littérateur Lord of the Ten Golden Pagodas and Mandarin of the Full Moons.*

(*Moonlight and Music.*)
Moon-faced gal on balcony floor
See young fellow down by door.
He singee song to pletty little feet,
But don't see robber acloss the stleet.
Big old dragon what livee in a cloud
See allee samee and laugh out loud.

(*Homicide and Highway Robbery.*)
Cloud come along and blottee out moon.
Fellow stop banjo; lain velly soon.
Walk off bully with love in his head.
Robber come along and fellow is dead.
Big old dragon what livee in a cloud
See allee samee and laugh out loud.

(*Crime is Punished and Virtue Marries Rich.*)
Bimeby little gal have awful fits;
Bimeby robber get choppee into bits.
Little gal mally a velly lich man,
Have a lot of little boys and spendee
all she can.
Big old dragon what livee in a cloud
See allee samee and laugh out loud.

64 WONG, AS A FREE-LANCE WRITER, SOLD THIS POEM TO *PUCK* IN FEBRUARY 1885. CALLING ITSELF A MAGAZINE OF HUMOR, *PUCK* NEVER SHOWED CHINESE EXCEPT AS CRUDE CARICATURES.

been one of about one-hundred young Chinese sent to Hartford, Connecticut, as members of the Chinese Educational Mission—an abortive attempt to train a cadre of future officials and engineers. Lee was recalled in 1884, at the end of his freshman year at Yale, but returned in 1887, enrolled again in Yale, and married Elizabeth Maud Jerome, described as a "New Haven heiress," in the first recorded marriage of a Chinese to an American in New Haven.

Lee's article was titled "Why I Am Not A Heathen?" He argued that those who persecuted Chinese were not true Christians. He said Christians were the only ones trying to help the Chinese in America and that improvement in the treatment of Chinese could be achieved only by Christians, concluding: "The final appeal is to be made to the Christian sentiment of the nation."[15]

(To complete his life: After graduating from Yale in 1890, Lee founded the *Chinese Advocate* as a journal for the Chinese Sunday Schools. One of his sons was killed in France in World War I. Toward the end of his life, he returned to China as editor of the *Canton Gazette.*)

Lee was wrong. The final appeal was to the racist sentiments of the nation. In 1892 Congress approved a measure drafted by California's Thomas Geary that extended the Chinese Exclusion Act of 1882 for another ten years, denied bail to Chinese in habeas corpus cases, and formalized passports to be used—inside the country as well as for travel—exclusively by the Chinese. A *Times* editorial called it "one of the most humiliating acts of which any civilized nation has been guilty in modern times."[16]

heathen alike hold but which Christians ignore. That is what keeps me the heathen that I am. And I earnestly invite the Christians of America to come to Confucius." His article was considered so provocative it was reprinted by the *Tribune,* which later printed three letters containing readers' comments.[14]

The next month, the *North American Review* printed a reply by Yan Phou Lee, who had reversed the Chinese order of his name to put his surname last, in American fashion. Lee had

58

In September the Chinese in California decided to fight the law and assessed each Chinese one dollar to meet the legal costs. In New York, members and supporters of a newly formed Chinese Civil Rights League nearly filled the largest meeting room of Cooper Union as one speaker described the Chinese as "victims of the demagogues on the Pacific Coast." One of the main speakers was Stephen Baldwin, head of the Chinese Sabbath School Association, which united forty of the estimated sixty Sunday Schools in New York and New Jersey.

Wong Chin Foo, who had never before shared a platform with New York's Chinese Christian leaders, was also there—charging that the law would suspend the guarantees of the Declaration of Independence.[17] In January 1893 he went to Washington, on behalf of the Civil Rights League, to testify in favor of a repeal bill before the House Foreign Affairs Committee. Making what was described as "a logical argument in perfect English, which had the close attention of the committee," Wong said he did not hope for additional immigration but only wished justice for Chinese already in the United States. He called the requirement for identity documents "cruel and unusual punishment," because it classed the Chinese with thieves and criminals, who were forced to be photographed for identification.[18] The bill never emerged from committee.

Oddly, although the Chinese Consolidated Benevolent Association of San Francisco organized a boycott of the passport-registration provisions, the case was pursued in New York. Three laundrymen volunteered as test cases: Fong Yue Ting of 1 Mott Street, Wong Quan of 4 Mott Street, and Lee Joe of 2077 Third Avenue. In May 1893 they appeared at the Federal Building in New York. They produced the photographs but the law also required a "reliable white witness," to certify the accuracy of their statements. Instead, they were accompanied by Guy Maine, a widely respected Chinese Christ-

NEWS FROM CHINA.

65 A FAMILIAR NEWSPAPER REACTION TO A MAJOR FOREIGN STORY: SEEKING A HOME-TOWN ANGLE. THE NEWS APPARENTLY BEING TRANSLATED FROM AN ENGLISH-LANGUAGE NEWSPAPER CONCERNS THE JAPANESE INVASION OF KOREA.

ian who spoke English and had appeared in local courts as an official translator. But, since he was not "white," the applications were rejected. All were immediately arrested, arraigned, and ordered deported.[19] A writ of habeas corpus was requested and denied, setting the stage for an appeal to the Supreme Court. Within two weeks a judgment was handed down.

The case entered history as *Fong Yue Ting v. United States*. The vote was five to three against the Chinese. The majority followed most recent precedents: that the nation was sovereign and could control both the entrance and residence of aliens and that the Executive Department must be allowed to exercise this sovereignty unhampered by the Judicial Department.[20]

The fight for Chinese dignity had to be fought in China, not in the United States. In 1892, the year the Geary Act was passed, Sun Yat-sen opened a drug store in Macao and surrounded himself with men from the Triads. In Honolulu

IN THE ENEMY'S QUARTER.

66 The text explained: "It isn't an altogether pleasant experience which a Japanese gentleman encounters in passing through the Chinese quarters of New York. He is in no peril of personal assault, indeed, but he is likely to be subject to jeers and jibes which affect him even more keenly than blows." But Wong Chin Foo praised the Japanese, saying they represented culture, learning and progress.

Western ideas have in the East to the extent never before known."[22]

In about 1895 Wong Chin Foo returned to Chicago, his original home in the United States, and again tried to publish a Chinese-language newspaper. When next he came to public attention, his name was linked to Sun Yat-sen's. Sun had gone to England, where, in October 1895, he was kidnaped by the Chinese legation in London. English friends obtained his release. The bizarre incident brought him to public attention for the first time. Reporters in London wanted to know why the Manchus would try to kidnap this obscure person. Sun boldly claimed to have been the leader of the Canton uprising, saying he was determined to establish constitutional government in China. He also claimed his organization was strong in the United States, with a center in San Francisco and headquarters in New York.

A Brooklyn *Eagle* reporter went to Chinatown for comment. "Chinamen who are very prominent in Celestial circles in New York City," he wrote, "were very reticent but when assured their names would not be made public...acknowledged there was such a society but not one would say he was a member." London newspapers referred to a letter from Wong Chin Foo in Chicago saying the movement in the United States was in good shape. At year's end Wong was interviewed at his newspaper. He said he had rented an office in Chicago for Sun's use in the United States and that funds and followers were being raised for an invasion of China from "a convenient base in the South Pacific."[23]

Wong had as little luck in publishing a Chinese newspaper in Chicago as he had in New York in 1881. It failed but, undaunted, he formed the Chinese Equal Rights League of America to campaign for repeal of Chinese exclusion laws and give Chinese the right to vote: "We want Illinois, the place that Lincoln, Grant, and Logan called their home, to do for the Chinese what the north did for the Negroes," he proclaimed.[24] Wong Chin Foo, the eternal rebel, was still fighting lost causes.

in 1894, Sun formed the *Hsing Chung Hui,* or "Revive China Society," transferred his base to Hong Kong, and made contact with the Triads in Canton. After an abortive Triad uprising in Canton in 1895, Sun fled to the United States and traveled across the country, contacting Triad members en route. He later wrote: "I stopped at a good many places, sometimes for days, sometimes for a couple of weeks....Though I worked hard there were very few who paid any attention to me. There were only a few individuals, at the most a dozen or two in each city, who were favorable to my ideas of revolution."[21]

One of those was Wong Chin Foo. The stirring in China revived his hatred of the Manchus. In August 1894, when Japan invaded Korea and went on to attack China, reporters flocked to Chinatown for reaction. Wong said he hoped the Japanese would win: "They are the real simon-pure Chinese, the Japs are, and they represent the culture and learning and progress which

Chinatown and Its Environs in the 1880s

In September 1881, a year after his appointment as deputy sheriff proclaimed him an ethnic cog in the Democratic machine, Tom Lee staged a Tammany-style picnic on Staten Island. About fifty men, including Tammany bosses Maurice Hyland and J. A. Dingle, assembled outside a saloon at the corner of Mott and Chatham and, at a blast from the bugler of the 69th Regiment, started in a procession of barouches to the Staten Island ferry. On the other shore, Lee led the way to refreshments at Mayer and Bachmann's brewery and on to the dancing pavilion at New Dorp, where "Mingo" DeLuce served a breakfast of fish, ham and eggs, eels, clam fritters, potatoes, bread, and coffee. With not a chopstick in sight, ethnicity was marked by an orchestra playing instruments a reporter described as a mallet, a truncated quarter cask, and a hollow half-globe, plus recognizable gongs and cymbals.

While some went swimming and others sat watching the waves, the more athletic competed in a hundred-yard race for a $250 purse offered by Tom Lee. After another of Mingo's substantial meals, the caravan filed back to the ferry and on to Chinatown, where lanterns, firecrackers, roman candles, and an attempt of the orchestra to play the Star Spangled Banner attracted two thousand cheering spectators.[1]

Tom Lee rented the basement at 2 Mott for $1,000 a year and another at 4 Mott for $750, using one for an export business in tea and silk and the other to manufacture cigars. In March 1882 Tom Lee's first son was born. He already had a daughter, Rose Lee, then two years old. The baptism of Tom Lee Junior was celebrated five weeks later with a reception and huge meal at the Lun Gee Tong at 18 Mott. The guests included two dignitaries wearing the flowered silk coats and scarlet silk skull caps with red coral buttons that signified mandarin rank. Recognized by both Tammany and the Chinese diplomatic mission to the United States, Tom Lee was in firm control of the Chinese in New York.[2]

In April 1883 Lee and his wealthy friends became the first Chinese to feel confident enough of their environment to buy property on Mott Street. Lee and Kwong Hong Long bought number 18 for $14,500, Kwong Hong Long (then at 5 Mott) bought number 10 for $8,500, Wong Acton (who had been located at 105 Park since his 1880 eviction by the Moravians) bought num-

ber 8 for $8,500, and Mon Lee and Company bought number 12 for $5,000. It was obviously a close-knit affair, since Wong Acton was also associated with Kwong Hong Long at 5 Mott.[3]

The purchases precipitated a challenge to Lee's authority. Charles Meyers, a lawyer claiming to represent "respectable Chinese merchants," filed charges alleging Tom Lee went to various merchants, showed his deputy-sheriff badge, and promised if they would pay him five dollars a week for each fan-tan table and ten dollars for each opium room he would guarantee freedom from police interference. As a result, said Meyers, thirty-seven gambling houses, lottery rooms, and opium joints had mushroomed along Mott Street, from which Lee gathered at least ten thousand dollars a year. Meyers specifically asked the police to close houses at 4, 6, 8, 10, 12, and 14 Mott where, he said, notices were written on white paper saying "Gambling Night and Day," with a three-cornered lantern serving as notice by night. Meyers said part of the money collected by Lee went to the police.

The district attorney, a Tammany appointee, refused to countenance an allegation of police corruption, but did take away Lee's badge and sent the other charges to a grand jury which, in May, indicted Lee for keeping a gambling establishment.

It was a charade. Under Tammany, gambling and prostitution flourished everywhere in the city. The gambling charges were laughed away and only one person was arrested: Ah Chun, who kept an opium room at 13 Pell Street. When questioned, Ah Chun said he paid Tom Lee ten dollars a month for the right to operate the place. With this, Meyers thought he had found a way to overcome the handicap of a lack of evidence. He sought Ah Chun in the Tombs and persuaded him to give an affidavit to having made regular payments to Lee for the right to operate an opium room without police molestation. To ensure the affidavit would stand up in court, Meyers had Ah Chun swear to it in the presence of Justice White of the Tombs court. Meyers showed his affidavit to the district attorney and Tom Lee was arrested.

He appeared for the trial on May 16 with former judge Horace Russell as his lawyer. The court interpreter was James Baptiste. Since all Chinese knew Baptiste was an officer of the Lun

Gee Tong and close associate of Tom Lee, Meyers brought his own interpreter. His precaution was in vain. Ah Chun, viewing a courtroom crowded with Lee's toughs, denied he had paid any money to Tom Lee. As for his affidavit, he said he had not understood it when it was read out to him. The charges were thrown out and Tom Lee was set free.[4]

Other charges against Lee were dropped and Lee was soon displaying his badge again. Ah Chun also escaped unharmed. It was not until May 15, after Ah Chun's arrest, that an ordinance was passed making it a misdemeanor to operate a room for the sale or smoking of opium. The judge directed the jury to find a verdict of not guilty.[5]

AS A GAMBLING AND ENTERTAINMENT CENTER

Few Chinese lived in Chinatown: houses were too valuable for commercial purposes to be used as living quarters. In a once-private house measuring twenty by sixty feet, a gambling room in the basement rented for $50 a month; a store on the first floor rented for $90; the privilege of using the hall for a small sales area cost $10; the second floor, often used as a restaurant, rented for $35; the third floor, which could be divided into portions as dormitory, rented for $45;and the fourth floor, perhaps used as a brothel, rented for $30, bringing an annual rent roll of $3,120. In another instance, a three-story building on lower Mott Street might bring an annual rent of $2,500 to $3,000, while a similar building just three blocks north on Bayard Street, occupied by Irish or Italians, might bring less than $500.[6]

Chinatown was transit center for the estimated fifty thousand Chinese in Cuba who, when returning home for a visit, came to New York, waited a few days, and took the train to California, where they boarded a ship. It also served the Japanese, Filipino, Hindu, Maori, Hawaiian, Malay, Annamese, and other Asian seamen whose vessels docked at Front Street a few blocks away.

For all, fan-tan was the game of choice. It was played on a long white table about four feet high and five feet wide. On this was placed a white mat or metal plate with the numbers one, two, three, and four in marked squares on the sides. The dealer sat on a high chair in front of number one. The cashier sat in front of number two. Some players sat on stools at three and four, but most simply crowded around the table. Near the dealer was a pile of Chinese copper coins with a square hole in the center. The dealer took a double handful, placed them on the table, and covered them with a concave metal lid. After

bets were placed, the dealer removed the lid, spread out the coins and began removing them four at a time, using a taper or curved stick about eighteen inches long, never touching the coins with his hands. Fan-tan meant "repeatedly spreading out."

The object was to guess how many coins would remain after the last possible group of four had been removed. If none remained, the winning number was four. The winner got back his money and was paid three times his bet less a seven percent commission. If a man placed a bet at a corner he was betting the two adjacent sides. If he placed a bet on one side, but not in the marked square, he was betting the two opposite sides. In these cases, the winner got his money back plus an equal sum less the usual commission. Often, buttons of various shapes and colors or dominoes were substituted for cash so, in the event of a police raid, no coins could be produced as evidence of gambling. In the more exclusive rooms patronized by professional gamblers, settlement was made in a side room or, if the amount was large, a loser would be allowed to make payment within twenty-four hours.

If the game had gone on for some time, and the house was losing money, a settlement was made with the players and if any of them wanted to run the game for their own profit, they could do so after playing a small rent to the company and a fee to the cashier for his services. In less-organized games, or those rigged to fleece the unwary, quarrels were frequent and an aggrieved player might attempt to seize any money displayed on the table.[7]

As a commercial enterprise, fan-tan was a pyramid, with about twenty-five bankers at the top. They would lend from one thousand to thirty thousand dollars to syndicates of two to ten persons who organized and supervised the room. The dealers and cashiers were tong men who made a good living as professional gamblers. Each room, or bank, had to feed its employees, including "steerers," three times a day and give its best customers meals, drinks, and a place to sleep. A steerer at the door, who chanted "fan tan inside, come and make your fortune," received a commission for each person enticed inside. There were also hangers-on who stood near the table and were the first to call out the winning number. A winner might give them a dollar if he thought they had brought him good luck. The hangers-on might also play for a beginner and earn a commission.

Although the sign outside read, in Chinese, "Open Day and Night," play was limited to a few hours in the afternoon, resuming at eight o'clock

67 OF THE THOUSANDS DRAWN TO THE BOWERY BY ITS THEATERS AND "MUSEUMS" OF LIVING CURIOSITIES, FEW VENTURED INTO CHINATOWN, ONLY A BLOCK TO THE EAST; ITS REPUTATION WAS FORBIDDING.

68 FAN-TAN. THE DEALER, LEFT, HOLDS THE CUP FOR COVERING THE COINS. THE CASHIER HOLDS THE STICK FOR COUNTING UNITS OF FOUR.

at night. On Sundays and holidays, when streets were crowded with laundrymen and others, the games might begin at eleven in the morning. Gamblers were fanatically superstitious. None dared start without bowing to an image of Kwan Kung, burning some incense, and consulting the fortune blocks or the sticks. Every room had a scroll and implements for this purpose. White was the color of mourning, hence associated with bad luck. The owners painted their walls white and used white decorations, if any, in an effort to bring bad luck to their patrons. Even the inscriptions at the shrine and the candles burned there were white instead of the customary red. Oranges were associated with purification rites, hence good luck. A piece of orange peel was kept in the box where the coins or buttons were stored. A gambler on the way to fan-tan would turn back if someone jostled him on the street or if a cart seemed to obstruct his way. He would not read a book—or even look at one—while gambling because the Toishan pronunciation for "book" sounded like the word "to lose." If a player accidentally touched another's

69 A BASEMENT GAMBLING ROOM.

money or counter while placing a bet he would immediately withdraw his own wager.[8]

Professional gamblers had a union, known at one time as the *Kai Yon*, or "Street Opinion Society." Once, reopening after a police shut-

64

日夜開皮

Game Open Day and Night.

70 This sign on gambling rooms actually meant late afternoon into the night.

down, the union raised house percentages to meet "extra expenses"—perhaps higher payoffs. If a member fell sick, the society would make a subscription book in his name and send it to members for contributions. If no member volunteered to nurse the sick man, someone would be selected by lot from among his clan or territory association. If he died, members would be responsible for his burial and the return of his bones to China.[9]

Wong Chin Foo, whose attempt to publish the city's first Chinese newspaper soon failed, and who later took to free-lance writing to support himself, wrote in an article for the *Times* that there were twenty or thirty professional gamblers in the city. They wore suits of Canton cut, lived in the most expensive lodgings, considered manual work degrading, never went to bed before two or three in the morning, and never showed themselves on the street until the same time in the afternoon. They even had their own

72 With others at work, gamblers were the conspicuously idle.

small safes with tens of thousands of dollars available for large games. The games were milked by the police and politicians. The man who came for the collections on behalf of the precinct received something for himself, and individual policemen, officers, and politicians dropped in regularly for a drink or gifts of cigars and fine teas. This cost from twenty to eighty dollars a month.[10]

Should an operator refuse, retribution was not long in coming. When the operator of a gambling and opium house at 17 Mott refused payment when his collector called, his place was raided within three days. In the Tombs awaiting trial, the collector called again, saying charges would be dropped if he paid $150, otherwise he would be railroaded to prison. Once again he refused, and he was tried and sent to prison.[11]

Almost all Chinese patronized lotteries, wagering small sums in the hope of a large profit. The most popular lottery was the White Pigeon ticket, or *Pak ko piu*. A syndicate using an auspicious name rented a room and divided it by a railing extending from floor to ceiling. Except when the lottery was in progress, wooden shutters blocked the view of the interior, where there was an office. Twice a day, at midafternoon and at nine or ten o'clock at night, the shutters were removed and an assistant began to sell chances based on

71 Gambling room at the corner of Doyers and Pell.

光緒拾柒年九月　吉　日

紐約東正襟公所

每著今因騙鬥後開貨用太多花議每贖式式電
伍銀以上者投例照抽雙閧亦然如不運例照抽
罰銀壹拾大員正倘有此手要逗樓作証銀若
嗣即謝花紅銀位大員餘銀歸入本堂若有賣兇
身銀帥不落珠碼無論行番稔角那蹟限壹拾
員先字告明以免後論各宜見諒

73 After gambling rooms were shut by the police and later reopened with an increase in the police toll, owners posted a "Notice to Fortune Seekers." The translation: The gambling houses are reopened again. As extra expenses must be paid, a new rule has gone into effect. Instead of the old percentage of 7 percent deducted from winnings of over fifty cents, a new percentage has been established. Henceforth a percentage of 7 percent will be deducted from all winnings and a percentage of 14 percent from all winnings over twenty-five dollars. Every gambling place must post this notice on the wall where it can be easily seen. Inspectors of the Gamblers' Union shall visit all gambling houses to see that this law is enforced, and any failure to comply with said law shall be punished by a fine of ten dollars, half of which shall go to the informer. Given under our hand and seal in the seventeenth year of Quong Soi, King, and the ninth month (October).

New York Bing Chang Union

the first eighty characters of the *Tsin tsz man,* or Thousand Character Classic, a book in which no two characters are alike—so familiar to Chinese the characters could be used instead of numbers.

A player who marked off any ten of the characters paid one dollar. He could either come to the office to make his selection or mark a ticket sold by runners who traveled to stores and laundries as lottery agents. When the shutters were taken down, individual sales were made and agents handed in tickets to be recorded as sales. An hour later, the manager rolled eighty pieces of paper, each stamped with an individual character, into pellets and placed them in a large tin pan. He mixed them and drew them out one at

a time, placing them in bowls marked 1, 2, 3, and 4. A player on the other side of the rail selected one of the bowls as the winning numbers for the night and received a small tip. The manager unrolled the numbers and pasted them on the board in the back of the office, with the spectators watching every move to guard against cheating. Five winning numbers paid $2; six paid $20; seven paid $200; eight paid $1,000; nine paid $1,500, and ten paid $3,000. The company deducted five percent for its costs.

More than ten numbers could be bought at a higher price. There was a book showing how much these would cost and what they would pay. Winners had to be paid the day following the drawing. Sometimes, companies had to suspend operations when their capital was suddenly depleted by a large winner, reopening when they had raised the money to pay off their debt. But, in the long run, the house won—the odds were sixty-five to thirty-five in its favor. In addition to the manager, there was a secretary who received the money and recorded bets and an assistant in charge of the board, marking the winning numbers with a brush and red ink.

Lottery agents had a union, charging from five to twenty-five dollars for life membership. Most of the tickets were sold through them, since they would accept bets as low as ten cents for a single number. They collected fees in advance, charging $1.15 for ten characters and turning in one dollar to the manager. Lottery managers were quick to reject any winning tickets they could claim to be improperly marked. The agents performed a valuable service by insuring customers against mistakes in marking tickets. For those who thought there was some order of winning numbers, and the future could be foretold by the past, sheets marked with the winning numbers dating back a month or more were displayed in most shops.[12]

Another lottery was a riddle game known in New York as Wah Way, based on a sheet of thirty-six blocks, each containing two characters: an animal, such as a bird, fish, spider, or tiger; and a mythological or historical character, a common occupation, or simply an object, like jade. There was also a human diagram marked with clues linking the thirty-six boxes with parts of the body. The *Wah Way* was conducted, like *pak ko piu,* by a syndicate using a rented room divided in half. Now there were no shutters. The day before the drawing, the pair of characters in one of the boxes was drawn on white paper, rolled up in a piece of black cloth, and hung on a wall or chain for all to see. A literate man, called a poet, composed a riddle in verse hinting at the hidden character, "The country has the (right) way. / All the people with rain and dew and moistened." Or: "The officers all forbear. / The people spread abroad with favorable winds." Bettors had to guess the meaning of the riddle. Or they might ignore the riddle and think of the part of the body. If someone's left foot itched, he might bet on the character shown at the left foot of the body diagram.

In the morning, agents circulated with the riddle and slips with the thirty-six squares and returned for the afternoon or evening drawing. A winner was paid at the rate of thirty to one, giving the house a 20 percent advantage. The agents were allowed to keep 10 percent of the money they collected and received an additional 10 percent from a customer who bought a winning ticket. At the time the winning riddle was announced, the riddle for the next drawing was also displayed, so agents could circulate both the news of the previous winning riddle and a new riddle to tempt laundrymen and clerks to try their luck again.[13]

George Walling, who boasted of "thirty-eight years as patrolman, detective, captain, inspector, and chief of the New York police," painted a lurid picture of a *pak ko piu* shop:

> If an inquisitive stranger puts his face into [a] shop...at once a look of ugly distrust comes into the face of the gambler behind the wooden fence. He now has the appearance of a venomous animal in a cage...and if the strange white man has been piloted in by a Chinaman, it is with no friendly glance that the latter is regarded. Next to an unknown American, the Chinaman hates one of his own kind who shows the American the

sights and oddities of Chinatown....He thinks he may be blackmailed by threats of police interference. If an American wishes to see an evil expression on a human creature's face he should penetrate a Chinese gambling den and loiter about until the keeper of the place and his satellites have worked themselves into an agony of nervousness.[14]

AS A RESIDENTIAL CENTER

Chinatown was a night town. Shops did not open until about ten in the morning. Even then, customers were few. Noticeable stirring began at about two in the afternoon when, as if at a signal, waiters jogged from restaurants with large trays of covered dishes balanced on their heads and disappeared inside shops. Curtains were drawn, and merchants and clerks had their meal. There was more activity later as lottery agents gathered bets and reported the results of the day's first drawing and as merchants and elders sorted out the affairs of community life. In the evening, under the soft glow of lanterns, all would be quiet. Gamblers and their clients would be packed into small rooms, the steerers would be calling softly to passers-by, and a few men would sit chatting quietly in doorways and smoking long-stemmed pipes.

The largest group living in the vicinity of Chinatown were cigar makers, with about three hundred so employed in 1885. The principal manufacturer was Mig Atak, whose factory at 91 Chatham Street employed twenty-five to one hundred men depending on the state of business. Sam You, or Charles Samuels, had a factory and shop at 495 Chatham. Hong Kee Kang, or William Hong—the Civil War veteran—had his factory at 500 Pearl. Other nearby residents were merchants, clerks, and employees of shops and small food processing factories along with a few in service trades, like barbers, doctors, and professional gamblers.[15]

Single men lived in dormitories. Since about 80 percent came from the Guangdong district of Toishan, they divided according to collections of villages dominated by a single clan. They called one another brother, cousin, or uncle, depending on their relative ages, but they were, at best, distant cousins.

A dormitory was generally operated by a partnership of two or three men. The cheapest house was found, generally in some dilapidated private house, and the cheapest portion was rented, either the basement or a loft on the top floor. The partners partitioned off a little space as a private room for themselves and divided off two or three cubicles for boarders willing to pay a little more for privacy. Two sides of the

74 MATCHED CHARACTERS ON LOTTERY TICKET.

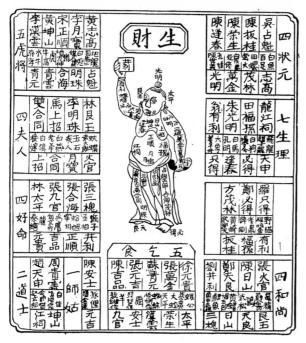

75 DIAGRAM TO HELP IN BETTING.

官原容 國有道 祥雲十三
百姓暢和風 萬民沾雨露

76 POEM AS HINT.

remaining space were lined with bunks in tiers of three, the upper level being reached by small boards nailed to the uprights as ladders. One room on upper Mott Street had twenty bunks for thirty men. Another, in a house on Park Street, had twelve bunks for twenty-four men. There was a large table and stools in the center of the room and a cooking stove at a wall. A bowl of sand was placed on the floor, where incense sticks were burned for the tutelary spirit—the ghost of the first person to die in the house. The bowl was kept on the floor because the Chinese believed humans shrank after they became spirits. Another bowl of sand was placed on the mantlepiece for use if other invocations were required or simply to burn incense to make the room smell sweeter. The Chinese never drank fresh water. A pot of boiling water, or water that had been boiled and was now tepid, was kept on the stove. Two teapots were on the table. One contained room-temperature boiled water with a slight tea flavor. The other teapot was encased in a wicker basket lined with felt or cotton, one or two inches thick, with only the spout protruding. The tea-flavored water in this pot remained warm for hours.

The average daily charge for a bunk and three meals was $2.50. Some dormitories, where men crowded three to a bunk, charged from $1.50 to $3 a week. In such cases, the men were probably employed in a place where employers provided a large midday meal and tea in the morning and evening, so the men were only charged for their beds. Meals were cooked on a stove using hickory or oak wood: The Chinese believed coal smoke spoiled the flavor of food. Breakfast for full boarders might consist of a tripe or fish chowder or steamed pork balls served with rice. Similar dishes, or a fried mixture of meat and vegetables, were served at midday, with soup as the final course. The evening meal was a snack of rice and one or two small portions of meat. The midday and evening meals were eaten with a tiny portion of *namadhaio* (rice liqueur flavored with different fruits). Sometimes gin was served, but again, in a bowl so small Americans were reminded of a thimble or a child's tea set. If a boarder had an excuse for celebration, he might provide the entire room with a special dish to supplement the final meal. The last hour or so was spent quietly, smoking tobacco, opium, or hashish and playing cards or mah jong for small stakes. The men were generally asleep by ten o'clock. The bunks were covered with fiber mats, sometimes with newspaper added for insulation. Pillows were round pieces of wood, sometimes with small legs like stools. Quilts were preferred to blankets. Boarders were expected to roll up their bedclothes and mats in the morning and place them neatly on a shelf over each bunk. The proprietors then washed each bunk with a bleach and disinfectant.[16]

LAUNDRIES

In 1885 there were about a thousand laundries in Manhattan (which then included much of what is now Bronx county), three hundred in Brooklyn, and 225 in nearby New Jersey. They employed 4,500 men. In 1888 the estimate for the same region had doubled to 3,050 laundries. A poor farmer, who could earn only sixty cents a day in China, could clear fifteen dollars a week as a laundryman in New York.[17]

Most laundries were operated by two men in partnership, sharing the costs and profits equally. In residential areas, where wives did the

77 LAUNDRYMEN AND A STROLLING PHOTOGRAPHER IN 1883. ALL ARE MEN WITH LONG QUEUES. A SECLUDED WOMAN PEEPS FROM A SHUTTERED UPSTAIRS WINDOW.

family wash, a man might operate a laundry alone. In areas of Manhattan with many rooming houses, where single male tenants needed a fresh shirt and collar a day, a laundry required as many as six men, of whom two or three might be partners and others hired for specific tasks, such as ironers or washers. Sometimes business was so brisk black women were employed for washing.

In an article for the *World*, Wong Chin Foo wrote that a laundry was a good long-term investment. In addition to providing a living, it could be sold for $350 when the man returned to China. One man, Chin Wah Sing of Mott Street, opened and sold thirty laundries over a period of four years, earning over $9,000. A laundry at 118 Chatham Street did so much business it was valued at $2,500. Another, on Flatbush Avenue in Brooklyn, was worth $2,200. An average laundryman was able to save enough money, sell his laundry, and return home with savings of from $1,500 to $2,000. Wong Sai Ung of Brooklyn went to China four times and, in 1885, was back on his fifth trip.[18]

A laundryman, as did all Chinese business-

men, adopted an auspicious name for his shop, such as Hop Sing (Deserving Prosperity) or Wo Loung (Success Through Concord), and wrote the name in red on his signboard. Despite his good-luck name, a laundryman in a residential area was merely tolerated as a human washing machine. His customers did not know his name and called him Mr. Sing or Mr. Loung, if not simply "Charlie." If there was trouble of some sort and his real name was disclosed, this was taken as another example of Chinese duplicity or secretiveness.[19]

It cost from seventy-five to two hundred dollars to open and equip a shop. The layout was the same throughout the country. For the conservative Chinese, once a practical and economical method was worked out it was repeated again and again. First came an outer room where customers were received and ironing performed. Rear shelves formed the wall of the second room, which was used for sleeping. The shelves did not reach the ceiling, and the entrance to the inner room was curtained instead of closed by a door, allowing a man in the sleeping room to hear if anyone entered the shop. Beds were narrow planks or army cots. Behind this was the drying room, which heated the sleeping room in winter but made it steaming hot in summer. A large coal stove was placed in the center of the drying room and tin plates lined the lower half of the walls. Iron wires were stretched in parallel lines across the room as high as a man could conveniently reach. A rear room contained the washtubs, tubs for boiling clothes, wringers, a cook stove, and a lavatory.

Mondays, Wednesdays, and Fridays were washing days. Tuesdays, Thursdays, and Saturdays were ironing days. One of the wash days, depending on when customers brought in most of the work, began at about six in the morning and did not end until midnight. Work on the other wash days might be finished at about eight or nine o'clock at night. The shop was closed on Sundays, but there were still a few hours work to be completed. The shop was cleaned, laundry sorted and marked for the Monday wash, and the income and expenses totaled for the week. Any helpers employed in the shop were paid and the partners divided the rest, leaving a small amount to start the next week.[20]

Laundry owners had their own association, as did the ironers and washermen who worked for them, generally as apprentices. In June 1884, during the brisk summer months, the leaders of the ironers and washers associations managed to raise wages, which previously ranged from $3.50 to $4.50 a day, to a minimum of $5. But the owners had their own meeting in October and wages plummeted to $3 a day, or $10 a week with food and lodging.[21]

Owner associations fixed prices and enforced them. In May 1883 Lung Poy moved from New York to Paterson, New Jersey, and opened the Hong King laundry. To build a clientele quickly, he set rates lower than those charged by other shops. One Sunday someone came to his store and said a friend from New York wished to see him at a house on Godwin Street. He went, entered a room, and was surrounded by men armed with hatchets and knives. They told him he must raise his prices. When he refused, he was knocked down, beaten, and hacked. His cries attracted neighbors, who called police. All of his assailants were named Moy. One, Moy Sin, was later sent to jail for felonious assault but was soon released. A year later, Moy disappeared after borrowing two thousand dollars to start a laundry on Pell Street. It was then revealed he was a gambler and "head of a large society." Moy's conduct would later be recognized as that of a tong thug.[22]

Laundrymen spent as much as 80 percent of their lives within their shops. Almost everything was delivered, so a man was a stranger even to other shopkeepers in the neighborhood. Early in the morning, when the rest of Chinatown was asleep, peddlers left Mott Street carrying more than a hundred pounds of goods suspended from the ends of a bamboo pole—food, clothing, soaps and bleaches, a variety of pins, needles, thread, buttons, and whatever else a laundryman might need. They had regular customers, visiting each several times a week. If a laundryman needed an unusual item, the peddler delivered it when next he came. The only other Chinese visitor a laundryman might see during the week was the lottery agent.

WOMEN AND SEX

There were few Chinese women, and even these were seldom seen outside their homes. A few women, bought as slaves in China, were smuggled into New York for use as prostitutes or to adorn banquets. They cost their owners—invariably tong gangsters—thousands of dollars, and there was always the risk of having them rescued by the Sunday School teachers who closely monitored Chinatown life. There were two such instances of rescue in the 1880s—both well publicized.[23]

Another reason to smuggle girls into New York was to serve as servants in the homes of wealthy merchants whose wives were small-footed—mothers and ornaments—not housekeepers. Servant girls might be seen hurrying along Mott or Pell on a family errand. When older, they were sold as wives or concubines for wealthy men and lived comfortable and secure lives.

Except for wealthy merchants, the greatest problem was in finding sexual outlet. Traveling prostitutes built a clientele of laundrymen, with their services recommended by one store owner to another. This was dangerous. The neighbors were ever-watchful. If a woman entered the shop and disappeared behind those mysterious curtains, rumors would spread. At best, the laundryman might lose many customers. At worst, his window would be smashed with a brick. Even if there was no trouble from neighbors, there was the ever-present threat of blackmail. Neighbors and police invariably sided with a white woman who claimed to be the victim of a wily Chinese.

In 1879 Wah Sing and Lee Ing, who owned a laundry on Third Avenue, were walking along 14th Street when a woman came up behind them, stole Wah Sing's wallet from under his blouse, and ran away. The men chased and caught her, retrieved the wallet, and tried to take

78 TRAVELING PEDDLER FOR LAUNDRYMEN.

her to a police station. She screamed, and a crowd gathered and began to beat the two Chinese. When Wah Sing drew a knife to protect himself, someone in the crowd fired a shot that struck him in the cheek. Wah Sing was taken to a hospital, where a doctor said the bullet had lodged in his jaw and could not be immediately removed. Lee Ing was arrested. He was released the next morning when the facts became clear.[24]

SHOPS AND RESTAURANTS

Aside from laundries, the major source of employment were shops catering to other Chinese. In 1888 thirty all-purpose stores were counted in Chinatown. Most catered to men from a single county or cluster of villages. They were also post offices. Customers were given envelopes with the address of the store printed in English. A family in Guangdong had only to add a man's name in Chinese characters and the letter would find its way to the right man in New York. Since letters were opened as soon as they were received, news from home was shared with the proprietor and other customers and would quickly circulate throughout the community.

The main store was Yuet Sing's at 202 Chatham Street, where foreign visitors marveled at wonders such as boned duck's feet, dried and wrapped with chicken livers; spiced duck pressed into cakes; duck's legs in oil; white sausages made from deviled oysters and dried pork; salted shad in oil; canned bamboo shoots; seaweed from Korea; small, salty black cucumbers resembling pickles; and two dozen varieties of sugar-cured fruits, including the most popular, ginger apricots.

In 1885 Wong Acton's store at 8 Mott was valued at $150,000. It also did an export business, sending to China "ginseng, fine prints and piece goods, cutlery, firearms, and other American manufactures." The wealthiest merchant was Wong He Cong (also spelled Qwong He Chung), at 32 Pell, said to be worth over a million dollars, with a large export business to Tonkin, Canton, and Cuba.[25]

Six restaurants were counted in 1885 and eight in 1888. The most simple meal—rice and separate dishes of chicken and fish—cost twenty-five cents. Tea and the final course of soup were supplied at no charge. In contrast, an American restaurant of the period charged sixty cents for its cheapest meal. If two men ate together, they could have duck for fifteen cents, perfumed pork for ten cents, a fish dish for ten cents, a noodle dish for ten cents, meat balls for five cents, and rice for five cents—fifty-five cents for the two of them. Namadhaio for two cost eighteen cents. Tom Lee's restaurant at 4

79 LAUNDRYMEN WHO VISITED CHINATOWN ON SUNDAYS USUALLY BROUGHT A FEW GROCERIES BACK TO THEIR SHOPS.

Mott was noted for its patés and dumplings. A restaurant at 11 Mott was known for its soups and stews and one at 14 Mott for its fancy dishes.[26]

Oddly, for Americans, liqueur was served from a teapot while tea was served in a bowl covered with a small saucer. The diner let it steep and then poured some into a second bowl for drinking and added hot water to the original bowl. This was repeated five or six times. It was claimed the last cup was as good as the first. Customers sat on high stools at round tables. The walls were hung with scrolls bearing such maxims as, "It is only the superior man who knows what he eats and what he drinks"; "It is here that heroes met and sages drank: Why should we abstain"; or "May you meet one at the end of the earth and find him a brother."

Wong Chin Foo, who delighted in countering American charges that the Chinese invariably lived cheaply, wrote that a first-class *gzuh*, or "spread," of forty courses might take two days to finish and cost fifty dollars. A second-class

80 THE STORE AT THE BOTTOM WAS IDENTIFIED AS YUET SING'S GROCERY AND GENERAL GOODS STORE AT 202 CHATHAM STREET (MODERN PARK ROW). A CUSTOMER IS DRINKING WEAK TEA FROM A POT KEPT WARM IN A WICKER COZY. THE INSET AT THE TOP WAS IDENTIFIED SIMPLY AS "A FRUIT VENDER'S ALLEY."

81 In August 1888, a reporter and artist from *Harper's Weekly*, whose Park Row office was a few blocks away, explored the exotica of Chinatown as if on a foreign safari.

82 A RESTAURANT IN THE REAR OF A STORE (SEEN THROUGH DOOR WITH WINDOW FACING STREET). WHAT LOOKS LIKE A TEAPOT CONTAINS LIQUEUR. THE MAN ON THE LEFT SIPS TEA FROM A BOWL POURED FROM ANOTHER BOWL, ON HIS LEFT, WHERE IT STEEPS UNDER A LID.

spread, he continued, with twenty-eight courses cost forty; a third-class spread of eighteen courses cost twenty five dollars, and the cheapest, with eight courses, cost eight dollars.

In the kitchen—in the rear of the dining room and open to the view of diners—whole pigs and plucked chickens and ducks were suspended from hooks in the ceiling. Live fowl protested their fate in cases on the floor. The earliest restaurants built their own massive stoves of firebricks with andirons at one end and an open pit at the other. A pig could be suspended by its heels and lowered into the pit for roasting. In later years,

the cooks used huge iron stoves. Since they cooked at high temperatures, there was a double wooden baffle in front to shield the cook when he was standing close to the stove. Panels could be lowered to feed the fire with hickory or oak. A metal box, open at the top, was used for roasting. Chickens, ducks, or a side of ribs were seasoned, spitted on irons, and fitted into slots in the box. A metal dome-like cover was placed on top and the fire was stoked under the range, where the roast rested. The metal distributed the heat so the meats emerged evenly done. For kitchens without an open pit, there

74

83 Restaurant kitchen. The round wooden containers on the rear shelf were for cooking dim sum. The waiter, right, is returning with dishes after a meal. The bottles contain liqueur.

was a larger box and lid for roasting whole pigs. Honey was rubbed into the skin to achieve the admired brown, sweet-tasting outer layer of meat.[27]

OTHER ENTERPRISES

In 1884, a *Times* article reported there was only one Chinese barber in New York. His name was Ti Chow, and he did a lucrative business on the top floor at 17 Mott.[28] By the late 1880s, there were a half dozen, including Chung Ah Lee, who worked in a long, narrow room on the second floor of 22 Mott. On Sundays customers were waiting from morning till night. To help pass the

time, they were offered tea, tobacco, and a bunk where they could smoke a pipe of opium. At a time when a shave in an Italian shop cost five cents, and ten cents in an American shop, the minimum charge at Chung Ah Lee's was twenty-five cents, while the deluxe treatment could cost as much as one dollar and take almost an hour to complete. The customer was seated on a stool or straight-back chair. His queue was unbraided, combed, and tied into a knot at the top of his head. A soft square of red silk was tied around his neck, his face and neck were sponged, and the short hair around the knot was washed. The

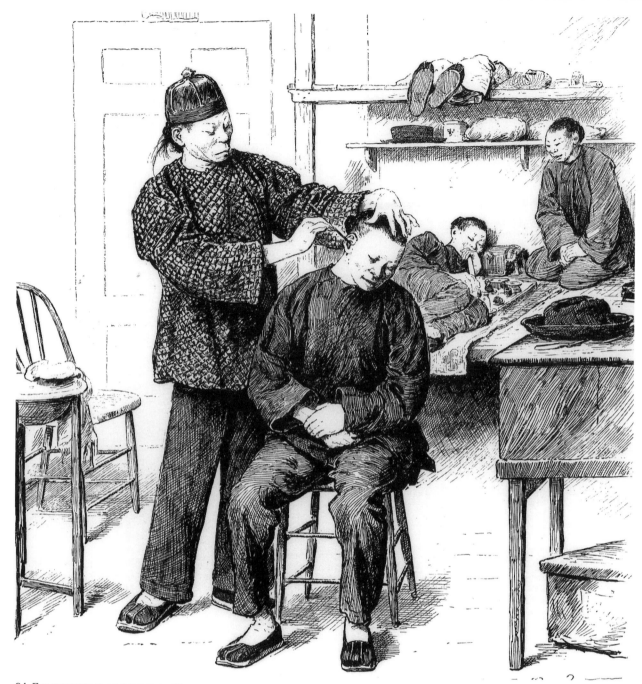

84 Ear cleaning at a barber shop. With many customers waiting on Sundays—a laundryman's only day off—opium bunks helped pass the time.

customer held a small basin under his chin to receive the scrapings as Chung shaved the entire front of his head with a small, moon-shaped razor, starting at the right above the ear, then moving around to the front and left. No soap was applied, only warm scented water. Next, Chung shaved the face and throat, temples, and back of the neck, and trimmed the eyebrows. Chung then mounted a high stool and took the customer's head onto his lap. He opened a case and took out an ear razor, with a blade about five inches long and less than a quarter of an inch wide. He also took out tweezers nearly a

foot long, a needle with a tiny crook at the tip, a small brush, and a wire with a cotton ball at the tip. First, he brushed the inside of the ear. Then he inserted the razor, twirled it, and again brushed the ear. Then he used the hook and tweezers to draw out any additional dirt and once again brushed the ear. At each step, he went deeper and deeper until it seemed the ear drum itself was gently tapped and massaged and the customer felt his ears pink and tingling. Next, the hair in the customer's nose was removed and his face, scalp, neck, and shoulders were massaged, pinched, rubbed, pushed, and

85 A SCENE JUST BEFORE INDEPENDENCE DAY, 1889. THE ACCOMPANYING TEXT TOLD OF FIREWORKS OF "CHEAP AND INFERIOR QUALITY" SOLD TO "THE NOT OVER-NICE CUSTOMERS."

pulled until they were moist and almost sore. His fingers were cracked, his toes pulled, and his arms and trunk twisted one way and another. Finally, as a soothing finish, his arms and neck were gently patted.[29]

One of the most respected professions was that of a scribe, who was on a social level with doctors and the richest of merchants, to be consulted on subjects literary, poetic, and practical, such as the auspicious name for a store or a child who was about to begin his education. There were ten Chinese scribes in the city in 1885, of whom three were considered artists. Since there was no font of type in Chinatown, the business cards, prayer cards, and New Year cards so much in demand had to be drawn by hand on a stone and printed on a lithographic press. The scribe's work ranged from ordinary announcements, such as the notice of the sale of a business, to more elaborate statements issued by the many associations and organizations in Chinatown. He conceived and designed the names of shops, drawing the characters on fine paper that was then pasted on a board for a carpenter to execute or on a window for a painter

to copy. He also sketched on transparent paper a man's name to be used by a stone mason who carved cemetery headstones.[30]

FUNERALS AND FESTIVALS

In 1883 the Chinese consulate bought a plot on a small hill at the far end of the Cemetery of the Evergreens in Brooklyn to serve as the community's main burial ground. Americans called it Celestial Hill. The slight rise was auspicious, since it was believed demons could only travel in a straight line. For a long time there was a large muddy pond at the foot of the hill and that too was pleasing because it was believed evil spirits were deterred by water. A large iron incinerator, shaped like a chicken coop, was permanently installed at one side of the burial ground for burning the effects of the dead. For a wealthy family, even this was insufficient. In November 1886 Mai, one of only four Chinese women in the city, died of consumption at the age of twenty-five. She was the wife of Chin Shun, an importer of Chinese and Japanese wares with a shop at 139 Chatham Street. Twelve carriages carried mourners up Chatham

77

86 "Celestial Hill" at the Cemetery of the Evergreens. At the top, mourners are burning effects of the deceased.

Street to the Bowery, across to the Grand Street Ferry, and on to Evergreens. An express wagon followed behind with trunks of her clothing, her bed, and her chair. All was burned in a pyre beside her grave.[31]

Celestial Hill was not a final resting place. In July 1888 three men arrived from San Francisco to collect bones for shipment to China. They set up a little wicker tent and exhumed sixteen of the approximately two hundred bodies interred there, pulling queues from skulls, scraping off any remaining flesh, and packing each set in a sealed tin box. These were consolidated in five larger boxes to be shipped to the Hong Chow Asylum in San Francisco for forwarding to Hong Kong and then to Guangdong. Their superintendent, Hop Ah Ton, dressed in American clothing and speaking good English, told reporters that bodies were exhumed three or four years after burial. He said his company charged $100 for

87 The Moon Festival. The text described the cake as "a dirty looking doughy substance made of melon seed, gee-ma nut, almonds and walnuts ground up and held together in a paste of quince jelly." The Joss House, with its familiar side-slanting entrance stair, is in the background.

79

each body, and the five large crates collected at Evergreens, weighing a total of 650 pounds, would cost $105 to send to San Francisco. Hop Ah Ton said that for the past two months he and his men had exhumed bodies in Los Angeles, Denver, Kansas City, Wheeling, Pittsburgh, and Philadelphia. During the three days the process was underway in New York, memorial ceremonies were held in private homes and association halls. When the bodies were shipped, the ceremonies duplicated those held for the departure of living persons.[32]

The spring festival in the third Chinese month and the autumn festival in the eighth month were occasions to remember and propitiate the spirits of the dead, although—to Americans—the feasting and music that accompanied the observance seemed hardly appropriate. In April 1883 dozens of carriages left the Yuet Sing store at 204 Chatham Square followed by wagons loaded with roast pigs, fowls, and provisions. They crossed the river by the Catherine Street ferry and continued on to Evergreens cemetery. After the food was placed in front of the graves, a venerable-looking man—perhaps Yuet Sing himself—took a piece of yellowish mock money, lit it with a candle, and threw it before the offerings. Then he lit a bunch of incense sticks, bowed three times, touching his forehead to the ground, and placed the sticks in the ground near the burning paper. He knelt and bowed three more times. An attendant handed him a small cup of namadhaio, which he poured on the ground, and again bowed three times. When all the others in the party had gone through the same ceremony, the food was put back on the wagons and returned to Chinatown, where feasting and music lasted into the early morning.[33]

The most noticeable feature of the Autumn Moon Festival—on the full moon of the eighth month of the Chinese year—was (and is) the consumption of moon cakes, made of rice flour with a mass of chopped nuts and fruits in the center and baked in an oven.[34]

GOVERNMENT

In June 1883 China opened a consulate at 95 Clinton Place (soon renamed West 8th Street). The first consul was Ou-yang Ming, who often claimed to speak little English but was thoroughly familiar with the language and American ways. He was one of 120 boys (as was Yan Phou Lee, mentioned earlier) sent by the Qing government to the United States beginning in 1872 as part of the Chinese Educational Mission. The idea was that they would return home and help modernize China's military and civil service.

They were scattered in small towns throughout Connecticut for preliminary studies with the intention that they would complete their education at Yale. But in 1881, after an inspector from Peking found the boys were becoming American in thought and manner, they were ordered home. Most, including Ou-yang Ming, obeyed, and some, like him, rose to high positions.[35]

After enactment of the Exclusion Law in 1882, China proposed that Chinese travelers between Cuba and China be issued an identity document by the Chinese consul-general in Havana, similar to the document required by Chinese in America who wanted to go to China and return. Washington agreed and a consulate was opened in New York to facilitate travel between Cuba and China. Ou-yang Ming, now a mandarin of the fourth rank, was sent to New York as the first consul. He was later promoted to the more important consulate of San Francisco and eventually became China's minister to Chile.[36]

Jann Ting-seong, another CEM boy, returned to the United States on his own and became one of the engineers who designed and erected the Brooklyn Bridge. He later invented the Jann coupling device for railway cars and other mechanical devices. Toward the end of his career, he managed the Dry Storage Battery Company in Brooklyn and was an engineer for the Croton Water Works.[37]

A *Tribune* reporter described Ou-yang Ming as of "medium height with a small moustache that covers about two thirds of his upper lip, drooping at the ends as represented in the familiar pictures of mandarins, and his chin showed a short growth of beard." He wore an upper garment of dark blue-figured silk, dark yellow silk trousers, black silk shoes, and a black silk cap. The consulate was a substantial four-story building with heavy mahogany doors. The walls of the large (then known as a "double parlor") reception room on the first floor were covered with gold-figured paper, with a blue-figured Brussels carpet. The ebony furniture was upholstered in crimson velvet and there were large porcelain vases on the floor by the mantels.[38]

Ou-yang Ming attempted to play a role similar to that of the American, British, and other foreign consuls in China: de facto rulers of their communities. In August 1883 he issued a proclamation telling the Chinese to obey the laws, not to quarrel, and not to go to courts but, instead, to settle their disputes through community mediation. The following January, he directed that after February 15 no Chinese would be allowed to open a laundry within three blocks of any other.[39]

YUNG WING'S HOUSE.

MANDARIN YUNG WING.

STUDY AND DINING-ROOM.

IN THE SCHOOL-ROOM.

PARLOR.

THE COLLEGE.

88 THE CHINESE EDUCATIONAL MISSION SCHOOL IN HARTFORD, CONNECTICUT.

In July 1884 the imperial flag—a dark blue dragon on a yellow field—fluttered atop 16 Mott as Cheng Tsao-ju, the Chinese minister to Washington, alighted from a carriage to be greeted by Deputy Sheriff Tom Lee, a line of wealthy merchants, and Wong Chin Foo. Cheng wore a dark blue silk jacket and black silk robe embroidered with golden dragons and other figures, silk trousers, black satin boots, and a black silk cap with a red button and peacock feathers. Ou-yang Ming was similarly dressed, but without the dragons and only a gold button on his cap. The minister complimented the Chinese on their good behavior, claiming that of the ten thousand Chinese in New York and environs, only eight had been convicted of crimes in the previous ten years and not one had been found guilty of intoxication, disorderly conduct, burglary, highway robbery, or other common crimes. Finally, as paraphrased by a *Times* reporter, Cheng admonished:

> Don't smoke opium, don't quarrel, don't litigate, and don't go into politics. American politics are to be avoided; they serve the professional politician only and injure others by reducing them to lower morality. I know you all obtain justice in the local tribunals. At the same time, if you have grievances, report them to me or to your consul and they will be righted.[40]

Early in the history of the Chinese in San Francisco, the *Chung-hua kung-so* (Four Great Houses; the name was retained when member organizations expanded to five and later to six) was formed as an umbrella organization and as an intermediary with the Qing government. As such, it was registered in Peking.[41]

New York merchants, in 1885, also registered a Chung-hua kung-so with Peking. Its main function was to keep a record of leases and other business contracts and to serve as neutral ground where strongmen might attempt to settle disputes peacefully. It was inaugurated with a procession from the old private house at 16 Mott to a room over Yuet Sing's store at 202 Chatham Street. Two Taoist priests, carrying a scroll of Kwan Kung, were followed by Huang Sih-chuan, who had succeed Ou-yang Ming as consul, merchants in flowing robes, and finally the Chinese orchestra. Half the mixed population of the neighborhood gawked at the sight.[42]

The move to 202 Chatham Street, also known as 10 Chatham Square—an old, three-story house with a small stoop and mansard roof—was temporary. In 1887 officials of the Chung-hua kung-so raised $16,500 to buy the building at 16 Mott. Tom Lee—listed as "Chairman of the

89 In about 1883, a brick building replaced an early frame house at 16 Mott. As the headquarters of the Consolidated Benevolent Association, it contained a shrine to Kwan Kung. To generations of tourists, it was the Joss House.

Chinese Municipal Council"—was in charge of raising $25,000 for a new structure. In March 1890, when the new building was ready, the organization was incorporated as the Chinese Charitable and Benevolent Association, later changed to the Chinese Consolidated Benevolent Association (CCBA).

For non-Chinese, 16 Mott was known as the Joss House. An attendant, described by Americans as a priest (actually, the man who interpreted the book of divination), was paid thirty dollars a month and allowed to keep the profits from the sale of twenty-five-cent packets of candles, incense, and mock money to be burned before having one's fortune told. He was also a messenger, distributing notices of monthly meetings in the form of slips of cardboard shaped somewhat like a bottle. The narrow upper portion was red and the lower portion yellow. Each notice contained the name of the member and the time of the meeting. These were collected at the door as a record of attendance. Members who failed to appear were fined one dollar. Officers, called councilors, were appointed or elected by the separate clan, district, trade, and professional associations. The entire community was then divided into two territorial organizations: Ning Young, represent-

90 TOURISTS THOUGHT OF IT AS A CHURCH OR TEMPLE, BUT THE SHRINE WAS SIMPLY A PLACE TO USE THE FORTUNE STICKS TO PROBE THE FUTURE.

ing Toishan, and Lung Sing, representing the remaining 20 percent of the community from other regions of Guangdong. Two men stood for election each year but, since the chairmanship rotated between the Ning Young and Lung Sing, both candidates would be from one or the other grouping. There was a similar division of the lesser posts of Chinese secretary, English secretary, and office manager.

Expenses were met by membership dues, recording fees, fines, and a "port tax." An indi-

vidual planning to leave the metropolitan area had to announce his intention by paying a tax. This simultaneously served as notice of his departure so he could be detained if he tried to leave without settling his debts. Agents of the association were posted at the dock when a steamship sailed for China and at the railroad station when trains left for California, to make sure no one escaped.

An *Evening Post* reporter described a typical scene in 1899: A crowded pier and "prodigious"

91 By 1890 the shrine was decorated with intricate carvings from Canton.

noise; "perhaps thirty Chinese, quiet, motionless, watching"; "papers are inspected and stamped and many pass through"; someone tries to run away and "a phalanx of blue-coated Chinese block his way"; "there is a row"; "a policeman

92 As a joke, reporters called notices on telegraph poles a "Chinese newspaper." It came to be accepted as a fact.

takes a hand"; he is "arrested for disturbing the peace, or is accused of some crime and arrested;" "the steamer sails without him."[43]

Notices of partnerships formed or dissolved, businesses for sale or already sold, or businesses sought or goods for sale were posted on a board in front of 16 Mott. To spread the news wider, individual notices were tacked on the wooden poles that dotted the streets. Americans called them Chinese "newspapers."[44]

The mandatory rotation of officers between the majority and minority community served to check corruption. The Benevolent Association collected more money than needed for its bare-bones existence. It was never clear what the excess was to be used for: Certainly not for "benevolence"—that was the function (although seldom performed) of family organizations. There was temptation for officers to misuse community funds, ostensibly as loans. There was a saying: "Officials can commit arson as they please, but the common people are not permitted to light their lamps at night." The Chinese felt bound to "officials" who had contacts with the American police and bureaucracy. The poor spoke of things that were rightfully theirs as "favors." All business licenses and sign permits—even a marriage license, should one be required—were favor papers. And since only "officials" or "gentlemen" could get or give favors, they were supported as a privileged class.[45]

The principal power of "officials" lay in their ability to manipulate the allocation of business sites and to fix prices. Laundries and other businesses were registered with the Benevolent Association. Registration became a valuable asset, making a business worth more than its lease or stock. The extra value was called *p'o Tai*, or "store foundation." The Chinese compared it to the goodwill recognized in American business practices and claimed it arose from the labor and careful attention a man had put into his business. When a Chinese sold a business, he demanded a large sum as "foundation money." Most of the haggling in the sale of a business involved the amount to be paid for *p'o Tai*. Often, a sale could be concluded only when the buyer and seller were of the same clan. The seller, who might receive less than he hoped for, was compensated in status as a man who had dealt kindly with his kin or clansmen.[46]

This was Chinese-made law. An incident that

84

began in September 1889 illustrates the complications of enforcing the registration practice where an American might be involved. John White owned two frame buildings at 15½ and 17 Mott. He rented them to Hoy Sing and Kwan Tung, owners of the import firm of Wing Ho Hing, for $3,800 a year. White decided to construct a brick building with the single address of 17 Mott and told Hoy Sing and Kwan Tung he would rent part of the building to them. They moved to temporary quarters pending construction. When the building was complete, White offered a new lease at six thousand dollars a year. They objected, and White leased the building to a Philadelphia firm run by several Chinese named Lee. Soon, the Lees notified White they had been threatened and would have to break the lease. When White tried to find out why the deal went sour, he learned of a notice posted on the bulletin board outside the Benevolent Association:

> Let this be known, that Wing Ho Hing and others have the right of occupation to the surface floor and second floor of store 17 on the street....Due notice had been given to that effect when the building was being torn down. Now the building is finished and ready to be delivered into the hands of tenants, a second notice is given in order to prevent future disputes.

White tried to have Hoy and Kwan arrested on a charge of criminal conspiracy, but a judge refused to issue the warrant. The *Times* said the boycott was controlled by the "Long Si Lee Tong, which inspires fear of death." The Lun Gee Tong's (to give its more customary name) strong-arm methods were soon evident. In October police were called to a basement laundry at 207 Fifth Street, where Lee Hing said three robbers had come into his laundry, knocked him down, gagged him, tied his hands and feet, slipped a noose around his neck, and attached this to his ankles so if he struggled he would have strangled himself. He claimed he became unconscious and would have died except that a neighbor came for his laundry and, finding the door open, went into the rear, cut the ropes, and tickled his nose with feathers until he regained consciousness.[47]

Lee Hing said he knew exactly who did it and where they lived. Detectives rushed to 17 Mott Street and found three men named Lee in the back room. They were the same Lees from Philadelphia who wanted to lease the new building. At Essex Market Police Court the next morning, a Chinese woman, who said she was the wife of one of the Lees, came to complain of a frame-up by the Wing Ho Hing partners. The case was dismissed with no further hearing. The unwelcome publicity in the newspapers following the complaint of White also embarrassed the Chinatown establishment by exposing their un-American practices. The Lees and Wing Ho Hing came to an understanding on *p'o Tai* rights and the Lees took possession of the two floors.[48]

In July 1888 Tom Lee again flaunted the power of the Lun Gee Tong with a picnic. His diamonds flashing, Lee promised a "bully time," with plenty to eat and drink. Reporters wrote "no Christians need apply," for an event that would "counter the flesh pots of Sunday School strawberry festivals." Two hundred Chinese, most of them in blouses and straw hats, the others in American trousers and shirts, accompanied by "Caucasian wives...also some young and middle aged Caucasian women, not wives" and about twenty non-Chinese, took carriages to the dock at East 31st Street and boarded the steamer *Pomona* for Bay Cliff Park on the south side of Staten Island. The band went along too, with Tom Lee using a chunk of wood to pound the largest gong of all—"brass, two feet in diameter, with curled edges." A German band was at the other end of the boat. Gon Hor, the gigantic past-grandmaster of the Chinese Lodge of Masons, used his size and authority to maintain order.[49]

The following October, the death of a long-time Lun Gee Tong official brought another display of the tong's strength. Lee Yu Doo was said to have been a general in the unsuccessful "Black Flag" attempt of former Taiping rebels to prevent the French seizure of the Tonkin region of Vietnam in 1883–85.[50]

At Naughton's funeral home (Kennedy had long since retired) on Mott Street next to Transfiguration church, the remains of Lee Yu Doo lay in an open coffin, with playing cards and mock money scattered on his chest. For ten days, teams of four men rotated watches at the corners of the bier. On the day of the funeral, an uncooked suckling pig and a fresh-killed goat were placed before the coffin, flanked on the sides by heaps of fruits and candies. Before this stood another table with a complete roasted pig and more heaps of food. A third table, with a huge vase of paper flowers, burning candles, and incense sticks, was placed in front. Mourners dressed in yellow, purple, and blue entered, bowed, and stood silently as the orchestra on either side beat gongs and cymbals, and someone occasionally uttered a piercing wail. Finally, the coffin was closed, placed in a hearse, and a procession of more than five hundred mourners

began, with twelve policemen clearing the way. Immediately behind the police walked Tom Lee, James Baptiste, Wong Chin Foo, and another official named Ha Bow. Behind them came an American brass band playing a dirge. Then came Lee Yee, riding on a large white horse. Lee was also said to have been a Black Flags general. He was dressed in a fawn-colored costume with a black turban, with an old-fashioned horse pistol stuck in his belt. He was followed by two other reputed generals similarly dressed. A tall Chinese on foot carried a placard inscribed "Lun Gee Tong CFMS." Masonic ceremonies had been performed at the funeral home and some of the marchers wore Masonic aprons.

A group said to be veterans of a Black Flag regiment had a broad band of black muslin around their foreheads and wore dark blue baggy breeches and blouses with light blue leggings. Others carried poles bearing twenty different symbols, among them a jar, a sword, an axe, and a flute. The hearse, pulled by four horses draped in black, was followed by twelve pallbearers in sky-blue robes. A man sitting next to the driver threw pieces of mock money for devils to devour. Eastsiders quickly seized them. General mourners and members of other societies brought up the rear.

An estimated ten thousand persons jammed Chinatown and neighboring streets, since the procession stretched for half a mile to the ferry. Other crowds lined the route through Williamsburg and out to Evergreens. After the usual chickens, rice, and wine were laid out, and the candles and incense burned, an enormous fire was lit and the dead man's personal belongings were thrown on it. The marchers filed by, stripping off their black turbans, white gloves, sashes, and tunics and tossed them into the flames, along with all the badges, flags, and insignia carried on the march. It was night when the ceremony ended. Scarcely had the Chinese left when a waiting mob rushed to loot the grave of food and trinkets left to propitiate lurking devils.[51]

The Six Chinese Theaters in New York

The Chinese of New York welcomed their first major theater company in June 1889 when, after performances in San Francisco, the *Swin Tien Lo*, or "Most Sublime Company," opened at the Windsor Theater on the Bowery. Actors were well paid, with stars earning from fifty to one hundred dollars a week and supporting players ten to twenty-five dollars. In addition, admirers honored them with gifts of money, food, tobacco, and opium.[1] The actors believed they were reciting sacred scriptures where each word and gesture had its precedent and any lapse verged on impiety, with punishment ranging from a fine or extra work to beatings. There were nearly fifty actors, including Tak-a-wing, who played female roles and was considered one of the greatest stars of his time, declaiming his lines in falsetto and walking with the peculiar gait of a woman with bound feet.

The plot of the main play—*The Faithful Vassal*, set in the Tang Dynasty in the early sev-enth century—was familiar to all Chinese. The aging emperor sends his son-in-law at the head of a large army against northern invaders. The parting of the prince from his wife, played by Tak-a-wing, was staged as a tableau, with the princess and her maids arrayed in elaborate costumes. It was considered a masterpiece of Chinese dramatics.

Because of mutiny and disaffection, the imperial army is defeated in its first battle. The prince is captured by Tartars but displays his literary abilities to such advantage that the Tartar king gives him his eldest and fairest daughter as a wife. Five years pass. News comes that persuades the Tartar king to release the prince on parole. He returns home to find the Chinese armies have been defeated and his relatives slain, except for the princess, who escaped with the aid of a faithful vassal, only to become lost in a wilderness.

Food is scarce, and the vassal, who gives

95 Announcement of the arrival of the Swin Tien Lo company.

what little there is to the princess, is about to die of starvation when the prince arrives just in time to hear the vassal's last words. The prince returns to Tartary with the princess and tells the king the story of the faithful vassal. The Tartar king is so moved that he becomes an ally of the Chinese emperor and sends the prince at the head of an army to seek vengeance. The prince slays his enemies and is proclaimed heir apparent, with both wives as queen consorts.[2]

The plays and performances were far beyond the comprehension of Bowery audiences. Newspaper reporters in effect wrote their own scripts. A *Times* reporter found another play set in the 10th century B.C. reminiscent of the comedies and melodramas of the Bowery stage:

> The action proves that several practical jokes that are still current antedate the Christian era. The two genii who were represented by the comedians pulled chairs from under each other and pretended to read books held upside down in a way that would not have been out of place in one of Hoyt's farces....The actors walk with swaggers and struts which would make genuine English "dudes" turn green with envy. One general had a bearing that was the exact counterpart of Pat Rooney in his most grotesque moments. ...Tak-a-wing...and his attendant slave were plastered on their cheeks with the most brilliant imaginable rouge. Their choicest and tenderest attentions to Tak-a-Wing's lover consisted in blowing his nose with their fingers, a deed performed with an observance to detail more faithful than pleasant....When [Tak-a-wing] tapped his comic would-be lover with his fan, one almost expected to hear the words, "Go away, you naughty man."[3]

A *Tribune* reviewer, saying "no written account can do justice" reviewed the prop man:

> The property man loses something about every ten minutes and comes in and hunts around under the chairs for it and walks down the footlights and peeps over into where the orchestra ought to be to see if it has rolled off the stage. The hero may be making love to the heroine, or the heavy villain slaying the royal prince, but the property man wanders in and searches for that "property" just the same. The heavy man and the leading lady step out of his way and get up and let him move their chairs and otherwise show that they are of minor importance....When the hero triumphs over the cruel father and beats him with a whip which looks like an exaggerated whisk broom, he raises it up to a great height and brings it down with a murderous velocity to within

about a foot of the victim's person; then he stops and hits a gentle conventional tap, the misguided old gentleman meanwhile working his shoulders up and down in great pain. After all, it is much like our own Western drama....The only man who seems to have marked out absolutely original lines for himself is the property man. The way he stands around and silently accuses the star of having stolen one of his chairs is absolutely unique.[4]

A month later the Most Sublime Company ended its tour. Chinatown got a company of its own in March 1893 when Chu Fong, a wealthy, English-speaking merchant, rented a large warehouse basement at 5 and 7 Doyers Street that had previously housed a Chinese Sunday School and hired thirty actors from California. New York's Sabbath laws prohibited theatrical performances on Sundays—the only day when great numbers of Chinese would be in Chinatown. Since the days of P. T. Barnum, theaters, variety halls, and dime museums that depended on holiday crowds had evaded the ban by calling their Sunday performances "sacred concerts." When Chu Fong did the same, a reporter noted that a Chinese sacred concert was "gymnastic opera boufee [sic]...run on the same lines as those of his Caucasian brothers."[5]

Then in July 1895, to the hoots and jeers of the audience, the police marched eight actors—still in their robes and paints— to the Elizabeth Street station, pointing to the costumes as proof the performance was a violation of the Sabbath. Chu Fong was arrested at his home, brought to the station, and released on bail. He managed to placate the police, and the theater reopened.[6]

The following January the police staged an encore. Five actors, including two "who were impersonating female characters on the stage [were] hustled off in their disguise." This time the issue went to trial. The prosecution produced Quan Yick Nam, a Chinese employee of the police, who testified that the Sunday performance was the same on other days. The costumes were shown as evidence that the performance, by any reasonable definition, could not be considered sacred.

The defense produced Mark Yet, a merchant and interpreter, who said that although they might seem "weird and gruesome," similar performances were given at joss houses and temples in China. Yale graduate Yan Phou Lee affirmed that the play was religious. William Fales, on leave from his post as an American vice-consul in Amoy, said he had seen similar plays hundreds of times in Chinese temples. He

96 Theater interior, 1896, with gaslights over the stage.

testified that the actors only seemed to be wearing strange and fanciful costumes—their dress was that usually worn by rich men of the historical period being presented. As evidence they were in accord with the Sabbath, Fales said Chinese plays were classified according to the moral concept explicated and the one being performed came under the category of "Virtue Rewarded."

Chu Fong tried to impress the court with his social standing. He produced a complimentary letter from Mayor William Strong, who had visited the theater during a tour of Chinatown in 1895. The expert testimony was dismissed and the mayor's letter was ruled irrelevant. Chu Fong was found guilty of Sabbath breaking, and his license to operate a theater on Sunday was declared void.[7]

Somehow, Chu Fong straightened out the licensing problem and reopened the theater, but when the visit of Chinese viceroy Li Hung Chang in late August and early September 1896 brought extraordinary attention to Chinatown, with front-page articles in all newspapers, the police again closed it down, despite a sign saying visitors

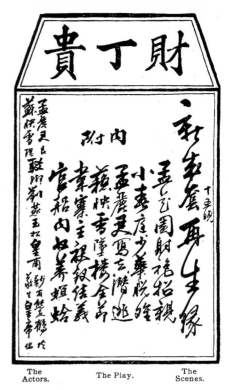

| The Actors. | The Play. | The Scenes. |

97 PLAYBILL FROM 1900.

98 THEATER ENTRANCE ABOUT 1906. NOTICE THE SIGN. IN CHINATOWN, AMERICANS WERE THE "OTHER."

would hear a sacred concert with recitations of the "moral precepts of Confucius, whose goodness all the world acknowledges."[8]

Chu reopened when outside attention diminished but gave up in May 1897. He said he paid one actor three thousand dollars, plus board and expenses, and had sustained a loss of seventeen thousand dollars in the face of the hostility of the police and gamblers: "The police say it brings Chinese to the area on Sunday to gamble. Gamblers say the Chinese go to the theater and don't gamble."[9]

Chu's sliding scale of admission prices had been one dollar at six o'clock, seventy-five cents at seven o'clock, fifty cents at eight o'clock, and twenty-five cents at nine. For any seats empty after ten o'clock, the price dropped to fifteen cents.[10]

The enterprise was bought by Chin Yu, a wealthy restaurant owner, who reduced the initial entrance price to fifty cents (twenty-five cents after nine o'clock) and managed to support a troupe of forty, including leading actor Lee Sung, who was paid two thousand dollars a year plus room and board.[11]

Chin Yu was succeeded by Charlie Gong, who operated the theater for many years and was known to reporters as the Frohman of Doyers Street. The stage was a simple platform without curtains or footlights. A few bars of gaslights hung a bit higher than the heads of the actors and a few feet in front of them. A fan worked by strings and gears stirred the stuffy air. The wall at the rear was elaborately painted in bright colors, with pictures of birds, animals, and dragons. Two rear doors for entrances and exits were covered by curtains. The orchestra sat in an alcove between the doors. Behind them was an embroidered picture of Confucius, said to be copied from a hanging in a temple in Peking.[12]

The actors did everything in pantomime. A hero mounting a spirited horse and riding off would lift one leg in the air, twirl around a few times, hopping and jerking up one leg, and make his exit. If a princess had to return to her sumptuous chamber, two servants would appear carrying silk curtains, and she would walk between them. A chair piled on a table was a steep mountain for the hero to climb. If he had to look out a window, he walked with his arms out, palms perpendicular, as if feeling a wall, and then moved his hands in a square, outlining the window. Finally, he stretched his neck through the spot and gazed into the distance.

Costumes were old brocades, sometimes embroidered with gold and silver. The colors were warm pastels woven in blended shades. An actor wearing yellow, with yellow banners emerging from his shoulders, was the emperor. A dignified old man always had a long beard hanging, strangely, from his upper lip rather than his chin. An actor with his face and neck streaked with red and black was a barbarian.

The audience sat in rows of benches that accomodated about five hundred persons. Some slipped out of their shoes and perched on the back of the benches, with their feet on the seats, to gain a better view of the stage. Hawkers wandered about selling sweets, oranges, bananas, and sugarcane. When Chinese newspapers began to be published, there was a stir as the night's editions were sold for reading during lulls in the action.

Audiences used to the Canton theater expected interludes of farce and acrobatics. For about two years in the 1890s a father-and-son team of acrobats, Dai Sa Kwong and Dai Sa Loon, performed at the Doyers Street theater and also appeared at the "concert saloons" of Coney Island. But when the son, Dai Sa Loon, began wearing flashy neckties and took an actress from the Coney Island stage as a companion, Dai Sa Kwong removed himself and his straying son to San Francisco.[13]

The arrival of the theater coincided with the development of tourist Chinatown. They were charged fifty or seventy-five cents no matter when they arrived and were shown to a box at the side of the house, or to another at the side of the stage. A sex farce was performed—like everything else—with broad gestures to illustrate the words, and in the beginning the presence of tourists posed a problem. Once, as the music picked up tempo indicating a climax of some sort, a notice was hung on one of the pillars. There were shouts as the actors left the stage and the orchestra played alone. A guide told the tourists that the audience was expressing its admiration for the musical solo. Actually the audience was angry. The notice said that, because of the foreigners, the rest of the scene would be played offstage.

A way was found around such contretemps. When tourists entered, the action ended and the orchestra hammered gongs and clashed cymbals, vamping until they were seated. Then generals with banners streaming from their shoulders burst on stage with a vast army of four or five men trailing behind. The orchestra picked up the tempo and the actors emitted squeals of hate and whirled and fenced. One actor would hold his lance above his head and another would strike it. The first would return the blow and this blow would be parried in the same way. A lance flew through the air, to be fended off at the last

99 Theater interior about 1906. Perhaps because of the state of photography, the actors woodenly hold their poses.

minute with the easy movement of an arm or leg. The actors would twirl and circle in a crouch with more blows, more parries, leaps, twirls, screams, and squeals until one would fall and die, only to stand up and make his exit. The orchestra would vamp while the prop man rearranged the set. If the tourists showed no signs of leaving, the stage manager, who sat near the entrance, would rattle a hard gourd indicating more was required, and two other champions would step forward to begin a new battle. When this battle ended, the guide might say that the joss house was about to close and they must hurry. All would exit, and the wearied musicians would put down their instruments and light cigarettes. After a few minutes the actors reassembled and, at another rattle of the stage manager's gourd, the play would resume at the spot it had broken off.[14]

A performance was not mere entertainment. There was a short, ritual play at the start of a lunar month, invoking the blessings of heaven and driving off evil spirits with a rattle of drums and the explosion of a few firecrackers. The play began every night at the prescribed time, usually half-past six or a quarter to seven. Since the Chinese were still busy closing their shops and having their dinners, there might not be anyone seated, but it did not matter: the ritual of the play had to begin at the appointed time.

Because there was no curtain to indicate acts,

reporters joked that a single endless play was being performed. In fact there was a separate play each evening, although each might be part of a historical series. The names of the plays posted outside in English were satiric: *In Darkest China*; *Dragon's Breath*; and *Seven in the Family, Kindhearted the Whole Lot.*

A rare description of a plot survives from 1903. A poor student of aristocratic birth is engaged to a pretty girl. They are separated by the slings and arrows of fate that littered the Chinese stage. The student is rescued and cared for by a rich mandarin, who recognizes his abilities and gives him his daughter as a wife. After long studies and promotions, the student, now an official in his own right, returns to the home of his adopted father and finds the girl of his youth serving as a maid. They recognize one another, and the old flame is rekindled. The former student says his new official position will allow him to have two wives. There is a show of jealously and hurt feelings between the two women, but the daughter of the mandarin agrees, providing she is recognized as the chief wife. The first love accepts this and they live happily ever after, or so it may be assumed.

The theater was Chinatown's only large auditorium and social center. As such, it could not escape the tong wars between the On Leong and Hip Sing tongs that erupted in New York shortly after the turn of the century. The theater was under On Leong control. On August 7, 1905, a string of firecrackers was set off near the stage. As the audience rose in their seats to see what had happened, Hip Sings seated at the front and rear fired volleys of heavy bullets. Four On Leong men were killed on the spot or later died of wounds. The audience ran into the streets. The police who clubbed their way through the crowds found chairs and curtains riddled with bullets, the floor littered with hats, coats, shoes, and parcels of food, and some terrified Chinese cowering under benches.

More than a dozen men were arrested for the killings, but no one was ever tried. Tom Lee, the On Leong chieftain, turned away a reporter saying: "The Chinese theater is just the same as a Christian Church. Decent Chinamen go there, say a prayer, eat an apple, just the same as an American man goes to Christian Endeavor."[15]

The theater lacked dressing rooms and other facilities for the actors and musicians. Instead, communal living rooms were rented in a house at 10 Chatham Square and a tunnel was opened to the theater so that actors could reach the stage in full costume.

The theater was again a target during a 1909 war between the On Leong Tong and the Four Brothers family association. Two gunmen slipped through the backstage tunnel, waited until the popular actor Dop Doy (Comedian) Hong left his room to get a drink of water from the hall bathroom and killed him with one shot at close range.[16]

The theater had already lost most of its customers as the community huddled down. The killing of Dop Doy was the final blow: it closed a few weeks later. An attempt to revive it as a Bowery variety house failed. The following March it reopened for Chinese plays, but that too failed. With a tong war raging, residents did not want to stay out late. Finally, in August 1910, the building was bought by the Rescue Society on Doyers Street, better known as the Chinatown Midnight Mission, to aid the Bowery's many alcoholic and homeless men.[17]

It was another fifteen years before Chinese opera returned to New York. In July 1924 a home was found in what had been Miner's Bowery Theater, noted for melodrama, light opera, and burlesque. The *Chuck Man On* Company—said to be the best in Canton—arrived from Vancouver and Seattle with thirty principals, an orchestra of six, and trunks filled with silk and brocade costumes. The plots were more contrived than the melodramas that had previously stalked the worn boards. One, whose title in English was given as *Shadows of a Great City*,

involved a priest who manipulated a go-between to make advances toward a respectable married woman. Her husband finds an incriminating slipper in her room, and she is accused of infidelity. When she throws herself into a river, the emperor happens to be passing by on his barge and he rescues her. The emperor and his consort reconcile the husband and wife, the evildoer is punished, and the play ends—five hours after it began—with Confucian harmony.

The heroine was played by a woman ballyhooed as a Manchu princess down on her luck. Chinese jammed the theater night after night, at prices ranging from one to five dollars. So eager were they that instead of remaining away for a leisurely dinner, as was the custom in China, many came before the opening curtain prayer at seven and sat until the last clash of cymbals at midnight. Not since Weber and Fields in the heyday of Miner's had there been such enthusiastic and rapt audiences.[18]

The company left New York after a few months. Its success encouraged entrepreneurs with On Leong connections to take a five-year lease on the London Theater at 235 Bowery near Rivington Street, three-quarters of a mile north of Chinatown. They renamed it the Chinese Theater and began performances in January 1925. Soon after its opening, someone fired three shots into the air. The audience ran out, and the police searched for casualties, but found none. The orchestra also fled, but the actors on stage continued to declaim their lines, true to the tradition that the performance was a religious act that must be completed.[19]

Other Mott Street impresarios leased the most fabled of Bowery theaters—*the* Bowery Theater at 48 Bowery—the oldest and most ornate still in use. It had opened in October 1826 and was once a stage for Junius Brutus Booth, Edwin Forest, and Lillian Russell. Later, Germans bought it and called it the Thalia, under which name it hosted Yiddish and Italian vaudeville until its final days as a Chinese theater. Most actors for the two Chinese theaters lived a cloistered and communal life on State Street in Brooklyn.

Audiences, numbering three to five hundred, wearing the standard summer dress of straw hats and silk shirts, drifted in after dinner and sat under house lights that remained on throughout the performance, munching melon seeds and sugarcane, guffawing at the sex jokes and expressing mild approval for bravura performances.[20]

The Bowery was roofed by an elevated train track, cut in the middle by trolley cars, and lined

100 THALIA THEATER ON THE BOWERY, ABOUT 1925, WHEN OWNED BY THE CHINESE.

with cheap shops, bars, flophouses, derelicts, and alcoholics. It took an adventurous tourist to look through the doors to the Orient:

> The Chinese are indifferent to gilding and stucco statuary. Exteriorly their theaters are as drab as doss houses. No paint, no flaring posters, no signs. You might pass several times before noticing that they were theaters. Interiorly they are so ramshackle that you would imagine rats running about among the legs of the indifferent audience. There are women as well as men; they are all Chinese and all eating seeds. What is being performed is bizarrely fantastic....The actresses, in brocade kimonos...wear ribboned head-dresses and engage in long dialogues in bird voices. A man with long black hair and a gold spear head fixed in the center of his brow takes advice apparently from his antique prospective father-in-law. They bow to one another countlessly....Hours of it! And, of the fleas mounting one's trouser-legs.[21]

The greatest test of the actors' resolve to maintain their traditions came in 1925 when federal agents and police swept through Chinatown in fruitless attempts to force an end to a raging tong war. Hundreds of men were arrested at random in homes, clubs, and restaurants. Among those swept up were entire audiences at the Thalia and Chinese theaters. Yet at both theaters the actors continued performing to empty seats.[22]

When the first sweep did not stop the killings, federal and local police staged another dusk-to-dawn sweep, cleaning out restaurants, dormitories, and clubs and taking away the audiences of both theaters, seizing the actors as well, still in their costumes.[23]

Like the earlier Doyers Street theater, the

101 THE LEAD MALE AND FEMALE ACTORS.

Bowery theaters were used for public meetings. The 1920s and 1930s brought repeated rallies in support of the Chinese republic and in protest against the Japanese invasion.

The old wood of the Thalia vanished in June 1929 in the flash of a careless fire. All that remained was a blank wall and three marble columns. A temporary stage was found at the Grand Street Theater, formerly the Jacob P. Adler Theater, until a new house was found at 201 Bowery and renamed the People's Theater.[24] On July 9, 1930, the bill at the People's Theater was *The Robber's Mistake*. Four shots were fired as the actor in the title role was miming his way across the stage, hiding behind invisible trees. The audience fled and the actors—a new breed, apparently—fled as well. Police found a tong leader dead under a seat.[25]

When the Depression came and waiters and laundrymen economized even more than usual, support for the theaters vanished. The five-year lease on the Chinese Theater was allowed to lapse. The People's Theater was also vacated. By the summer of 1931, the cymbals and gongs were again silent.

The sixth and last Chinese theater opened in New York by accident. The Tai Wing Wah company, consisting of twenty-seven male and seven female actors and six musicians, arrived from Hong Kong in 1940 and was installed in an old movie house on East Broadway, directly under the Manhattan Bridge. It was stranded when the war began in the Pacific, and the troupe spent the next ten years at what was called the New Canton Theater. The auditorium seated nine hundred but only a few hundred men came on any night, paying from 50¢ to $1.40 for a performance lasting from seven o'clock to midnight. On weekends, when there were special performances of the best of the classics, the performance lasted to one or two o'clock in the morning. As usual there were no intermissions, and the

house lights remained on as the audience read the evening papers hawked in the aisles or went out on errands, returning for what they knew would be a bravura part. Most were men, although there were a few women with restless children who might run up and down the aisles or lean their elbows on the stage and mimic the actors. Children were rare, and the indulgent bachelors liked to have them around. At the end of the night, the audience left behind mounds of gnawed sugarcane, orange peel, and the shells of litchi nuts and sunflower and watermelon seeds.

The actors earned twenty-five dollars a week plus room and board. The stock company was supplemented by occasional stars, who worked a circuit across the United States and Canada and were paid as much as one hundred dollars a week. Six microphones scattered around the stage were the only concession to modern times. The plays were still the classical fare of warlords, kings, princesses, villains, and clowns strutting in time-worn brocades. Whether there was an audience or not, the actors moved with unhurried dignity, never omitting a syllable, gesture, or grimace. In *The Hunter and the Ghost* a young lady mincing across the stage, dabbing her cerise-shaded eyes and tracing her words with fluttering hands, told of troubled dreams in a falsetto voice as the orchestra crashed and shrilled amid the desolate lofts and bargain stores under the rattling old bridge.

When Sid Win Wing, the manager, was asked the plot of a drama called *The Girl Is the Hero*, he replied: "This warlord in Shantung, thousands of years ago, he saw a girl. He killed her enemies. He married her. I don't know the story exactly but the actors do." The company survived, growing more tattered and undisciplined, until 1950, when the theater, by then called the Sun Sing, was refurbished and reopened as a movie house featuring the latest imports from Hong Kong.[26]

The Birth of the Restaurant and Tourist Industry

At the turn of the century, with more than seven thundred thousand Irish, English, Germans, Italians, French, Spaniards, Russians, Greeks, Poles, Hungarians, Scandinavians, Japanese, Syrians, Egyptians, Armenians, Bohemians, Rumanians, Turks, and many other nationalities jammed into lower Manhattan,

Chinatown was the center for fewer than ten thousand mostly males living, working, and marketing on Mott Street from Chatham Square to Pell Street and tiny, crooked Doyers Street: three small blocks that could be strolled in a few minutes.[1]

Yet decades of lurid newspaper stories had

THE OPIUM CURSE.

STARTLING FACTS WITH REGARD
TO THE EVIL IN THE
UNITED STATES.

102 THERE WERE TWO CHINATOWNS: THE REAL AND THE FICTITIOUS. WITH RARE EXCEPTIONS, AMERICANS, FED ON GENERATIONS OF EXOTICISM AND SENSATIONALISM, KNEW ONLY THE UNREAL.

created the myth that this drop in New York's ethnic ocean was the place where evil lurked. An 1890 article in *The Illustrated American* titled, "Opium Curse," promised, "Startling facts with regard to the evil in the United States:"

> Our eyes became accustomed to the darkness, and successively the form seemed a human being, a man, a Chinaman. It might have been a wax figure, for all the life it displayed. The flat felt hat was drawn over the yellow face, as if it had been jammed on by some other person than the wearer, and not disturbed afterward. The stiff blouse gave no hint of surrounding a living body within it. The tubular trousers might have been sections of stovepipe. The Chinaman was not even leaning against the wall. But his very silence and immobility spoke power well controlled, and of strength of purpose hard to turn.[2]

Actually, opium was more of an American disease than an affliction of the Chinese. Opium, in the form of laudanum, was widely used as a soporific for cholera, food poisoning, and parasites of many kinds. H. H. Kane, a New York doctor who specialized in treating American addicts, claimed the Chinese used less opium, as a straight drug, than Americans, and rec-

ommended the Chinese opium pipe "as a therapeutic agent" to wean addicts from the habit.[3]

While the Chinese stereotype epitomized evil, it also epitomized exotica, thanks to which the slumming craze opened new opportunities at a time when the future of Chinese laundries hung in the balance. At first, Chinese laundries had the advantage of location: They were everywhere, in little neighborhood stores. Then steam laundries established agencies in groceries and

103 TO THE WRITER AND ARTIST OF THIS EXPOSÉ, DOYERS STREET "WAS MORE LIKE A WINDING ALLEY IN AN OLD-WORLD TOWN THAN A STREET IN AN AMERICAN CITY."

104 Mott Street became "the center of the opium trade in New York."

ceeds, some of the natives kick off their slippers, their bare stockings peering through the rungs of their stools. The odor of fuming cigarettes fills the air; an incessant babble prevails; every few moments you will see a Chinese pick up a bone or a bit of refuse food and deliberately send it flying under the table to the dirty floor! A greedy cat munches away under one of the tables. Were it not for the red banners on the walls, the eating house would be as bare as a barn; and assuredly, it is as uninviting as a pig-sty. Yet the visitors to Chinatown love it dearly, and laugh and chatter there in a corner; the ladies, especially, on their first visit, cannot prevent themselves going into ecstacies over the tiny teacups. Thus, today, the "slummers" eat, drink, and are merry in their new experience with strange dishes.[4]

other stores where laundry could be left and later picked up. Moreover, when piped water was installed in the kitchens, a woman could heat water and do "soft washing" in her home, sending out only shirts, collars, and cuffs for the "starch laundry" business. This was the hardest of laundry work, with the smallest profit margin for time invested.

Ordinarily, Chinese restaurants did not attract "foreign" customers: They were not on the ground floor, like solid American restaurants, but up two or three flights of stairs, and there were no menus, and the smells seemed awful, but it was all this that made them exciting for the young of the Gay Nineties. A description of a safari into darkest Chinatown appeared in the July 1893 issue of the magazine *Once A Week*:

> Through a narrow hall and up dirty stairs brings one to the Chinese Delmonico's restaurant. A good dinner consists of nine courses, served on bare wooden tables and eaten with chopsticks. The meal begins with sweets, half a dozen bits of sugared ginger heaped on a small eggshell compote; the ginger is dyed a brilliant scarlet. In rapid succession follow dried nuts, candied apricots, and other delicacies....Some of the patrons have before them huge bowls of steaming rice, which they eat by bringing the dish to their lips and then literally shoveling the food into the open mouth....As the dinner pro-

A generation of Sunday Schools and festivals and picnics had taught the Chinese about American tastes and manners. When slumming disclosed a profitable niche, entrepreneurs were ready and able to exploit it. Chop suey (developed in the West, although no one can be sure where or when) proved the means. In 1896, a *Leslie's Illustrated* reporter enthused:

> Chow chop sui calls Americans to Chinatown. An American who once falls under the spell of chop sui may forget all about things Chinese for a while, and suddenly a strange craving that almost defies will power arises; as though under a magnetic influence he finds that his feet are carrying him to Mott Street. A good meal of chop sui, some duck, or *op*, some boiled chicken, or *gai*, rice, and tea costs about fifty cents [while] chop sui, rice, and tea alone could be had for thirty cents.

The reporter thought bird's-nest soup tasted "like steam from a locomotive mixed with the odor of oily smells" but said pigeon with mushrooms "instantly appeals to American tastes and could compete with the cooking of a best Parisian chef."[5]

In 1896 Chan Kew, whose "Evangelical Band" was supported by parishioners of the Central Congregational Church in Brooklyn, invited a few adventurous women from the church to din-

97

THE CHINAMAN AND THE THREE WOMEN TOOK TURNS IN SMOKING THE ONE PIPE.

"MAMIE," SHE CALLED, IN A FRIGHTENED WHISPER, "ARE THEY GOING TO RAID US?"

105 TWO OF THE PROMISED "STARTLING FACTS."

106 "AMERICAN OPIUM SMOKERS—INTERIOR OF A NEW YORK OPIUM DEN," AN ILLUSTRATION FOR AN 1881 *HARPER'S WEEKLY* ARTICLE BY H. H. KANE. THE LOCATION WAS NOT GIVEN, BUT SEVERAL OPIUM ROOMS WERE OPERATED BY AMERICANS IN THE BACK STREETS OF THE UPTOWN THEATER DISTRICT. THE CHINESE WAITER, A TOUCH OF EXOTICISM, DID NOT SIGNIFY OWNERSHIP. NO CHINESE WOULD DARE OPERATE SUCH A ROOM OUTSIDE THE POLICE-PROTECTED BOUNDARIES OF CHINATOWN. KANE ESTIMATED THERE WERE 4,000 AMERICAN OPIUM SMOKERS. HE CONSIDERED OPIUM SMOKING HARMLESS, SAYING THE DRUG "PRODUCES A PLEASANT CONDITION OF DREAMY WAKEFULNESS...APPROACHING THE *DOLCE FAR NIENTE* OF THE ITALIAN."

ner in Chinatown to see for themselves that evil did not lurk behind every lamppost. He escorted his guests to a restaurant on the third floor of a Pell Street building, where they were shown to ebony-colored chairs with marble seats. The room was lit by lamps with tinkling colored glass and the walls were hung with ornaments of silk and shells. Gone was the cat darting for bits of food on the floor. Gone too were the Chinese, except as waiters. The first dish, called "Pineapple Chicken," consisted of "peas in pod in brilliant natural green, dark, rich mushrooms, large pieces of preserved pineapple, and small pieces of chicken." Next was "chop sui, not so aesthetic a dish as to appearance, but very delicious to taste. Beef, pork, and bean sprouts are its principal parts. The beef and sprouts only are in evidence." Chan Kew said rents were terribly expensive on Pell Street. A large store on the ground floor rented for at least one hundred dollars a month and a small front room rented for at least twenty-five dollars.[6]

The growth of the restaurant industry, and the almost simultaneous birth of the tourist trade, was spurred by the visit, in 1896, of

107 Until the "slumming craze" of the early 1890s, Chinatown restaurants were designed for the Chinese, who favored stools and bare wooden tables.

108 Others, like modern fast food restaurants, served a quick bowl of yotcamein (soup garnished with pork, hard-boiled egg, and onions): a dish familiar to Americans who had lived in the West.

99

109 Li Hung Chang in New York. Because his was an unofficial visit, he was received by President Cleveland at a private house in New York. Lower right, being carried up the steps of Grant's Tomb, still under construction; center left, the fireworks in Chinatown.

100

the Chinese viceroy, Li Hung Chang. A *Harper's Weekly* reporter hailed him as the most distinguished visitor since Lafayette, "not excepting His Highness the Prince of Wales."[7] Newspapers, focusing, as always, on trivia, built enthusiasm with descriptions of his royal insignia (a yellow jacket and many-eyed peacock feathers) and toyed with the rumor he carried his coffin with him and—if so—would he keep it in his room or would he prefer to have it safely stored during his visit? When Li arrived on the steamer St. Louis on August 28, hundreds of ships sailed out to Sandy Hook to provide an escort. At the Battery, Li entered a carriage and was paraded up Broadway to the Waldorf Hotel behind a detachment of the 6th United States Cavalry.

The high point was a visit to Grant's Tomb, then still under construction. In 1879, after leaving office, Grant had traveled around the world, and Li had honored him in Canton with a seventy-course dinner. Before a crowd of twenty thousand, four policemen carried Li in a litter to the steps of the tomb for the wreath-laying ceremony.

Li was too regal to notice the merchants of Chinatown, but they were not without influence. They persuaded the city to divert the viceroy along Mott Street enroute from one appointment to another. The street was jammed, and fire

escapes were packed to the danger point. All was respectfully silent until he passed; then came the explosion. Strings of firecrackers were draped from the cornices of five-story buildings with ropes and pulleys attached so when the bottom bunch was touched off, the string could be lowered so the explosions would continue at ground level. Bunches of firecrackers were lit and tossed out of windows and the sidewalks and streets were blanketed by colored paper and shrouded in smoke.

Newspapers described the decorations in loving detail; American and Chinese flags in every other window; lanterns as big as watermelons; others two feet wide at the top and a foot long, tapered down from the middle, with thin ribs covered with delicate white silk painted with flowers and designs; a butterfly with green, black, and yellow wings and a pink thorax nailed to the door at 19 Mott; a dragon flag twenty feet square suspended over Pell Street; a miniature house, complete with balcony and figures within, suspended at 33½ Mott; a string of bell-shaped white lanterns of silk, with mellow lights from the candles inside, strung across Mott; somewhere else, a large ship made of many-colored worsted wool with tassels hanging from the keel.

"Don't believe them," wrote one reporter, "when they say our cities are lacking in picturesque-

110 An example of the elaborate carvings and furniture.

111 Banquet menu from a first-class tourist restaurant, about 1890.

ness. Go over and look at Mott Street ragged out for Li Hung Chang and you will see an odder, more colorful sight than you would find in Europe."

They did come. The press of souvenir hunters was so dense that some merchants charged five cents just for a look around. When a Chinese boy in holiday clothes was seen, with his tiny braided queue falling down his back, a shout went up and the crowd came running. His father snatched him up and ran to safety.[8]

Chinatown was filled every night by crowds who bought slippers, paint pots, bracelets, punks, backscratchers, chopsticks, tea, soapstone earrings, fat Buddhas, and monkeys that saw, heard, and spoke no evil. Some items were as cheap as ten cents; few cost more than twenty-five cents. Costumed figures made of wood, clay, plaster, or papier maché, and dressed in rice paper, grass cloth, silk, or satin, were sold in a group of two or three in a glass box for $1.50. Chinese lanterns were a favorite. They had four, five, or six sides, with ground or painted glass set in a framework of teak or ebony ranging from simple sticks of wood to rich carvings and inlays, gilded or lacquered. If that were not enough, rows of beads, wooden

balls, monkeys on silk ropes, bells, or networks of lace were suspended from the frames. The lanterns burned candles, or kerosene lamps or could be attached to a gas fixture. In some, wires were set inside with cardboard figures of monkeys, deer, or tigers that moved with the heat, casting shadows on the glass.[9]

Souvenir shops, however, were incidental to the restaurants. They competed through elaborate decorations and furniture of teak, ebony, or ebonized ironwood imported from China. A guest was offered a square stool, twelve by eighteen inches, with an inset of marble or granite on the seat. The frame might be carved and inlaid with mother of pearl. The stool cost the owner five dollars. There were also massive chairs, weighing as much as fifty pounds, with substantial arm rests and a foot rest usually covered with a bamboo sheath. The seat had a reversible panel with a warm side of Canton flannel for winter and a cool side of Singapore mat for summer. The legs and arms were carved and inlaid with mother of pearl, silver, polished marble, and even jade. The most elaborate, with jade insets, cost as much as two hundred dollars. Tables of teak or ebonized ironwood, four or eight inches higher than a standard table, had

102

tops of marble or granite with the sides and legs richly carved, the legs ending in a dragon's claw grasping a glass or stone globe.

Guests were often shown through the kitchen on their way to the dining room, so they could see that everything was spotless and the ladies could examine Chinese cooking methods. Hickory and oak logs were now too expensive and the cooks had switched to coal. Otherwise, little had changed from earlier decades. Ordinary cooking was done in shallow woks with places on the massive range for roasting spitted chickens, ducks, or whole pigs. The price per dish ranged as high as $1.50 or $2 for chicken breasts and mushrooms or bird's-nest soup.[10]

Some shops ignored the tourist invasion. At Wo Kee Company, in the basement and first floor of 8 Mott, business was for the Chinese trade, with imported teas, spices, nuts, various roots and herbs, tiny-brown-and white sausages, dried long and slender eels, dried and smoked ducks and chickens, dried oysters, and sugared melon seeds—all displayed in boxes, baskets, and pans on the floor and counters. Elsewhere there was cloth for making coarse working jackets and quilted silk for dress coats and, here and there, bracelets, ivory ornaments, dainty porcelain cups,

113 Children at Doyers Street mission.

silver pipes, cork-soled shoes, Chinese playing cards, buttons, beads, games, and pictures.

Another pioneer, Wing On Company at 12 Pell, dealt mainly in imported teas, groceries, silk, and general merchandise. The best-decorated store was managed by Sang Chong at 28 Mott, with elaborate carvings over its counter and lanterns hanging from the ceiling. Kwong Yuen Shing and Company at 32 Mott specialized in fancy goods, but to reach the gorgeous silks and satins at the back of the store, a customer had to pick his way past baskets of every-day produce.

Some stores stayed open until ten o'clock at night for the benefit of laundrymen who shopped after work and liked to eat well. A man could be seen with a bag or basket of loubuck (like a squash or turnip), dung kua (a melon), gray mats of seaweed, duck eggs wrapped in a mass of gray clay, canned oyster oil (used for making a sauce), dried oysters, shark fins (to be cooked with chicken), a string of the ever-popular little mottled sausages, dried cuttlefish, or a specialty like ducks feet tied with a bit of ducks liver inside a pig's stomach.[11]

The busiest shop on Doyers Street was Hee Jan's bakery at number 16. The entire establishment was fitted into an area eight feet wide and fewer than twenty feet deep. A helper kneaded dough by bouncing up and down on one end of a long pole, pounding the dough in a trough at the other end. He used the same pole to press dough into thin strips, only this time he placed the dough on the work table and pressed down on it with the pole. In the fall, Hee Jan devoted much of his time to mooncakes stuffed with fat, chopped meat, nuts, and raisins for the autumn festival. Another of his preparations was a confection that looked like a brown orange—a globe three or four inches in diameter, with a shell of sweet, tough dough. The inside was hol-

112 Pressing dough in Hee Jan's bakery.

114 THE DAUGHTER OF AN ACTOR WAS "RESCUED" BY A MISSIONARY TO PREVENT HER FATHER FROM BINDING HER FEET.

low except at one point, where there was a teaspoonful of plum marmalade. No one could figure out how he made the dough expand into a sphere. Another dainty was a long, thin bar of jelly and crystal sugar, covered with a thin layer of flavored cake and dipped into sesame seeds.[12]

At 1 Doyers, Wang Kai Kee, artist, engraver, lithographer, and sign painter, crammed his shop into an area only six by fifteen feet, a good part of which was taken up by his lithography press. The walls were covered with pictures and signs and other samples of his work were scattered on every table and shelf. The confusion gave little indication of his social standing. As a scholar, he was on a level with doctors and above the richest of merchants. He drew sketches for sign carvers, inscribed visiting cards on small sheets of red paper, drew up petitions and memorials, and was available for advice on any subject, literary or poetic.[13]

Two shops specialized in children's clothing, one on Pell Street, nearly opposite Doyers, and another on Mott near Chatham Square. Prize items were small, round caps with a hole in the top for ventilation. They were made of silk or satin of every color and embroidered in floral

patterns. The most expensive were embroidered in silver and gold and set with semiprecious stones. Some bore poems or ancient sayings appropriate to childhood. Many of the caps were made by a woman who lived on Doyers Street and received commissions from as far away as Cuba and Puerto Rico.[14]

Chinese medicines were sold by at least eight pharmacists. Astringents with magical properties included stag horns, dried red-spotted lizards, silkworms, moths, tortoise or oyster shells, or the bones and teeth of what were said to be dragons. As purgatives there was copper verdigris, pearls, bear's gall, and the shavings of rhinoceros horns, or so it was claimed. Other remedies were less exotic. An oil with a heavy flavoring of menthol was used as a linament for rheumatism, neuralgia, and headaches. If someone had eaten too well, he was given a lozenge of peppermint, sugar, charcoal, and lime.[15]

Traveling dentists arrived every three or four months and opened clinics for as long as their services were in demand. They pulled teeth with their thumb and forefinger, a feat learned in boyhood and perfected with constant practice. The dentist drove wooden pegs into a board and spent at least half an hour a day pulling them out. He also attached a tooth to a heavy weight and lifted this regularly to be sure he could always retain a firm grip on a small object. The tendons and blood vessels of his hand bulged and his forearm seemed as hard as wood. The dentist alleged toothaches were caused by worms and kept a few white grubs in a jar as proof. If a patient refused to have a tooth pulled, the dentist eased the pain with a mixture of opium and oils of peppermint, cinnamon, and clove, rubbing the mixture on a man's gums, cheeks, and even his neck. He also cleaned teeth, using a brush of split bamboo and a paste containing the ground shells of cuttle fish. He was poorly paid: an extraction cost only twenty-five cents.[16]

James Naughton had expanded to the houses at 31, 33, 35, and 37 Mott Street, doing business as a livery and boarding stable as well as a funeral parlor. An adjacent store sold the paraphernalia of funerals: tinsel garlands, artificial flowers, perfumed candles, sticks of incense sometimes three feet tall, and mock money in all denominations. Earlier, the Chinese used perforated slips of paper in imitation of coins with a hole in the center. By 1900 they used brown paper stamped to represent dollar bills, silver paper to represent silver dollars, and paper printed in black, red, and gold to represent American double eagles. A hundred thousand dollars in mock money cost twenty-five cents. For one dollar a mourner could buy a miniature palace of bamboo and paper, complete with furniture, food, silks and satins, cows, horses, boats, mandarin robes, and a green sedan chair such as only the highest officials were allowed to use. These palaces were burned either in front of a dead man's house or at the grave.[17]

Necessity, in the form of a shrinking laundry trade, spurred the search for a wider restaurant market. In early 1902, a *Tribune* reporter chronicled the trend:

> In the last year or two a surprisingly large number of Chinese restaurants have made their appearance in uptown districts. The tawdry outward decorations of red and blue lights and huge Chinese characters are in every case the same. The same, too, are the unattractive entrances and the general dilapidation of the establishment. Nothing about them seems attractive and yet these places thrive and their number increases with astonishing rapidity....There is also a free and easy atmosphere about the Chinese eating house which attracts many would-be "Bohemians." Visitors loll about and talk and laugh loudly...."Yockaman," "chop suey," and "chow main" are the pièces de résistance....Twenty-five cents worth of some kinds of chop suey, served with rice, will make a toothsome dish for two people. Tea is served free of charge and the quantity is not limited....Negroes are in disproportionately large numbers.[18]

Blacks, who found it almost impossible to eat in restaurants outside their segregated neighborhoods, were welcomed by the discriminating Chinese. Since most New Yorkers refused to eat in a room with blacks, some chop suey places had only black customers.

By 1903 there were more than a hundred chop suey restaurants between 14th and 45th streets, from Third to Eighth avenues. As Longacre Square (now Times Square), became the theater district, the Chinese played to the after-theater crowd with pseudo-Oriental glitter—colored lanterns, silk and bamboo hangings, and polished wood tables. The floors were carpeted and the waiters were dressed in clean uniforms.[19]

Still, nothing equalled the lure of Chinatown. In the words of Harriet Quimby, the city's best-known guide to the new and exciting:

> None of the foreign quarters...attract so much attention on the part of the sightseer as this one. At all times the streets are kaleidoscopic....When the dining hour arrives the scene is varied by the appearance of waiters who pass hither and thither bearing trays of assorted bowls, all tightly covered, balanced on their heads. They are carrying dinner to merchants who cannot leave their shops. Then there are boys who scurry along with baskets; and little girls with painted faces who sway on their wooden shoes as they carry their little burdens of steaming hot pork, or perhaps, a roast duck or chicken from one of the restaurants.

The restaurant "much patronized by members of the Smart Set"—she wrote—was the Oriental, on the three upper floors of a building on Pell Street. The top floor was reserved for banquets. The other two were divided into smaller rooms furnished with ornate furniture and gilt carvings. Each room was dominated by a fantastic colored dragon peering down with shiny, green eyes.[20]

As restaurants flourished, so did manufacturers of noodles and other staples, wholesalers of restaurant supplies, delivery firms, and farms to supply special meats and vegetables.

As early as 1878, when the Chinese population numbered only about a thousand, a venturesome pair established a farm in the then-virgin lands of the Bronx.[21]

Major farming did not develop until the middle 1890s with the expansion of the restaurant trade. One pioneer was Shen Ho Joe, who was said to have lost a great deal of money at the fantan tables and sought to escape the snares of the city by renting a few acres on a high bluff in the Steinway area of what is now Astoria, Queens. Shen Ho Joe was so successful he was able to sell out to four others and retire to China.

The farmers marketed a variety of cress—used for flavoring soups—while their American neighbors were just stirring from winter lethargy. A variety of white and green kale was ready by the middle of April, along with small, sweet peas. Then came a succession of gourds and roots, the most imposing of which was a hairy squash that—if left on the vine—grew to forty pounds, but was usually harvested when it weighed only a few pounds. Restaurants served the squash candied and glazed as a sweet, tasting like a citron or mild lime. Other crops were water chestnuts, a Chinese variety of sweet potatoes, and a variety of parsley that gave off a strong smell when crushed. Vegetables, to be cooked after they were soaked in water and sprouted, included lotus bulbs, soy beans, and various other beans.

Farmers divided their land into small squares and harvested about fifty varieties of plants from a single acre. Since each was planted according to its growth period, sowing and harvesting was constant. Several men—generally close rela-

115 RESTAURANT FAVORED BY THE "SMART SET."

116 A FARM ON LONG ISLAND IN ABOUT 1905.

tives—worked from dawn to nightfall, and even after dark with the use of lanterns if there was an urgent order for the next morning. Their neighbors sneered at the ramshackle huts the Chinese called their homes, but the Chinese were never sure of their rights as aliens ineligible for citizenship. They only rented the ground and, in winter, moved to be near Chinatown, so there was no incentive to build or improve their quarters.

They first tilled the ground carefully, bending over, picking up, and tossing aside each rock or pebble or weed. Seeds were gently thrust, one at a time, into water-soaked soil and covered with a thin layer of soil over which was spread a layer of brownish, liquid fertilizer that undoubtedly contained—in Chinese fashion—nightsoil. Water from wells was allowed to settle and warm in large barrels. If it developed a greenish mold, so much the better. The farmer slung a yoke across his shoulders, filled two pails with water, and slowly walked down the rows, gently spilling water at the roots of plants. For some, even this was considered too harsh; water was applied with a dipper. Farming was a labor of love repaid with a rich and steady harvest.[22]

THE TOURIST TRADE

Despite the lure of its restaurants and souvenir shops, tourism did not become a major Chinatown industry until the second decade of the twentieth century. Before that, its dim, narrow streets and sinister reputation was too forbidding. But then, the sinister itself—or rather, the manufactured image of sin and lurking evil—became a prime lure.

Tourist flocks grew larger after World War I, to the indignation of, among others, S. J. Benjamin Cheng, a student at Columbia University, who wrote a 1922 letter to the *Times*:

> Every day and all year round there are special sightseeing motor cars decorated with Japanese paper lanterns bearing a huge signboard in front standing right in the midst of the business center of New York City and with a couple of people walking around shouting desperately, "Chinatown, O, Chinatown, one dollar down to see Chinatown." What do you think that a Chinese or any red-blooded human will feel when he passes by such a car and hears such shouting?[23]

Maria Moravsky, a Russian immigrant, mocked: "I was even afraid to entrust my laundry to a Chinaman [and] I shuddered at the mention of chow mein."[24]

A reporter for the *Times* magazine section took his own tour, conducted by a detective, who pointed out such sights as the "wizened little Chinaman" who sold newspapers:

> That bird used to be a gun toter for one of the killers down here during the tong war. The killer would go out and mark his man and then this little mule—that's what we call a Chink—would pop up and slip him a gun just before he wanted to shoot. The killing bird would let go at his man and pass the gun back to his toter who lost himself in the crowd. A dozen people might see the shooting and who did it, but there'd never be a sign of a gun. No, the Chinks aren't so dumb, it's a hard job to prove anything on one of them....This is the old arcade. It's probably seen more shooting than any other part of Chinatown....Bricked up? I'll say so. When the tongs were having their battles, the killers of one of them used to lie up here on top of this arch in the arcade and take a shot at every member of the rival crowd who passed by in the sunlight of the street outside. Then they'd pop into a tunnel and come up in half a dozen places—maybe a hundred yards away.

The Rescue Society on Doyers Street, where three hundred homeless men (none Chinese) curled on hard benches or the dirty floor every night—once the innocent home of the Chinese Opera—was now pointed out as "the biggest hop-smoking dive Chinatown ever had."[25]

Chinatown became a made-to-order scenario and set for the infant movie industry. Actors trying to film a scene on Mott Street were pelted with vegetables, especially since the movies used Japanese to portray Chinese. Charlie Lee, an import-export merchant, told a *Herald* reporter he thought the tongs should stop the cameras.[26]

Another movie film crew was attacked in 1932 when a Fox Movietone unit staged a raid on a purported Doyers Street opium den as part of a series of shorts on police adventures. Men of the Narcotic Squad were filmed dragging prisoners from the building. The Chinese who gathered saw the alleged prisoners were blacks wearing Chinese clothes. They also saw the crew filming a closeup display of opium pipes, supposedly captured at the scene, but actually brought from the Elizabeth Street station. As the crowd swelled, the crew and actors were pelted with melon rinds, tomatoes, eggs, and a few bottles and tea cups. The Emergency Squad was called and hustled two Chinese to the station where, for their temerity, they were manhandled before release.[27]

In reality, the modernization of Chinatown and Chinese was relentless. When the Reverend Lee To became the first Christian chairman of

117 FOR TOURISTS, DOYERS STREET AT NIGHT HAD THE THRILL OF THE ORIENT WITH THE REASSURANCE OF A FAMILIAR POLICEMAN.

118 CHUCK CONNORS, WITH TRADEMARK DERBY AND PEARL-BUTTON SUIT, WAS A HANGER-ON IN DOYERS STREET SALOONS WHO EARNED TIPS BY SHOWING THRILL SEEKERS TAME WONDERS LIKE THE JOSS HOUSE. FOR AN ADDED TIP HE WOULD SHOW THEM AN OPIUM DEN COMPLETE WITH A "FALLEN WOMAN."

119 PHOTO-JOURNALIST JACOB RIIS TOOK A "FLASH" PICTURE OF AN OPIUM SMOKER.

120 BUT IT WAS NOT SINISTER ENOUGH, SO A FIGURE WAS ADDED.

the Benevolent Association in 1919, one of his first acts was to throw out the image of Kwan Kung. Rather than making enemies, in 1921 he became the first chairman to be re-elected for a second consecutive two-year term.[28]

Still, the tourist trade was one of the few means of livelihood for the Chinese and so Mott Street was not left bereft of a Joss House. The Chinese kept petitioning for a post office, explaining that mail links with China were a vital part of their social and business life and that they needed a post office where their language was understood. California-born Ng Que was appointed part-time postmaster in 1916 and rented a room at 13 Mott measuring seven feet by eight feet, four inches. Of course, he could not hope to pay the rent and make a living from selling stamps, so he installed an image of Kwan Kung in a room in the rear. When Kwan Kung was evicted from 16 Mott, this became the only place where old-timers of doubtful decision could cast the divining blocks or shake out a fortune stick. Here too, the perforated money burned during funerals was for sale, but most of Ng's income came from fees paid by tour guides plus tips from the visitors.

Ng had three daughters, all of striking beauty, who took turns helping their father. The guides led their flock through an alley—adding to the mystery—to visit the Joss House. As they exited through the substation, the guide would ask Ng,

121 THE RESCUE SOCIETY ON DOYERS STREET WAS IN CHINATOWN BUT NOT A PART OF IT.

109

122 Open tourist bus in 1923.

weekday night, two hundred young men and women struggle with English composition, American history, modern European languages, and science. The American-born Chinese have a passion for education, as witness their enrollment in our local universities."[30]

123 A wall of notices touted as the Chinese newspaper.

124 What attracted this couple to a dingy basement?

as priest of the sacred shrine, to bestow his blessings. He did so happily, raising his arms with the dignity of a sage, since the guide's fees helped send all three daughters to college. When he died, one daughter became postmistress of what was billed, again for tourists, as "The World's Smallest Post Office."

A second Joss House opened in 1926. Poy Yee, with a useless law degree from California, raised five sons by operating a room on the second floor of 5 Mott. It's attraction was a huge plaster Buddha of no artistic or religious merit. Tourists were invited to pat the Buddha's ample belly "for good luck." Lacking daughters, Poy Yee hired "pretty young women who lectured on Chinese gods and customs, reading the latest jazz song sheets while waiting for the next batch of the gullible."[29]

The exotica was make-believe. As Will Irwin, the historian of Manhattan in the 1920s, wrote: "The only worshipers who knock their heads on the floor and burn punk-sticks to the Gods of the Upper Kingdom are a few seafaring men off the steamers in the harbor, or old fellows past learning new ways....The sight most typical of modern Chinatown is the assembly-room of the Baptist Mission in Doyers Street. There, any

Then came the Depression. In 1930 alone, more than 250 restaurants were forced to close, with a corresponding loss for the restaurant-supply industry.[31] But restaurant owners were

American cabarets that depended on liquor sales for their profits were forced to close, but Chinese restaurants with music and dancing survived because they made a profit out of food alone. A first-class Chinese establishment could offer a complete lunch or dinner, with music and dancing, for $1.50 to $2. One, in the heart of Broadway, replaced a cabaret where Irene Castle had danced at the height of her vogue. In its latter guise, shop girls with bobbed hair and cloche hats went for a quick lunch and danced in pairs for lack of midday beaux.[32]

A *Times* reporter added:

> These Chinese places are to be found in many parts of town, not omitting the reaches of Broadway, where the lights are the brightest. They have orchestras and dance floors and terraces of tables above, with subdued lights and alcoves or booths and waiters in evening dress. Indeed, the air is quite the air of the more pretentious sort of real night clubs and the decorations suggest a silken luxury....Naturally these places are well patronized by classes and types of persons who are not reckless spenders.[33]

With repeal, the pendulum swung the other way. Chinese restaurants could not face the

always quick to adjust to the changing times and fads. Some years before World War I, when cabarets became popular, the chop suey restaurants that beckoned the after-theater crowd cleared away tables and added musicians for dancing, attracting a somewhat less-than-elite clientele with dragon motifs and white-gloved waiters. With prohibition, the elaborate

126 MENUS FROM ABOUT 1939.

competition of nightclubs offering a show, fast dance music, and liquor. The Cotton Club was built on the site of Young's, one of the largest Chinese restaurants in New York. Ever flexible, Chinese entrepreneurs migrated to find a new clientele. The Fulton Royal, on Flatbush Avenue Extension and Fulton Street in Brooklyn, opened at a cost of eighty thousand dollars with a seating capacity of seven hundred, offering a show that cost three to four thousand dollars a week to produce. It was a huge success. Waiters made $300 to $400 a month, but it had to close after seven years because of dissension among its shareholders.

Sumptuous restaurants were the exception. It seemed near every subway stop there was a small neon sign inviting tired office workers or shop clerks to stop for a dish of chop suey or to take some home. The Chinese were compelled to seek side-street or other out-of-the-way locations where rent was cheap and there was little competition from American restaurants. Customers called the waiters Charlie. When other Chinese said, "He's a Charlie," they meant he was a waiter. The day started early and ended late. If there were no customers, a waiter had to help with the cleaning. For all this, he received twenty-five dollars a week plus food and small tips. The overhead had to be kept low. A lunch of soup, chop suey, rice, and almond cakes was thirty-five cents in 1938. For forty-five cents, a customer got soup, chow mein with mushrooms or beef with Chinese vegetables, rice, coffee, and ice cream. A ten-cent tip was munificent.[34]

But no one felt it was a real Chinese meal if it was not consumed in Chinatown. It wasn't just the food. The lure of the exotic and the repetitive tong wars added spice.

The Sunday School Movement

Sunday Schools were established in the United States in the 1790s as part of the "Great Awakening" revival of pietism to bring religion to the poor, particularly "unchurched" Irish and German Catholic immigrants. A prime example was Louis Pease and his Five Points Mission.[1]

Seldom free of Eurocentric prejudices, Christian missionaries saw the Chinese as exotic and perhaps childish and too prone to surrender to evil influences and thus needing guidance on the way to salvation. This was blended with simple humanity; a willingness to extend kindness and personal contact. The missionaries' infantalizing would later prove a hindrance to growth, but in the early, flagrantly racist years of their encounter with America, where others greeted the Chinese with curses and fists, it was the helping hand of a few Evangelical Christians, mostly women, that was essential to social and economic survival. Perhaps more signficant, the Christians began the process of Americanization (as distinct from the "melting pot," which never applied to the early Chinese). Aside from religion, which they could accept or reject, or simply be indifferent to, the immigrants were being acclimatized to American mores and attitudes: what was regarded as proper or improper in human and social relations.

Pease and his successors could spare little time for the Chinese who came to their Mission, so that day-to-day work was left to Sara Goodrich. By 1875, when the House of Industry was swamped with new immigrants and could no longer support a mission that served only a few, Miss Goodrich, with support from her Fourth Avenue Presbyterian Church and "private benevolence," established a new mission at 525 Pearl Street, near Centre Street. She estimated that there were three hundred Chinese in New York working as cigar makers, laundrymen, and peddlers, plus between-voyage sailors. Her school provided English-language classes every evening, with religious instruction in Chinese on Sundays by Arthur Folsom, the returned missionary from Canton.[2]

By 1878, when the refugees "influxed" from Kearney's San Francisco, the Chinese had become exotic decorations to charity fairs. At a Washington's Birthday reception by the St. John's Guild, ladies served tea in little Chinese cups from booths with "pagoda roofs" while "Chinese boys in national costume...added greatly to the picturesque effect." "A Chinese concert of the most delightfully discordant and hideous character" afforded "unmistakable proof that they were 'real' Chinese." The orchestra was also featured at a "Martha Washington Reception" at the Academy of Music. After ten minutes, "the more nervous...begged to have it stopped," and the musicians were "given fre-

127 MOTT STREET SUNDAY SCHOOL. THE WOMAN AT THE BLACKBOARD IS PROBABLY NETTA MILLWOOD.

quent intermissions."[3]

A year later, defenders of the Chinese felt they had the perfect man to answer charges that the Chinese were vicious and depraved. He was Moy Jin Kee, the son of a Canton doctor, who had been hired by H. C. Parke, a dealer in Chinese and Japanese goods on Front Street. Moy had been educated in English-language schools in Canton and later lived in California.[4]

Moy asked C. S. Brown, the current superintendent of the House of Industry, to start a new Chinese evening school. Brown agreed, with his daughter as teacher, but two months later became uneasy, fearing "roughs in the neighborhood" might harm Chinese who came to the school. Moy proposed transferring the school to Mott Street, saying he would bear all the expenses. He quit his job with Parke and rented the ground floor of a house at 14 Mott, furnishing it with an old bureau and old benches and plain pine boards stretched across trunks. He had been living on Canal Street, remote from the main cluster of Chinese. To be closer, and to save money on lodging, he moved into a room in the back of the school.

It opened in May 1879, with Moy dressed in a navy blue blouse turned up at the wrists to "reveal snowy white and very large cuffs," broadcloth trousers, and "a pair of polished gaiters." Brown estimated there were a thousand Chinese in the neighborhood and said the school would convince them they were among friends.[5]

A *Sun* reporter visited the school, in "what was once the parlor of a fine dwelling," where "sisters from various churches in rustling silks" showed sixteen Chinese the pages for lessons or songs, noting that Netta Millwood, their teacher, "walked alone and unprotected and was never molested."[6]

Two weeks after it was opened, the school was closed and Moy Jin Kee was in jail, described as "the first Chinaman arrested in New York for theft." He had come to New York to visit his brother, who was a servant in the Sackett Street home of George Washington Reid, the publisher of the Brooklyn *Daily Eagle*. His

113

brother had anglicized his name as Jin Fuey Moy. When Moy Jin Kee visited him, he brought presents of chinaware and silks for the girl servants. This aroused the suspicions of Mrs Reid. With good reason: Moy's salary was six dollars a week, out of which he spent four dollars a week for room and board, leaving him little after carfare and incidentals. Mrs. Reid told Parke of her suspicions. He examined the articles and found they were from his store.

Moy had other troubles. He had told a newspaper reporter there were only twenty real Chinese in New York and the rest were "coolies" or "Tartars." When word of this circulated, his school was boycotted and Moy had to take refuge with Brown at the House of Industry, which was where police arrested him.[7]

The *Sun* carried a long editorial asking for pity and mercy. The Methodists were eager to avoid embarrassing publicity. Parke was persuaded to drop the charges and Moy returned quietly to China where—chastened by his experiences—he resumed his studies and was later ordained as a Methodist minister.[8]

The Christians tried to retain their bridgehead on Mott Street. Various denominations contributed for its reopening, with classes every evening, except Saturday. On Sundays, there were morning and evening Sunday School sessions. Netta Millwood was in charge, assisted by any volunteers who might show up. An average of fifteen Chinese came every night, ranging in age from eighteen upwards, but finally the Protestants admitted that the school was in the wrong place: "The greatest hindrance to our work is the existence of so many gambling and opium dens, fifteen or twenty of these being in full operation every Sabbath." In July 1881 the work was transferred to the Seventh Street Methodist Church where, under Netta Millwood, it continued for many years.[9]

Earlier, in 1878, Augusta Carto, the widow of an English missionary who had worked among the Chinese in Oregon, persuaded the pastor of the Trinity Baptist Church on East 55th Street, near Lexington Avenue, to allow her to use his auditorium for a Chinese School. She began with about fourteen laundrymen and seven women teachers, and had her first public reception during the 1880 Chinese New Year observance.[10]

In September 1879 S. L. Parsons and "a returned Chinese missionary," Mrs. M. D. Culbertson, started what they called

the "Brooklyn Chinese Sunday School" with twenty-five pupils "mostly from laundries...nearly all in native dress." Parsons said each student had a "lady teacher" and that several had learned to write since the school opened.[11]

In 1881, for the second year in a row, Mrs. Carto celebrated the Chinese New Year with a reception at the auditorium of Trinity Baptist Church. She stood at the door introducing guests to students dressed in neat dark suits, some with imposing watch chains across their vests. The pastor, S. L. Simmons, said the Chinese were often assaulted by neighborhood ruffians.

Mrs. Carto drew special attention to Ah Wing, who was taking drawing lessons at Cooper Union. She said she once persuaded the secretary of the Baptist City Mission to write a factory owner on Ah Wing's behalf. The manufacturer replied that any Chinese who came into his factory would be taking his life in his hands. The evening ended with a Chinese supper. A *Tribune* reporter noted some guests were upset since the Chinese walked around the tables with baskets of delicacies, using their hands to place them on plates. The guests "grew very merry over their curious feast" of strange patés and jellies and when most of the meal "was transferred to pocket-handkerchiefs for domestic inspection, [the] Chinamen were surprised because their labor of love did not meet with more praise than laughter."[12]

128 SELDOM NOTICED, THE HOUSE OF INDUSTRY CONTINUED TO OFFER SANCTUARY AND EDUCATION FOR CHINESE BOYS IN AN OTHERWISE HOSTILE WORLD. THE PICTURE DATES FROM 1899.

114

By 1883 there were ten Sunday Schools in New York and eight in Brooklyn, with an enrollment of about six hundred pupils—a sizeable number since the Chinese population of the twin cities was fewer than three thousand. There was also a Chinese Young Men's Christian Association at Sara Goodrich's Chinese Mission, now located at 119 White Street. With so many schools, a Chinese Sunday School Union was formed as a coordinating council, with a full-time paid secretary.[13]

A *Times* reporter explored the blossoming evangelization: "The maintenance of a Chinese Sunday School is difficult. A school must have a

129 ORCHESTRA AT THE 1883 SUNDAY SCHOOL PICNIC EXCURSION TO IONA ISLAND.

teacher for every student....The Chinaman is earnest, not for religion but to learn English. He gives undivided attention and expects his teacher to do the same." The students expressed their gratitude with "chests of tea, beautiful fans, and Chinese and Japanese vases. In one case a teacher was given a gold ring with engraving on it done in San Francisco, the design being elaborate." He quoted a "lady of social position and refinement:"

> I took up this work as a matter of duty, with a strong prejudice against these people. It is now a work of love. Before this near contact with them I saw only stolid indifference in their faces, they now beam for me with intelligence. And more deep and heartfelt gratitude than they express for any little favors shown them I have never met. This work is a most inspiring revelation to me. I have come to love these Chinamen for their many beautiful qualities of heart and I respect them sincerely for their admirable qualities of head.[14]

In June 1883, at the prompting of the influential Moy clan, students invited their teachers to an excursion up the Hudson to Iona Island. The idea spread, so that about 850 passengers, including three hundred Chinese, crowded the steamer. The main attraction was the Chinese orchestra and its mysterious instruments, except for which, a reporter commented, the picnic "sounded no note of heathendom."[15]

Harper's Weekly called it "the most notable Sunday School picnic ever held in the United States of America."[16]

In March 1885 Richard Bassett, the secretary of the Chinese Sunday School Union, reported that, with fewer than five thousand Chinese in New York and Brooklyn, the number of schools had risen to twenty-eight, with an average weekly attendance of seven hundred. In a show of strength, three hundred Chinese attended a service at John Hall's Fifth Avenue Presbyterian Church. One of them, in a prayer in English, asked God to enlighten Americans to make them kindlier disposed to the Chinese.[17]

The first independent Chinese church in New York was founded by Huie Kin, who would become the most respected Chinese in the city. In 1868, when he and three other Huie boys migrated from Toishan, their clan organization received them at Oakland, California, and, among others, found a job for Huie Kin as a houseboy. He was then fourteen. He learned English, was baptized in 1874, and at twenty-six he entered Lane Theological Seminary in Cincinnati. After completing his studies, he was

called to New York in July 1885 to work with Presbyterian Sunday Schools.

Sara Goodrich had died about two years earlier, and her White Street school had closed, but by then there were three other schools at Presbyterian churches in Manhattan. In October 1885 Huie Kin started another in a rented parlor at 15 University Place.

He found three enthusiastic helpers: Yee Kai Man, who changed his name to Guy Maine; Chew Mon Sing, who took the name of Joseph M. Singleton; and Tom Ah Joe. He had left home after he was baptized, at the age of twelve, over the strenuous objections of his father and, after several years at sea, came to New York, where he found work as a servant in the home of a Brooklyn doctor. With the help and encouragement of the doctor's wife, Tom Ah Joe entered a medical school and returned to New York to practice medicine under the name of Joseph C. Thoms.[18]

Huie described Chinatown as "a little Monte Carlo but without its glamour," with Tom Lee as its "uncrowned king:"

> We were young, full of ardor to fight the wrongs of the world and decided to wipe out the evil business, even though we knew that the most powerful organizations were behind it and the city police...were maintaining a tolerant attitude toward it....We went into the gambling houses dressed as ordinary workmen, mingled with the habitués and got to know the proprietors or operators by sight. With the incriminating information in hand, we had warrants issued and even took part in the raids, quite unaware of the personal risk we were running.

When threats did not deter them, Huie, Guy Maine, Singleton, and Thoms were offered a share in the profits. This too did not work, and twice Huie narrowly escaped deadly ambush. Huie and his band appeared in some of the cases at the Tombs, and managed to obtain a few convictions. "I do not believe," he later wrote, "any permanent good was done by our activities, but we did stir things up so that the police had to close all the gambling houses."[19]

If so, they did not remain shut for long. In 1887 police massed thirty-five men to raid a room at 39 Bowery guarded by a heavy oak door with a wicket through which visitors could be screened. When the wicket slammed shut, they chopped down the door with axes and confiscated implements to prove fan-tan and opium smoking were taking place. The proprietor was identified as Lee Toy, also known as Charlie Toy, a close associate of Tom Lee. Lee Toy and sixty-seven others were brought before a magistrate but the charges were dismissed because they were not caught in the act of gambling.[20]

A week later the police raided a basement room at 41 Bowery, next to the place they raided earlier, and connected to it through a door in the rear. This time the detail numbered forty, and they had to chop through two doors, only to discover a third so thick their axes could not penetrate. They brought up a battering ram, forced their way in, and made some arrests, with the same result: All were freed for lack of incriminating evidence.[21]

"SCANDALOUS" MARRIAGES

In September 1891 parishioners at the school founded twelve years earlier by Augusta Carto at the Trinity Baptist church on East 55th Street were uneasy at reports that suppers held after the classes led to a great deal of socializing between the Chinese and their teachers. Henry B. Hudson, who had replaced J. B. Simmons as pastor of the church, ordered an end to the suppers. Then, when the congregation voted to end the classes as well, Pastor Hudson agreed, telling a reporter he believed the classes were doing the "heathen" no good but might result in harm "in other directions."

Reporters soon discovered the root of the trouble: Lizzie Field, a teacher at Trinity Baptist, was engaged to Wing Lee, a laundryman from Brooklyn, and had left her home to move in with Mrs. Carto on East 51st Street. When reporters went there for comment, both Mrs. Carto and

130 ENGLISH LESSONS AT "THE CHRISTIAN UNION FOR CHINESE WORK" IN BROOKLYN IN 1883. VARIOUS DENOMINATIONS MAINTAINED TWO LARGE PARLORS, A LARGE SITTING ROOM, A KITCHEN, AND SMALLER ROOMS FOR AN ESTIMATED FOUR HUNDRED CHINESE IN BROOKLYN. APPARENTLY THE ARTIST FOUND THE YOUNG, SLIM-WAISTED TEACHER THE MOST NOTEWORTHY FEATURE: AN ATTRACTION THAT WOULD SOON FEED SCANDAL.

Miss Field denied the rumor. Mrs. Carto called the charge that the Chinese insisted on young teachers malicious gossip. She said there were twenty-five teachers at her school and all were over thirty and many were widows or old maids "well beyond the age of giddy girlhood."[22]

The following October, a deacon at Trinity Baptist was put on formal trial and expelled for "tattling, backbiting, and railing." Pastor Hudson called him a "babbling old woman who had spread tales for years and kept the congregation by the ears."[23]

With her school closed, Mrs. Carto moved to Brooklyn and so did Lizzie Field, with the intention of marrying Lee Wing. Oil was thrown on the fire when the Reverend Valentine Lewis, a Presbyterian minister who had worked for twenty years among the Chinese in California, Boston, and Tahiti, wrote letters to the *Daily Eagle* calling the Chinese licentious, vicious, and unfit companions for the young ladies who taught them.[24]

A half-dozen churches held meetings to reply to Lewis and defend their schools. Pastor R. B. Hull of the Greenwood Baptist Church in Brooklyn said he had worked for twelve years with Chinese Sunday Schools in New York and Brooklyn and had never known a Chinese to insist on the exclusive attentions of a young and pretty teacher. He said there were thirty-five Chinese students at his church and thirty-five teachers, but twelve of them were men. Of the twenty-three females, ten were married women and three were daughters who accompanied their mothers to the classes. Pastor Hull said he had baptized seven of his Chinese students, five of whom were "leading exemplary Christian lives" in New York, while the remaining two had returned to China as Christian missionaries.[25]

Soon Pastor Hull's own church was embroiled in a scandal involving the same mother-daughter combination he had seemed to feel was a protection for innocent young females. Mrs. Stephen French, the wife of a prominent Brooklyn contractor, had taught for many years at various Chinese Sunday Schools. Her latest was the Greenwood Baptist Church, where her daughter, Grace, joined her. In May 1892 nineteen-year-old Grace French eloped with Lee Tad, also known as Edward Lee. He was about twenty-nine and a salesman for a Chinese firm dealing in teas and laundry supplies, with a taste for silk hats and diamond stickpins.

Her family took the elopement as a blot on its good name. French told reporters his daughter must have been drugged and threatened to track Lee down and kill him. Mrs. French, who had visited her daughter, was upset but understanding.

"Do you think your daughter was drugged when she married the Chinaman?" a *Daily Eagle* reporter asked.

"No, there's not a word of truth in that. She married him with her eyes open and it is her affair. She has her life to live."

"Were you opposed to the match?"

"Certainly I was."

"Don't you like Lee?"

"I think he is a good young man but the terrible prejudice against the Chinese is what makes me revolt at the idea of my daughter marrying a Chinese man."[26]

Mrs. French supplied her daughter's address on Gates Avenue in Brooklyn. The reporter discovered that the ground floor was occupied by a laundry operated by Lee Wing, the man who had married Lizzie Field from the Trinity Baptist Church. They lived in an apartment above the laundry. Augusta Carto lived in an apartment on the same floor. Edward Lee, it turned out, was the brother of Lee Wing, who lived with his bride on the top floor.

Grace Lee, "slight, fair-haired with dimpled chin, blue eyes, pearly teeth, and fine-molded features," was shy. The interview was monopolized by Mrs. Carto, described as a "stout, vigorous Englishwoman."

"What did you find in Mr. Lee that made him more attractive in your eyes than other young men?" the reporter asked. The new Mrs. Lee blushed and Mrs. Carto replied:

> The same attraction which all young American girls find in Chinamen. They are so polite. Talk of the French! The French are nothing to them in politeness. They are so deferential to women, so patient, so good-natured, so thoughtful, so grateful. Chinamen don't drink, smoke, or chew tobacco. They don't use opium, don't gamble, and have none of that sarcasm that so offends young women in American men. Of course, I speak of those Chinamen who have been converted to Christianity. Then Chinamen make the most tender and constant husbands. They are devoted to their wives and children.[27]

The marriage did not last. On 22 November 1894, a notice appeared in the *Eagle:* "My wife, Grace E. Lee, having left my bed and board, I hereby give notice that I will not be responsible for any debts of her contraction. [signed] Edward W. Lee."

It developed that a child had been born and the couple had moved to another house in

131 This *Harper's Weekly illustration*, captioned "A Wedding in Chinatown," is pure fiction. The ornate building across the street at 14 Mott had just been built for an expanded Consolidated Benevolent Association. The Joss House, with its high stoop, is at 16 Mott. There seems to be a wedding party outside, as if the Joss House was a church, but Chinese marriages took place in homes, while European women, if they married Chinese, did so in churches or at New York's City Hall. What is being sketched is not a wedding, but the recurrent theme of miscegenation. The accompanying article dwelt on intermarriage between Chinese and Irish women, with children "whose features betray their intermingled blood."

Brooklyn. They began to quarrel, and one day Lee returned from work to find his wife had returned to her parents, taking the child, her piano, and some bric-a-brac. He sold the rest of the furniture, and he and his brother opened a new laundry in the Williamsburg section of Brooklyn. Ten years later, Grace Lee asked a judge to annul her marriage on the grounds that her husband had a wife and two children in Canton when he married her. She produced a man from Mott Street who said he knew Lee Ot (as his name was now given) when they were boys together. The judge ruled that this was not sufficient evidence.[28]

The Lizzie Fields and Grace French marriages coincided with the Chinese boycott of the registration provisions of the 1892 extension of the Exclusion Act and the subsequent unsuccessful appeal to the Supreme Court of the United States to declare the act unconstitutional. Shen Woon, the Chinese consul, was worried at the extent to which public opinion was inflamed. One day before what would have been the eleventh annual Sunday School picnic, he called Christian leaders to his office, now at 26 West Ninth Street, and told them to lower their profile. They complied: The outing was canceled, although invitations had already been sent out and a steamboat was stocked with refreshments for the planned trip to Cold Spring Grove on Long Island.

The picnics were resumed in June 1894, when seven hundred Chinese and eight hundred teachers and friends boarded a steamer for a subdued day of eating, hymn singing, and playing baseball at Roton Point, with rules created on the spot and no one keeping score.[29]

By 1901 the excursions grew so large they were divided into two sections. But with the tightening grip of Exclusion, the numbers of possible students was contracting and schools were disbanding. Then, when a young woman was murdered, the movement was reduced to a few churches.

THE ELSIE SIGEL MURDER

One of the guests on what was, by now, a single excursion in July 1909, was Florence Todd, superintendent of the "Chinatown and Bowery Rescue Settlement and Recreation Room for Girls" at 10 Mott Street. Although her interest was the non-Chinese prostitutes who occupied many of the houses in Chinatown, Miss Todd planned to join the excursion, along with one of her helpers, twenty-two-year-old Elsie Sigel. Her grandfather was General Franz Sigel, who fled to the United States after the German revolution of 1848 and was instrumental in rallying German Americans for the Union during the Civil War. He died in 1902. When an equestrian statue of Sigel was unveiled in 1907 at Riverside Drive and 106th Street, an estimated hundred thousand people watched a parade "that had not been equaled in many years."[30]

Elsie Sigel's father was Paul Sigel, the general's second son. Her mother had, for seventeen years, taught at a Chinese Sunday School at St. Andrew's Church at 127th Street and Fifth Avenue. Although her daughter never taught at the school, Elsie apparently found Chinese attractive. When she was eighteen, she met a man she knew as William Leon, the owner of a chop suey restaurant at Amsterdam Avenue near 191st Street. Leon sometimes joined Elsie and her mother at church services. Later, when Elsie volunteered to help Miss Todd in Chinatown, she was attracted to another Chinese—Chu Gain—a Christian who was manager of the Port Arthur restaurant at 9 Mott.

Elsie left home on the morning of June 9. When she did not return that night, her family, fearing a scandal, did not report her disappearance. On June 12 her mother received a telegram from Washington, reading "Don't worry. Will be home Sunday noon." It bore the initials "EJS." Still worried, Mrs. Sigel went to Chinatown, where Miss Todd and Chu Gain said they had not seen her. She spent the night at Miss Todd's mission. The excursion was the next day and she hoped Elsie would appear unannounced. Chu Gain was also worried. Monday morning, before the boat sailed, he hurried to the *Herald* to insert a notice: "EJS. Mother ill. Come home dear one."

William Leon was also known as Leong Lee Lim, Leon Ling, Leung Lum, and William L. Lion. He no longer owned a restaurant and lived in a small room on the top floor of a house at 782 Eighth Avenue, where he worked as a waiter in a second-floor restaurant owned by a "cousin," Sun Leung. When Ling—to use the name by which he was called all during the search—did not show up for work on June 10, Sun Leung knocked on his door. There was no answer. Mrs. Sigel, searching for her missing daughter, also knocked on the door, and there was no reply.

Sun Leung knocked at Leon Ling's door every day until the afternoon of June 18, nine days after Elsie Sigel disappeared, when he noticed a strong smell and called the police, who forced the door open and saw a small, rusty steamer trunk bound firmly with rope cut from an awning—twice around the front and twice lengthwise. They cut the rope and the lid sprang up, revealing the body of a woman crammed inside. They thought it was a black woman

120

and—in the nature of the times—dismissed the death as unimportant. Leaving quickly to get away from the smell, they sent a routine notice to the coroner's office. Several hours later, the coroner identified the body as that of a white woman dressed in undergarments. Now detectives were called. A picture of Leon Ling, dressed in the uniform of a cadet of the Chinese Empire Reform Association, was on the dresser. Detectives found fifty letters in a drawer signed "Helen." One read, "You seem to be growing cold to me. Just think of the sacrifice I have made for you—my family, my friends. For God's sake, don't desert me."

There were also twenty-five letters from Elsie Sigel. One read, "I am writing this while mother is away from home. She would not let me if she knew it. Don't think, Willie, that I will give you up for anybody. I will always remember the dear times we had together. I will see you soon."

The letters had return addresses. A detective went to 200 Wadsworth Avenue in Washington Heights to ask for help in identifying the body. Nine days had passed since her disappearance and the Sigels had yet to notify police of a missing person. Elsie's father was at the Port Arthur restaurant asking Chu Gain to intensify the search. When the police reached him there, Sigel could not bring himself to go to the morgue: he asked Miss Todd to go. She did at 1:24 on the morning of June 19.

By daylight, recently appointed Captain Michael Galvin and dozens of men from the Elizabeth Street station were combing Chinatown, asking everyone: "Do you know Leon Ling?" Reporters were told Ling was a member of the Chee Kung Tong, perhaps even a high official, but one informant, wearing diamond rings and a diamond in his shirt front, said Ling was nothing but "a cheap grafter."

Chu Gain, as the only Chinese closely involved, was arrested and subjected to the new "third degree," in which an accused was denied sleep and subjected to constant questioning. Chu said he had been in the United States since 1901 and attended a Sunday School in Hackettstown, New Jersey. He said that about three weeks before Elsie disappeared he received two letters in Chinese signed "Chief." One threatened to "cut him into mincemeat" if he did not stop seeing Elsie.

Paul Sigel said there had been a party at his house the night before Elsie disappeared. A half-dozen Chinese were present, including Chu Gain. Leon Ling was not invited but forced his way in. He saw Chu Gain and shouted something in Chinese. Paul Sigel believed Ling threatened

to kill Chu. Elsie left home at ten o'clock the morning after the party, saying she was going to the Bronx to visit her grandmother, the widow of the general. When she did not return by nine that night, Mrs. Sigel called the Bronx and learned Elsie had never been there.

A "dragnet" (another new word in police journalism) was spread across the country. A report from Pittsburgh said Leon Ling had recently addressed a Sunday School class, berating the Chinese for their wickedness. In St. Louis, four Chinese were arrested when they stepped off a train, but released when they proved they had come from Chicago to pick up some merchandise.

A Chinese federal government employee was trailed by detectives as he traveled by train with his wife and was arrested when the train arrived in Washington. He was released after proving he was not Ling. A policeman in the Bronx dragged a slimly built man to the nearest station house, where he was identified as a Japanese. Police in New Jersey picked up a man who proved to be a Japanese butler for a Morristown family.

The Sigel family felt disgraced. It was not until June 20—two days after Elsie's body was discovered—that Paul Sigel went to the morgue to make a positive identification of his daughter. He told reporters, "This should be a lesson to young girls not to mix with other than their own people." Four days after the body was discovered, her corpse was taken directly from the morgue to a new plot in Woodlawn Cemetery, a considerable distance from the vault where General Franz Sigel was interred. There were no flowers, and the services ended quickly. When a reporter went to the Sigel home, her father said he had no further interest in the matter and that it concerned only the police department.

The backlash affected Chinese Sunday Schools throughout the country. Although not a Sunday School, Miss Todd's home was closed when a wealthy uptown woman withdrew her support. A school in Pittsburgh that once had forty Chinese students was reduced to six and was soon expected to close. New York Sunday School leaders announced a reward of five hundred dollars for the arrest and conviction of the murderer. The Oriental Club, an association of modernized Chinese, also voted to raise a five-hundred dollar reward. A manifesto from the Chinese embassy in Washington, printed on imperial yellow paper, was pasted on the walls of Chinatowns throughout the country:

> For the body of a young lady to be thus discovered in the lodgings of a Chinaman throws disgrace on the whole body of our people in this country....If any one should

learn of the whereabouts of these two men he should at once report to the nearest police station, so that they may be arrested and brought to trial. In this way you will help to remove any stigma that may be attached to our people on account of this case.

The reference to "two men" included Chong Sing, who had a room next to Leon Ling and who disappeared at the same time. Four days after the body was discovered, a *Times* headline proclaimed the arrest of "THE MAN THE WHOLE WORLD IS SEEKING." Chong was traced through a photograph to a town near Amsterdam, New York, where he had found work as a cook in a private home.

He was taken directly to a police station and seated before a detective and an assistant district attorney. "You killed Elsie Sigel," an assistant district attorney shouted, jabbing his finger at Chong Sing's face. As the endless questioning went on, the floor around his chair was "littered with cigarette butts." Chong said Leon Ling killed Elsie Sigel because he was jealous of Chu Gain. He said he heard sounds from Ling's room and looked through a keyhole and saw them struggling on the bed. He said when he later looked through the keyhole, he saw Elsie Sigel with a handkerchief stuffed in her mouth.

Chu was taken to Ling's apartment, where detectives showed him he could not have seen what he claimed through the keyhole. "After another hard day under the merciless third degree," Chong Sing admitted Leon Ling had called him into the room and he saw Elsie Sigel on the bed with a handkerchief over her face. He asked Ling about blood on the floor and was told she had bitten her tongue and accidentally choked to death.

Elsie Sigel was a large woman, heavier than Leon Ling. Detectives said Ling alone could not have crammed the body into the trunk and held it shut while it was tied with rope. Chong insisted he had not helped in any way. He was taken to the Tombs and held as a material witness in prohibitive bail of one hundred thousand dollars.

All ships leaving New York were examined and their Chinese crews questioned. Chinese arriving in Vancouver to board ships for China were also questioned. Chinese said to resemble Ling were held in Chicago, Pittsburgh, Norfolk, Virginia, and Ravelstoke, British Columbia. A Chinese arrested in Pennsylvania confessed he committed the murder. So did another in Massachusetts. Police decided they were not telling the truth. A Pacific Mail steamship that had been searched before it left San Francisco was searched again when it docked in Honolulu.

Leon Ling was never found and Chong Sing was released the following September. All questions went unanswered. Above all, how did Leon Ling escape, and who sent the misleading telegram from Washington, obviously designed to delay the search for the missing girl? The fact that her body was crammed into the small trunk and tied securely was evidence he had at least one accomplice. Was there a tong connection? Since the police knew little about the inner workings of the community, this avenue was never explored. Even if it had been, it is unlikely anyone would have been of help.

Captain Galvin issued an extraordinary order that no Chinese could leave the city without permission. Several who tried to buy railroad or steamer tickets were turned away. But the search for the killer was obviously fruitless. Moreover, within a month a new tong war began, and the police could not spare resources for the search for killer; the Elsie Sigel case entered the record books as unsolved.

THE CHINESE GUILD AND HOODLUM ATTACKS

With their laundries throughout the city, and attending churches in white neighborhoods, the Chinese were vulnerable to constant harassment. In April 1881 Yung Ley Teep was returning to his laundry after Sunday School at the Third Reformed Presbyterian Church on West 23rd Street when, at the corner of Spring and Marion streets, he was surrounded by a gang. His hat was knocked off, he was jostled from one to another, struck down, kicked, and finally stabbed several times. He died at St. Vincent's hospital two weeks later. He was twenty-two. He had arrived in New York eleven months earlier and joined the church's Sunday School soon thereafter, missing only three Sundays. The church held an elaborate funeral service. The main speaker was John Hall, New York's most eminent minister. The congregation of his Fifth Avenue Presbyterian Church was the city's wealthiest. "They are charged with being uncivilized and immoral," Dr. Hall said in his eulogy, "but the people who prefer these charges are often themselves iniquitous. If this is to be called a free country all should have equal protection under the law, whether they are black or white, Mongol or Indian."[31]

In 1885 Ong Ah Mon attended a Sunday School at a church near his laundry at 148 East 134th Street and then went to Chinatown to complete preparations for his return to China. He had lived in New York for six years and managed to save a few thousand dollars. He planned to return home, marry a girl chosen by his family, and return to the United States. It would be an unhurried day. The third annual excursion was scheduled for the next day. He planned to be there and would not open his laundry, and so did not have to return early to prepare work for the next day.

On that Sunday, four sailors from the USS *Omaha* and a man in civilian dress lurched along the Bowery insulting every Chinese in sight. The civilian, David Quinn, was the most boisterous and the sailors tried to restrain him. At the corner of Chatham and Mott, Quinn pushed aside his companions, drew a revolver, and began shooting at any Chinese close to him. His first bullet struck and killed Ong Ah Mon. His second and third shots wounded two others. A policeman ran to the scene, clubbed Quinn to the ground, and rapped his stick on the sidewalk—the standard telegraph of a policeman requiring assistance. The police commandeered a vendor's cart, put Ong's body on it, and took it to Naughton's funeral parlor next to Transfiguration church assuming, rightfully, that he would handle the funeral.

Quinn was taken to a hospital, his wounds from the clubbing dressed, and then taken to jail. At Naughton's, Ong's body was laid out with a long, red scarf wrapped around his face to hide the wound. A pair of satin slippers rested in the coffin near his head. His clansmen scattered playing cards, mock money, and bits of evergreen over the body. With low, barely audible incantations, several men approached, shook Ong's hand three times, and left. That was the extent of Chinese services. The body was taken to the Bowery Mission at 36 Bowery for Christian services. A minister from Calvary Chapel extolled the Christian patience that enabled Ong "to bear the taunts of his persecutors without retaliation even unto death." When pallbearers carried the casket in procession along Mott and Bayard streets, the police had to restrain a hooting, jeering crowd. At Evergreens cemetery, a crowd waiting to seize the leftovers of the Chinese burial service was so unruly the police had to force their way to the grave.

Quinn was twenty-one and poorly educated. The slaying was obviously a drunken act. Normally, Quinn would have been charged with unpremeditated murder and would have received a light sentence, but the Chinese consulate hired William Beecher, the son of Henry Ward Beecher, and a prominent churchman and attorney in his own right, to ensure a vigorous prosecution. Quinn pleaded guilty and was sentenced to life at hard labor.[32]

Usually, the bullies were satisfied with blows and kicks. In November 1893 Yun Lee, a student of Jane's Methodist Episcopal Sunday School in Brooklyn, was set upon on his way to the church, knocked down, and kicked. When the superintendent of the school went to help him, he too was beaten. A policeman was called but declined to chase the hoodlums when they ran away. Two years later, in a series of attacks on Chinese attending the same church, one man had part of his ear cut off by a sharp stone. The Chinese were so frightened most refused to come to the class. The next Sunday, Sing Kee, of Third Avenue and 92nd Street in Manhattan, was hit with a club and knocked down. The following morning, E. B. Woods, a New York lawyer who was assistant superintendent of the school, went with Sing Kee to the local police precinct to get an arrest warrant for his assailant. Only then did the attacks stop.[33]

The merchants and tong leaders who controlled Chinatown offered no protection. Only one organization consistently brought help—the Chinese Guild (*Pao Liang Wei*: "Society for the Protection of the Good") of St. Bartholomew's Episcopal Church in Manhattan. The Guild was organized by Guy Maine, one of the men who in the early 1880s had joined Huie Kin in his futile attempts to close down Mott Street gambling. Maine, who could speak fluent English although he had no formal education, organized the Guild at 23 Saint Marks Place in 1889.[34]

Members—who numbered 466 the first year—were charged annual dues of two dollars. This covered a third of the Guild's expenses, including Maine's small salary. The church contributed the balance. His days, and parts of his nights, were filled with helping laundrymen cope with the courts and city departments; with leases and landlords; with settling disputes; translating writing letters; visiting the sick; and, above all, seeking police protection.[35]

The guild's lawyer was William C. Beecher. His value was demonstrated in September 1890, when two robbers cut a member in the face with a knife, nearly blinding him. They turned out to be repeat offenders and, when found guilty, were sentenced to twenty years in prison. In 1891, when membership had risen to 612, Maine said the number had to be limited, otherwise it would go up to a thousand. That year brought 1,014 separate cases, including eighty-seven instances of broken windows and thirty-six cases of assault and battery.

In 1893 Maine wrote that their work was hindered by passage of the Geary Act, which extended the original 1882 Exclusion Act:

The scholars seem to have no desire to further advance their knowledge of English and religion. I know men who hardly missed a Sunday in the Sunday School for years who are idling away their time on Sunday in public parks and on the streets. When pressed for reasons, their simple reply is: "I have no mind to study."

In 1895 Maine returned to China to see his mother after an absence of seventeen years. His place was taken by Dr. Jin Fuey Moy, the brother of Moy Jin Kee. Jin Fuey Moy had been a servant in the home of George Washington Reid when his brother was arrested for theft. In 1880, when he was eighteen, the Reids sent him to Pennington Seminary in New Jersey. He graduated three years later. After several years as a missionary at Sunday Schools in New York and Philadelphia, he entered Jefferson Medical College in Philadelphia. He married an American woman in 1889 and, a year later, got his degree as a doctor. He returned to New York in 1892 and worked for a while in what was called the Chinese Hospital, which Dr. J. C. Thoms opened on Hicks Street in Brooklyn.[36]

Thoms and Jin Fuey Moy were examples of the many harsh repercussions of the 1882 Exclusion Act, which made persons of the Chinese "race" ineligible for citizenship. In turn, this meant that trained Chinese were not able to practice their professions, since most states required citizenship as a basis for licensing as doctors, lawyers, or in other professions. The first New York test of the law involved Hong Yen Chang, a graduate of Yale and the Columbia Law School, who had lived in the United States since he was eleven or twelve years old, had no queue, dressed as an American, and who said he intended to live the rest of his life in America. When Hong applied for admission to the bar in 1887, a judge of the New York City Court of Common Pleas granted his application and administered the oath of citizenship.

There was a New York precedent for getting around the obstacle. In 1881, when a British attorney wanted to practice law without first receiving citizenship, the legislature passed a measure to "waive alienage." Thousands of immigrants were then arriving in the United States and it became a common procedure to allow professionals to begin early practice.

In Hong Yen Chang's case, the legislature again "waived alienage," but when the State Supreme Court made a routine examination of applicants for the bar, Hong was rejected by a vote of two to one.[37]

From then on there was no doubt that Chinese were barred from licensed professions. In one of the many perversions of racism, although Joseph C. Thoms and Moy Jin Kee could not treat white patients, they could treat Chinese, but this was of limited valued since most Chinese clung to traditional medicines. The Chinese Hospital Association of Brooklyn was incorporated in 1890 "for the exclusive treatment of Chinese" as a clinic where Thoms and Moy could practice their skills. With little support, it closed in about a year.[38]

When Moy replaced Maine, he too tried to mitigate the harassment of laundrymen. In an annual report, he told of a twelve-year-old who broke a laundryman's window three times in a single week and was not punished. In another incident, a group of boys grabbed a laundryman, threw a rope around his neck, and dragged him through the street. The leader was arrested and sentenced to thirty days in prison.

Moy hired a detective to complain to precinct captains. One replied: "If we arrest all these boys every time when they annoy a Chinaman we would have our hands full. Besides, what's the use? The magistrate would reprimand and discharge them on the following morning and the offender would return home and repeat the same thing over. You cannot secure a conviction to save your life."

Guy Maine returned from China in 1897 and left a record of a typical day:

7:10 A.M. To Brooklyn to settle business dispute between two members.

9:30 A.M. Got transcript of judgment of $105 for member.

10:15 A.M. Filed transcript in court and placed in hands of sheriff.

11:30 A.M. Took member to Gouverneur Hospital for dressing of wound.

12:45 P.M. Took two wounded men to Police Station to have assailant apprehended.

1:30 P.M. Went to Delancy Street to see landlord about lease.

2:40 P.M. Went to corner of 44th Street and 2nd avenue about alteration of store.

3:30 P.M. Went to 57th Street police court for warrant of arrest of man who broke window of member.

4:40 P.M. Went to West 48th Street to see landlord about having water meter installed.

5:15 P.M. Went to 43rd Street and 8th avenue to see member ordered by Health Department to have trap connections in store.

The major event of 1897 was what newspapers called the "Abducted Chinaman Case." It was an example of the ability of tong leaders to use a bribed police force as cat's paw. In October

"Too muchee bad boys alound here; allee time callee me names; fixee up little supplise-party!"

"Hey, Chinaman, Chinaman!"

"Supplise-party workee first-latee!"

"Heap chilly day when Hop Sing gettee left!"

132 PUCK'S FREDERICK OPPER, AS DID THE GENERAL PUBLIC, SAW THE BOYS WHO TORMENTED LAUNDRYMEN AS MERELY MISCHIEVOUS. CONTRARY TO WHAT HIS SKETCH SUGGESTS, A CHINESE WHO ATTEMPTED TO RETALIATE WOULD BE INSTANTLY ATTACKED BY NEIGHBORS.

Maine learned one of his members, Jin Bin, had been taken from his laundry on Second Avenue and all his belongings seized. Jin Bin had previously sought the Guild's protection in a dispute with the Chinese Laundry Union, *Dop Sing kong-so*, about undercutting prices. The union was incorporated in 1894, ostensibly "for buying, selling, operating, managing, and controlling laundry businesses." Maine referred to it as tong.[39]

A policeman from Staten Island came to New York with an arrest warrant charging Jin Bin with the theft of a watch. He secured the services of a marshal, seized Jin Bin and his stock, and hauled him back across the bay for a quick, quiet trial. When Maine arrived at the police station in Castleton, Staten Island, Jin Bin had been convicted and was scheduled to be sent to jail the next morning for a term of six months. Guy Maine arranged for a donation for his bail and to hire a lawyer to obtain a new trial. After repeated adjournments, it was shown that Jin Bin had been attending Sunday School at the

133 Choir of the Chinese Guild of St. Bartholomew's Church.

time he was accused of stealing the watch. He was found not guilty.[40]

In the same year, Maine tried another way to discourage attacks on laundrymen. He had a notice posted in windows of almost every laundry on Seventh, Eighth, and Ninth avenues offering a thirty-dollar reward "For the arrest and conviction of persons who break these windows, or for the molestation of the Chinamen in these premises." The attacks petered off but, since authorities were not willing to prosecute the boys who were arrested, the attacks resumed, and the notices were taken down.

In 1898 the Guild moved to the ninth floor of the new St. Bartholomew's Parish House on East 42nd street. Maine reported 201 dues-paying members and the usual dealings with landlords and city departments, window smashing, assaults, and robberies. In November three men wrecked laundries in Long Island City, injuring several Chinese. When they were arrested and brought to court, thirteen laundrymen appeared as witnesses and the men were fined five dollars each—a rare case of the usually timorous laundrymen defending their rights.[42]

In 1900 Maine greeted the new century with a telephone installed in his home in Jamaica, Long Island, making it easier for him to work harder. He received one call at 7:30 in the morning and was in court by 9 A.M. to press charges against a boy arrested for assaulting a member. On another day, he was in court early to press charges against three men who robbed a member the previous midnight. That was the year of the Boxer Rebellion, with lurid stories of Chinese killing missionaries. Maine wrote: "The anti-foreign outburst in China has been the cause of our extra work in court matters...as the rough element and mischievous boys have taken the opportunity to annoy and abuse the Chinese for misdeeds that they had taken no part in."

The worst incident occurred in July, when a mob attacked a large laundry on West 53rd Street, smashing windows with bricks and filling the store with empty tin cans and vegetables. A Chinese who came out with a flatiron retreated when he was chased by the crowd. Another Chinese came out with a club and beat one of the attackers until the mob came to his help. No police arrived. Order was restored only when Joseph Kennedy, a Spanish-American war veteran, borrowed a broom handle and chased the crowd away.[43]

Maine described 1901 as his "most difficult year....Almost every day we are called to represent members in the prosecution of their tormentors before magistrates. The frequent breakage has caused the insurance companies to refuse a risk, even at a high rate of premium on plate class." Once again the signs went up offering a reward—this time twenty-five dollars—for the arrest and conviction of anyone breaking laundrymen's windows or otherwise molesting them. As in the past, they did no noticeable good.

But a year later he reported relief, in the form of a new Children's Court. Children who broke windows could be put under bond to keep the peace, bringing a sharp decrease in attacks on long-suffering laundrymen.

There were other changes: the Guild's room was furnished with silk hangings and furniture from China and there was a new, fully vested men's choir. A reporter called it the first of its kind in the United States: "The members of the choir are uneducated in music and cannot read notes, but the hymns written in the Tonic Sol Fa system in Chinese characters are read by them with ease, and are sung with good effect."[45]

CHRISTIANS AND REFORM IN CHINA

The greatest changes of all were brought on by the stirring of reform in China. In Canada, in July 1899, the exiled Confucian scholar, K'ang

134 REFORM ASSOCIATION MEETING ABOUT 1910.

135 Chinese Guild Cadet Corps.

Youwei, founded the *Baohuanghui* (Protect the Emperor Society), better known as the Chinese Empire Reform Association. Later that year, an attempt to form a New York branch was suppressed by the Chinese consul general. As a *Tribune* reporter reconstructed events: "His influence was so strong that those interested in it were persuaded to give it up. They were afraid that membership would hurt their business." He

quoted the consul general as telling "the big tong which virtually runs things in the quarter 'It is easy to destroy but hard to build up again. Reform for China must be worked out under the present rulers.'"[46]

The next attempt succeeded, thanks to Joseph Singleton and Guy Maine. Singleton, like Thoms and Moy, had been a court interpreter and was known to judges, lawyers, and politi-

136 Quon Yuen Shing store.

cians. In partnership with Dek Foon, another Christian leader, Singleton established a small banking firm under his own name at 24 Pell Street. In 1902 he formed a branch of the Reform Association, with himself as president. Its headquarters, at 20 Mott, flew a flag with two red stripes and three stars representing "education, equality, and unity." The office was later moved to 7–9 Mott.[47]

In 1902 Guy Maine persuaded Major George McVicker of the 69th National Guard Regiment to drill his cadets with cast-off guard rifles. In his 1903 annual report, he wrote that five thousand men had joined the Reform Association. Reformers had also organized a Christian Chinese Burial Association, with a plot in Kensico Cemetery, and bylaws stating: "No heathen rite or ceremony shall be allowed at any time at the burial or on the grave of the deceased."[48]

Singleton was a skilled New York ethnic politician. In February 1903 he invited local judges and justices, with Judge Warren Foster (who had just achieved fame as mediator of a tong war) acting as toastmaster, to an elaborate dinner at the Chinese Delmonico's.[49]

The following May, Singleton and Maine linked the Chinese with the persecution of Russian Jews in Kishniev in Moldavia. They went to the Jewish Relief Committee and offered to help, saying, "We believe in liberty and want to aid those who suffer from bigotry." They arranged a benefit performance at the Doyers Street theater. The actors donated their services for a play set in the time of the Qing conquest when the Chinese were first made to wear queues. It earned $280 for the Jewish Relief Committee. Later, Jewish leaders arranged a reception and dinner at the Chinese Delmonico's and presented medals of appreciation to Singleton, Maine, Dek Foon, and another reformer, Jue Chue.[50]

Liang Chi-chao—the theoretician of the K'ang's reform movement—came to New York in the same month and Singleton arranged a packed house at the Doyers Street theater to hear his lecture. Liang's goal during a stay of six weeks, with visits to other eastern cities, was to raise funds for the Reform Association. He also persuaded merchants to raise forty thousand dollars to help underwrite a bank in Hong Kong—with a branch in New York (known as *Wah Yick* or *Huayi*)—to finance a Guangdong railroad project.[51]

The main participant was Lee Yick Deep of the firm of Quong Yuen Sing—the leading Chinese financier and philanthropist of the city. Among other things, Lee raised funds for the

137 HOMER LEA.

138 K'ANG YOUWEI.

129

Canton Christian College. When the Sunning Railway was built, opening the interior of Guangdong from the port of Canton, the line was supplied with steam engines and cars bought "for a song" after the electrification of the Third Avenue (Elevated) Railroad.[52]

In June Liang was guest of honor at another dinner at the Chinese Delmonico's arranged by Singleton, with nearly a hundred Chinese guests dressed in dinner jackets and none with queues. One of several American speakers claimed that "five hundred pigtails had fallen in the last month."[53]

The new century brought two newspapers set in moveable type. (Wong Chin Foo's short-lived newspaper was lithographed). The *Chinese Weekly Herald*, a four-page, four-column tabloid priced at five cents an issue or two dollars for a one-year subscription, appeared in February 1901. It required 12,700 separate ideographs. Its first editor was Chu Hing. Its owner and business manager was Kengo Moriya, a Japanese.

Its first editorial read: "We are here as strangers among a race ignorant alike of our language, our manners, and our customs, and apt to make our very virtues of frugality and industry weapons to scourge us and exclude us from those civil rights which are accorded to the meanest and basest of other nationalities."[54]

The following June, the paper asked its readers to sign a petition to Congress to allow the Exclusion Act to expire in 1902. Copies were posted on walls and bulletin boards: "We ask you, representatives of the American people, to abolish an arbitrary and unjust statute which is an insult to China and a stigma to the fair name of the United States." An American reporter commented: "There is something pathetic about the faith some of the Chinese have in this petition. There will be a great disappointment if it does not bring about the desired effect." And that's what happened. With the strident support of Samuel Gompers and the American Federation of Labor, the backing of President Theodore Roosevelt, and such other support as a resolution of the New Jersey legislature warning against opening the gate "for millions of dangerous and undesirable persons in invading the country," the Exclusion Act was not simply extended, it was made permanent.[55]

Within a year, the *Weekly Herald* had subscribers in almost every city and town east of the Mississippi and a few in Cuba, the Panama Canal Zone, and England. Many sent it to their villages as news of what was happening around them. After the first year, its editor was Lee Po Wong, a first-degree scholar from Peking's Imperial University. He became one of the most respected men in the city and, in 1902, was elected head of the Benevolent Association.[56]

In May 1904 the *Chinese Reform News*—financed by Jue Chue, Lee Yick Yue, and John Chant, three of the wealthiest Chinese in the city—became the second newspaper printed on moveable type. It was an eight-page weekly, with editorial and composing rooms on the top floor of a new building at 5 Mott. It sold for five cents a copy or two dollars a year for an annual subscription. Tong Chew, its editor, had been an instructor at a Reform Association college in Yokohama, Japan. He did not speak English. K'ang Youwei's daughter, K'ang Tongbi, who was a student at Barnard college, wrote an editorial for the first edition: "Our Emperor is virtually a prisoner in Peking....The tyrannical Empress Dowager must be deposed and the true ruler placed upon the throne. In this lies the hope for the success of our plans for reform."[57]

In 1905 K'ang Youwei himself began a triumphal tour of the United States. The reformers announced that cadets trained by Major McVicker would greet Kang in New York with a military display. It was bad enough—with a tong war then raging—for the Chinese to be drilling with rifles, but what of the international aspects: What right did Chinese have to train insurrectionists on American soil?

At about that time in Los Angeles, Homer Lea, a would-be general who had volunteered for action during the Boxer Rebellion, began training young men as a cadre to lead an uprising in China. However, Maine, in his annual report for 1903, described his corps as "the first of its kind." Later romanticized writings about Lea's cadets must be accepted with caution. A claim that New York cadets were trained "on Canal Street by Sergeant Jim Bradley" is obviously false: Any Chinese who dared to establish a presence on Canal Street in the early 1900s—especially for military training—risked lynching.[58]

When Major McVicker assured everyone the Chinese were merely drilling to build their bodies and minds, city officials allowed drilling to continue, but only indoors. When K'ang Youwei, accompanied by Homer Lea and others, arrived toward the end of June, the First Chinese Regiment marched and executed the manual of arms with small American and Chinese flags instead of rifles.

A few days later, the overhead fans in the dingy Doyers Street theater stirred the air as a perspiring, overflow crowd heard K'ang—dressed in the silks of a mandarin—deliver an impassioned, hour-long address contrasting such ancient achievements as the invention of gunpowder, printing, the mariner's compass, and cannon with China's present degradation, which he blamed on the Dowager Empress.[59]

The New York cadet corp was quietly disbanded after K'ang's departure, and some of the men returned to China. There was a military parade in Shanghai the following June, and Major McVicker was sure some of the men he had trained had become drillmasters.[60]

Sun Yat-sen was also in the United States in 1904. When he arrived in San Francisco and sought entry on a forged passport, the Qing government alerted immigration authorities to detain him for expatriation to China, where he faced a death sentence. Fortunately, Sun smuggled a message to a Christian minister, the Reverend Wu Pan Chao, founder and editor of the *Chung Sai Yat Po* (East-West) news, who mobilized forces within San Francisco's Chinatown to obtain his release.[61]

Sun's narrow escape made him a figure of legend among the Chinese. It happened that Huie Kin and his wife spent their vacation at the World's Fair at St. Louis and went on to visit friends in San Francisco, where they were introduced to the man everyone was talking about.

In 1902, when the Chinese consulate moved from a large building at 26 West Ninth Street to an office on lower Broadway, Huie Kin's Chinese Mission took over the vacated consulate. To help pay the rent, and meet the need of Chinese students (who would have trouble, for racist reasons, in finding rooms), the Huies turned the third and fourth floor into lodging facilities.

Sun told Huie he was going to New York and Huie invited him to stay at the mission. Two students from Yale and Columbia—Wang Chung-hui and Wang Chung-yao, the sons of a prominent Christian minister in Hong Kong—were also staying at the mission. Sun and the two Wangs, one of whom later became a prominent jurist in China, had long talks. Huie Kin recalled, "What they were working on nobody in the house had any inkling of, but we were later told that the first draft of the Constitution of the Chinese Republic was made there."

More likely, Sun was elaborating the program of his newly formed *Tung Meng Hui*, the pre-

139 St. Bartholomew's Chinese Guild school.

131

decessor of the Kuomintang. The Chinatown establishment regarded Sun as a dangerous revolutionary and, while in the city, he made no public appearances and Huie Kin was warned his mission would be boycotted unless Sun was evicted. Huie ignored the warning.[62]

A week later, Sun sailed for Europe, where agents of the Chinese government tried to kidnap him. That was two weeks before K'ang Youwei's visit to the city. It seemed triumphal, but this was an illusion. K'ang's movement was plagued by doubts about investments in private banks, book publishing, restaurants, real estate, and other businesses. When the Emperor Guangxu died in 1908, Singleton and Maine organized a condolence meeting at the Chinese theater, and mourning drapes were hung outside 16 Mott. It was simple courtesy. By then Kang's call for moderate reform had been drowned out by cries for revolution.[63]

CHRISTIANS IN CHINATOWN

In 1906 Maine reported average attendance at the St. Bartholomew's Sunday School—the largest in Greater New York—was only fifty, all of whom, except one, wore Western clothes, and most of whom had shaved their queues. In 1909 the Guild moved to 20 Chatham Square, on the rim of Chinatown, with the rent for their room paid by its members. By then there were only twenty-one schools in the entire metropolitan area and thus the annual excursion had become a single excursion.

Now, Chinatown itself would be the center of Chinese Christian life. Missionaries had already regained the foothold that was lost with the failure of Moy Jin Kee's Mott Street room in 1879. In 1892 the Baptists, led by Helen Clark, founded the Morning Star Mission at 17 Doyers Street, with Fung Y. Mow as its Chinese pastor. Fung, educated in a Baptist school in San Francisco, came to New York in 1883. His wife, a doctor, ran a dispensary on the third floor of the mission.[64]

Then a new Chinese missionary—Chan Kew—persuaded two dozen Chinese Christians to assess themselves one dollar a month each to support an "Evangelical Band" to roam the streets seeking converts. They rented a small room at 8 Pell for their headquarters and were pleased when as many as 115 men came to Sunday night services. Chan received the enthusiastic support of Isabel Shirley who, as far back as 1879, had formed a Chinese Sunday School at the Central Congregational Church on Hancock Street in Brooklyn.

Like Drs. Thoms and Moy, Chan had a degree but could not practice his profession. He had been ordained at the Moody school in Northfield, Massachusetts, and later received a law degree. In 1903 Chan married Mae Vorhees of Brooklyn, the great granddaughter of Fitch Randolph, who donated the land for Princeton University.[65]

Huie Kin had married Louise Van Arnam, a missionary student from Troy, New York, in 1889, and in 1895 became the first ordained Chinese minister in the city. Two years later, he moved his Chinese Mission into the Lenox Mansion at 53 Fifth Avenue, designed and decorated by the same architects who had built the ornate First Presbyterian Church on the opposite side of the street. It had previously housed the Presbyterian Board of Foreign and Domestic Missions. The Huie's turned its ornate art gallery into a meeting room.[66]

In December 1901 the Huies and women of their Chinese Presbyterian Mission organized the first Chinatown kindergarten in a long, narrow room on the first floor of 11½ Mott, with a piano donated by the Steinway company. Pupils, ranging from three to ten, were evenly divided between single and mixed parents. Since Chinese women did not go out, the youngest—and girls of all ages—were brought by their fathers. Business in Chinatown was conducted at night, and children, who stayed up with their parents, sometimes did not have their breakfast before noon, so classes began whenever twenty or so had arrived. They joined hands and formed a ring and danced around singing a good-morning song. In the early weeks, a hundred or so lonely, homesick men stood outside to listen to the children sing their school songs and hymns like "Jesus Loves Me." The men often joined in the chorus.

Girls were dressed in the brightest colors, with long, full trousers of colored cambric and a loose blouse of silk brocade. Their hair was tied in a glossy braid, interwoven and extended with strands of heavy, multicolored silk so that the end almost touched the floor, and they wore a band of gold-embroidered silk around their foreheads, with little tabs on each side, partially covering their ears. At the end of the day, when the children assembled for dismissal, they said, "Goodby: Be always kind and true," and bowed three times and exploded with whoops of joy and ran for the door, all trying to crowd through at the same moment. The kindergarten was later transferred to the Morning Star Mission on Doyers Street.[67]

Even the Transfiguration church finally admitted it had a mission at its door. Previously, the church reflected the anti-Chinese sentiments of its Irish parishioners. For instance, when in 1899 Manhattan Borough President James Coogan suggested Pell Street be widened to one hundred feet to provide access to Columbus Park (which had recently replaced the Five Points slums), he received the full support of the Reverend Thomas McLoughlin, pastor of the Transfiguration church:

> "I don't think anybody can speak more authoritatively on Chinatown and I will say that there is not a viler nest of iniquity than that section around Park and Doyers streets and Chatham Square. I can see from my house seven gaming houses. They are guarded by the police. Sometimes there are arrests, but rarely convictions. Gross immorality is everywhere prevalent.

Coogan's proposal and McLoughlin's screed were hooted down as further examples of Irish malice.[68]

But the Irish left, and the church fell on hard times. By about 1900 it had reduced its masses, auctioned its piano, and raffled off paintings and clocks. The clock in the steeple was stopped because it cost $690 a year to run. The church could not afford even that. The Italians who formed an increasing percentage of its parishioners were not used to supporting a church: In Italy, that was the government's responsibility.

In October 1908 a French priest who had worked in Canton for fifteen years opened a mission house at 103 Park Street, bringing with him two Chinese assistants. Unfortunately, when this mission was suspended in 1919, it left no record of its work.[69]

In 1910 the Peking government made a last-minute effort to woo overseas Chinese by opening, with the help of local merchants, primary schools in San Francisco, Chicago, and New York, and Transfiguration church was happy to get some revenue by renting two dingy rooms for classes. The principal was a Peking University graduate studying at New York University. Another student served as an assistant. Most of the local money was contributed by the philanthropist Lee Yick Deep.

Classes began at four in the afternoon with a hymn to Confucius sung to the accompaniment of a flute, and lasted until seven-thirty at night. More than fifty children, including some from Brooklyn and Newark, were taught the standard curriculum of a Chinese elementary school: writing, reading, Chinese history, and Confucian morality.[70]

The church was not the happiest location for a school. In July 1910 parents and students went down the block to the Port Arthur restaurant for tea, ice cream, and rice cakes to mark the end of the scholastic year. There were thirty-two boys in knickerbockers and four girls wearing dark dresses, with their braids tied over their ears in bright red ribbons. As Pastor Ernest Coppo finished a lecture on the evils of fratricidal strife, shots were heard. A rival tong man who strayed onto forbidden Mott Street was killed just outside the restaurant.[71]

During normal school hours, Chinese children went to Public School 23 at Bayard and Mulberry streets, where there was a special English class for Chinese and Italian students. There were also a few Chinese students in other schools, in all thirty-five for the city as a whole. Invariably, they were singled out as polite and industrious: Chinese children were drilled to guard themselves in the presence of Americans lest they provoke ridicule or hostility.[72]

Preschoolers went to the kindergarten founded by Huie Kin and later transferred to the Morning Star Mission on Doyers Street. This was jointly sponsored by Baptists, who conducted a Sunday School and adult education classes, and Methodists, who conducted the kindergarten. The kindergarten superintendent was Mary Banta. In 1904, while serving as a missionary at the Forsyth Street Methodist Church, Mary Banta was asked to organize an English class for the Chinese. She went into homes and laundries, persuaded twenty men to come to her first class, and thereby discovered her vocation.

Lee To, the superintendent of the adult work, migrated to California in 1887 when he was nineteen and was baptized three years later. In 1892 he went to China to study at the Baptist Academy in Canton and returned again to the United States, where, for eight years, he was in charge of the Baptist Home Missionary Society's work in the West. He came to New York in 1907 for study at the Baptist Bible Teachers' Training School, after which, in 1910, he was appointed superintendent of the adult side of the Morning Star Mission. He was also associated with the Mariner's Temple, which combined several earlier Baptist missions among immigrants on the Lower East Side of Manhattan. Lee To and Huie Kin were regarded as the strongest Chinese ministers in New York.[73]

In May 1908 Huie moved his mission to 222 East 31st Street, a large building previously occupied by the East Side Republican Club. It came complete with a library, reading rooms, a gymnasium, and even a bowling alley in the basement. The Chinese YMCA established a dormitory on the third floor accommodating twenty-five men. The beds were quickly taken

140 LEE TO: A 1916 PHOTOGRAPH.

141 HUIE KIN AT ABOUT THE TIME OF HIS RETIREMENT IN 1927.

by Chinese students at New York colleges. In 1909 they made the mission the headquarters of a Chinese Students Club. The group's first annual report in 1911 counted a membership of seventy-five, most of whom were students at Columbia and New York University. In 1910 Huie formed the first Chinese Boy Scout troop.

In December 1910 Huie's mission, whose roots reached back to 1868 and Lycurgus Railsback and Sara Goodrich at the Five Points House of Industry, was incorporated as the First Chinese Presbyterian Church of New York—the only Chinese church in the United States outside of California.[74]

(Huie retired to China in 1927 and was succeeded by K. Chong Young. The kindergarten, YMCA, and YWCA were dissolved. When Huie died in 1934, in his eightieth year, the church was renamed the Huie Kin Memorial Presbyterian Church. The building was later demolished, but the First Chinese Presbyterian survives in a two-hundred-year-old former Dutch Reformed church on Henry Street.)

For a week in April 1911, some of the sparkle returned to a Chinatown drained by tong wars and police repressions. Huie Kin, Consul Y. Y. Yung, the Chinese Merchants Association, the Reform Association, the Students Club, and the Chinese Athletic Bowling Alliance (another group at the First Chinese Presbyterian Church) joined in a week-long fair to aid famine victims in China. They rented the room of the rescue society on Doyers Street, brightened it with bunting and asked visitors to pay an admission charge of twenty-five cents for such pleasures as singing by tots from the Morning Star kindergarten dressed in "native" costumes, jugglers, acrobats, and a drill by the Boy Scouts. The guests then trooped along Doyers, sparkling with lanterns, to the Mandarin Tea Garden.

More than half the young ladies who sold trinkets, embroidery, and china at booths around the sides of the restaurant were of Chinese and American parentage. Still, all were dressed in embroidered, many-colored coats and trousers and wore their hair waxed down over their ears and decorated with jade ornaments, fancy combs, and flowers. The Students Club and the Bowling Alliance ran a tea room and the Boy Scouts bustled about reminding guests that one dollar would feed an entire family in China for a week. All Chinatown restaurants pledged a week's receipts to the cause. The fair raised ten thousand dollars.

This was the first time that the entire community had united for a charitable purpose. It was also the first time the Chinese ventured out

142 SUN YAT-SEN. HE WAS PROBABLY PHOTOGRAPHED IN 1911 AS HE WAS HURRYING HOME THROUGH EUROPE TO LEAD THE REVOLUTION IN CHINA.

of Chinatown to publicize the needs of their homeland. The fair ended with a parade around City Hall and back to Chinatown. Eight men manipulated a sixty-foot lion imported from San Francisco for the occasion.[75]

This venture was an indication of political reform stirring among the Chinese in New York. When the Qing dynasty was overthrown in 1911, they were ready.

Chu Fung Wing, generally known as Mon Lee, had come to New York in 1871. He sent his eldest son, Chu Su Gunn, to China to complete his education and then to Japan for further studies, where he picked up the revolutionary ideas of Sun Yat-sen. After another trip to China, Chu returned to the United States, where, in San Francisco, he was associated with Young China, the political organ of Sun's movement. In 1907 he returned to New York and, with six others, including Wang Kai Kee, the city's leading scribe, and his English-speaking wife, formed the Young China Association as a base for Sun's activities in the East. In 1910 the Association had an office on Pell Street and had about one hundred members.[76]

Sun himself came to New York in April 1911, staying at the Hotel Arlington on West 25th street. The Young China Association rented the Rescue Society room for a lecture by Sun on the future of China. More significantly, he was also invited to speak at the Benevolent Association. Only now, with revolution months away, were the conservative leaders of the Chinatown establishment willing to opt for change.[77]

The Wars of the Tongs

The notion, in historical and social studies, of "meaningful silence" has its roots in Pindar's statement: "What is without god is best passed over in silence."[1] Why should anything be passed over? Doesn't silence itself have meaning? Meaningful silence is at the heart of contemporary discussions of Japan's acts in occupied China and the role of almost two thousand years years of Christian anti-Semitism in legitimating the Holocaust. The 1992 observances of the five-hundredth anniversary of Columbus' "discovery" of America were accompanied by denunciations of the meaningful silence concerning the slaughter of indigenous peoples.

Nevertheless, the notion is problematic. Any opening is potentially infinite.[2] Therefore, should there then be silence? But, if so, why? Silence obscures who benefits. Did someone force the Chinese to do lion dances in the streets and decorate their restaurants with dragons and beaded curtains? The Japanese were equally persecuted—even put in concentration camps—but they quietly dispersed and took to gardening as a means of survival: there were no Japantowns. A closing-off of areas of discussion makes comparative history impossible by putting each group in a box to be discussed only on its own terms.

Tongs in Chinese American studies have been shrouded in meaningful silence. Often, if they are discussed at all, there is an attempt to explain them as necessary to defend Chinese communities from racist attacks, but there is no record of a tong opposing Americans: Attacks were always against other Chinese.

The subject cannot be avoided in any historical study that lays claim to objectivity. For almost a century in the West, and about fifty years in the East, tong culture and tong warfare shaped a major part of Chinese American life. Gangsterism, often labeled by newspapers as "tong fighting," still plagues Chinatown and its satellites in the metropolitan area.

Tongs, either as separate organizations or as elements within clan, territory, and merchant groups, enforced the laws and regulations of a largely autonomous society. But, since enforcement was never even, tong membership was indispensable as a protection against other Chinese. A laundryman or small restaurant owner was vulnerable in almost everything he did. He lived in his shop, which was illegal under municipal codes that said commercial premises could not be used for residential purposes. His business was staffed and managed by fellow Chinese, and replacements could be found only through smuggling or other evasions of the law. A man could be destroyed by a report to immigration, health, or housing officials. He needed a tong, or connections with a tong, to protect him.

Tong wars had a long history on the West coast, but were unknown in New York until 1900. The reason? The On Leong Tong (as the Lung Gee Tong had been renamed) gained a monopoly of the blackmail, gambling, and other illicit activities by buying the protection of Tammany Hall, the unchallenged ruler of New York. The police would not let a rival tong take root. Then Tammany's hold was loosened by reformist rivals and the way was opened for a rival tong—the Hip Sing.

A struggle between Tammany and would-be reformers began in 1892, when the Reverend Charles Parkhurst of the influential Madison Square Presbyterian Church launched a crusade against police-protected brothels and gambling houses, saying they flourished "almost as thick as the roses in Sharon." Parkhurst continued his broadsides for almost two years, railing against "polluted harpies, a lying, perjured, rum-soaked, libidinous lot." He spoke of New York as "hell with the lid off," leading to later descriptions of attempts to restrain corruption as "keeping the lid on."[3]

Governor Rosewell Flower—the Democrat whose oratory as a Congressman fed anti-Chinese hysteria in 1882—closed his ears, as did the Democratic State Legislature. But in November 1893 the Republicans gained control of the legislature and, the following January, State Senator Clarence Lexow was appointed to head a committee to investigate Parkhurst's charges.

Lexow, on Parkhurst's advice, chose John Goff, a former assistant district attorney, to conduct the investigation. Goff, in turn, picked two young lawyers as his assistants—William Travers Jerome, who would become one of the most controversial district attorneys in the city's history; and Frank Moss, who had been active in the municipal reform movement since 1885.

Month after month, madams, saloon keepers, abortionists—even bootblacks and fruit peddlers—testified that the police extorted weekly payments as, in effect, licenses to carry on their businesses. A share of this toll was passed up to higher police officers and they passed a share on to Tammany Hall politicians. The annual exactions totaled millions of dollars.

Representatives of an association of saloon keepers in Yorkville, on Manhattan's upper East Side, testified they had formed their association at the suggestion of a detective to simplify the collections. This was the reason for the On Leong monopoly: Tammany and the police preferred a single collection agency.

THE SAGA OF GEORGE WASHINGTON APPO

Some of the most damning testimony came from George Washington Appo, the son of Quimpo Appo. In his face, Appo resembled his mother. For most of his life he used the name George Leonard, so that few knew his father was Chinese, but he resembled Quimpo Appo in body: small and wiry. After his father's arrest, George was left with a woman in a Donovan's Lane hovel, where he picked his first pocket at the age of ten. Appo was first arrested at fourteen and was sent to the ship Mercury, which served as a "hard school" for wayward youths. About a year later he rescued a drowning comrade and was released for good conduct. He returned to Baxter Street and nine months later was sent to prison for two-and-a-half years for picking pockets. He was so small that a special uniform had to be made for him. In May 1876, a month after gaining his freedom, he was shot by someone whose pocket he had just picked, and lay for months in Bellevue Hospital, close to death. He recovered, was tried and convicted, and sent to jail for another two-and-a-half years.

143 CHARLES PARKHURST.

After his release, he shifted his amateurish pick-pocketing to Philadelphia. He was arrested in 1882 and tried to kill himself by drinking a vial of laudanum. He recovered, was imprisoned, freed, and jailed again, including a full year in solitary confinement. Freed, he returned to New York in early 1885 and operated scams listed as "bunco, dice, short cards, flimflam, and fake jewelry."

In February 1893 he was shot and blinded in one eye at a hotel in Poughkeepsie, New York. He was taken to a hospital and he again attempted suicide. Lawyers at his trial entered a plea of insanity, saying it might be hereditary, citing the fact that his father was already confined to the Matteawan Asylum for the Criminally Insane. This was rejected. Appo was found guilty and sentenced to one year in Sing Sing. He again tried to kill himself. He was released in 1894 for good behavior and returned to New York.[4]

Appo was convinced the men who tried to kill him had been hired by James McNally, who operated the con game in which Appo was involved at the time of the attack. Appo wanted revenge. He contacted Frank Moss and volunteered to tell what he knew about McNally and police corruption. In June 1894, as the court listened fascinated, Goff led Appo through an intricate, cant-filled description of the "greengoods business"—based on the purported possession of plates to print genuine dollar notes of various denominations. The operators sent letters throughout the country offering to sell money printed from the plates at a 90 percent discount. Victims were shown a tin box of genuine notes, which, at the last moment, was switched for an identical box containing bits of torn paper. Appo was a "steerer." When a victim answered one of the fliers, Appo met him at the train or ferry station and led him to a store where the money was switched. He then escorted the victim back to the train or ferry, warning him not to open the box until he was safely on the way. It was a lucrative business. McNally—an opium-den operator and former Sixth Avenue pimp—grossed eight thousand dollars a day, to be split between the men involved in writing and distributing the letters and others who bribed the police, postal clerks, and others not to interfere.[5]

Three months after his testimony, Appo's throat was cut and he was taken to a hospital. The police called it attempted suicide. Appo said a former greengoods man had given him a narcotic drink and tried to kill him. While he lay in his bed, a stranger appeared in his room, hit him

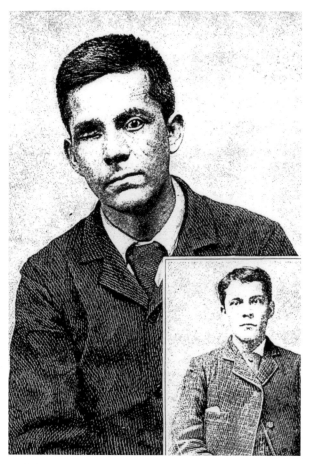

144 GEORGE APPO AS A YOUNG MAN AND AS HE APPEARED DURING THE LEXOW HEARINGS.

in the face, and tried to gouge out his remaining eye. Appo said the stranger was a policeman in civilian dress. When he got out of the hospital, he appeared in *In the Tenderloin*, a play based on his life, written by Edmund Price, the diamond-draped lawyer who defended Tom Lee in the early 1880s. The play soon closed and Appo was back on the streets.

During the hearings, McNally (and others who knew they would be called) took extended vacations in Europe. He returned in 1895 when the hearings ended. In early April Appo was arrested on a charge of trying to stab a policeman who had arrested him for disorderly conduct. It was a frame-up. He was in his cell only five minutes when McNally entered the station house through a back door, confronted him, and called him a squealer. Appo was released on bail. He fled (obviously for safety), was discovered in Buffalo, and returned to New York, where he pleaded guilty to assault. He was sentenced to six months in prison. After his release, he was arrested for stealing an overcoat from a saloon at Eighth Avenue and 116th Street. He served a year and nine months in Sing Sing and returned to New York, a hopeless wreck.

One night, he was standing at the corner of Mott and Chatham Square. He had just been in a fight and had a long knife in his hand. Someone brushed against him and Appo lunged and stabbed, inflicting a serious wound. At police court the next day, he said he could not remember anything. The authorities now decided to put him away as they did his father. He was declared criminally insane and sent to Matteawan where, apparently, father and son were never reunited.

THE HIP SING TONG

Compared to Appo's testimony, the story as told by another witness drew little notice, but it was a turning point in the history of the Chinese in New York: It ushered in the Hip Sings. The tong was first recorded in the East a few years earlier, in June 1889, when Chinese gamblers were put on trial in Philadelphia. The ethnologist Stuart Culin, then living in Philadelphia, recorded that the Hip Sings copied Triad rituals but were shown at their trial to be "merely an association for the purpose of blackmail."[6]

That was how they got their start in New York. For the first ten years after the ban on the immigration of laborers, the Chinese in New York were spared the vindictive application of the law customary in California. However, in July 1893—acting under the tightened Geary Act of 1892—the Treasury Department appointed J.

Thomas Scharf, a former Confederate colonel, to the new post of special Chinese inspector for New York. Previously, customs officials glanced at a document presented to justify admission, compared a man with the picture on his papers, and waved him along. Scharf insisted the document be verified. If a man was said to have lived at a certain address in New York or some other eastern city, Scharf would not let him off a ship until proof was received that such a place existed and such a man was known there. He rejected one man because his passport appeared to describe him as five feet one-half inch. When measured, he was found to be five feet six inches. A lawyer argued it was a clerical error, since fractions of inches were never used in passports, and that it must mean five-and-a-half feet. It was a few days before the Chinese was allowed to land.

When a ship arrived from Havana with actors for Chu Fong's recently opened theater, Scharf charged this was a device to evade the exclusion of laborers and threatened to arrest Chu Fong as a smuggler. On another occasion, he boarded a British ship, ordered the captain to muster his thirty Chinese seamen on deck, and walked the line examining each one closely, saying he believed one or two would desert, and he wanted to recognize those who might be seized. A reporter called this "asinine."[7]

A Chinese who Anglicized his name as Warry Charles was the first to seize this opportunity for blackmail. Charles, thirty-seven, had lived in New York for fifteen years. Although he was married to an American woman, and took part in Sunday School activities, he was linked to the tongs: He was the interpreter for Moy clan members who, in May 1883, were tried (and one convicted and imprisoned) for assaulting a laundryman in Paterson, New Jersey.

Charles volunteered his services to Scharf, ostensibly out of Christian zeal to fight corruption, only to be arrested in July 1893 for blackmail and charged with accepting seventy-five dollars in marked money from a Mott Street merchant on the threat that he would prevent the entry of the merchant's partner, due to return from a visit to China. There had earlier been complaints that Charles was demanding blackmail, and a detective planted the marked bills. Scharf appeared as a character witness at his trial, and Charles, while admitting he had received the money, said it was to rent a room to be used as a billiard parlor. He was acquitted and was next seen escorting his wife and children on the renewed Sunday School excursion in June 1894.[8]

Mock Duck, the next tongman to surface, would become the most notorious Hip Sing gangster in New York. In 1893, when he was only nineteen and new to the city, Mock Duck appeared at the arrival docks with papers supporting the claims of a man who had been stopped by Scharf. Scharf accused him of being a leading smuggler of Chinese into New York.[9]

When preparations for the Lexow hearings began, the Hip Sings—in the person of Wong Get—stepped forward as allies of Parkhurst's Society for the Prevention of Crime. Wong, who said he had been in the United States fourteen years, was called to the stand following George Appo. He testified that in January 1894, when he opened a gambling house at 18 Doyers Street, Tom Lee came with his gold deputy-sheriff badge stuck on his suspender and demanded sixteen dollars a week—fifteen for the police and one dollar for his own expenses. Wong Get said no Chinese doubted the police were involved because a policeman accompanied Tom Lee or his assistant, Lee Toy, when they came to collect the weekly payments, although, for appearances sake, the policeman waited outside when the money changed hands. Most of his day on the stand was taken up with an involved story of how he refused to pay Lee Toy, after which a detective came and broke down his door. He then went and paid the money and the detective came back with a screwdriver and put the door back on its hinges.[10]

The widely publicized evidence of utter Tammany corruption finally roused the public. In November 1894 a Republican-Reform fusion ticket headed by William Strong—a merchant and banker—with John Goff for Recorder (as the city's principal judge was then known) won a landslide victory. Goff received more votes than Strong. Six months later, Strong became the first mayor to make an official visit to Chinatown, leading four carriages of municipal officials to the Ling Hing Hung building at 20 and 22 Pell Street, whose crowded occupancy was manifested by ninety-six separate gas meters. The speech of welcome was made by Mock Duck.[11]

Mock Duck's real name was Mock Sai Wing. Born in San Francisco and educated at a Christian school, with a cherubic face and liquid eyes, he seemed a perfect ally of Parkhurst's Society for the Prevention of Crime. The Hip Sing Tong filed for incorporation in November 1896, giving its purpose as, "To establish and maintain a permanent place of meeting for the members away from the baneful influences of the opium dens and gambling joints where reli-gious observances, social amusements, recreation, and intercourse may be enjoyed and the study of the English language may be pursued."[12]

Their charter notwithstanding, the Hip Sings were busy in the pursuit of blackmail. When Scharf blocked the cheap ocean route to New York (in December 1894 he had bragged that only six Chinese had been admitted over the previous six months), the Chinese changed to the rail route across Canada, entering the United States at Malone, New York, and taking the train south to Grand Central Station in New York. Scharf hired Wong Get as an interpreter and arrested scores of Chinese at the station. They were held for close questioning, only to be later released.[13]

Scharf's post was eliminated in October 1897. In a summing-up article for the *North American Review* in January 1898 (preceded by, "That for ways that are dark and tricks that are vain the heathen Chinee is peculiar"), Scharf charged that five hundred thousand Chinese had entered the United States since passage of the 1892 Geary Act, nine-tenths of them illegally. He also claimed there were seven hundred thousand Chinese in the country. (The 1900 census counted a little more than one hundred thousand.)

A final note was written by Max Kohler, who had been an assistant federal district attorney during the Scharf era, and who later gained eminence as a specialist in immigration law, using his skills to defend newcomers against increasing restrictions and harassment. In a book reviewing his career, Kohler recalled:

> When I was in office, a Chinese inspector would arrest sometimes fifty Chinamen at a time, coming down on the New York Central from the Canadian border station, Malone, and claimed his associates up there used to admit them irregularly. He said he wanted to investigate each case carefully himself, after the arrest, before any trial, and ultimately requested the discharge of nearly all the defendants, which was granted. After I was out of office, reputable Chinese persons told me that his interpreter collected so much per head for nearly every man thus discharged.[14]

Inevitably, the On Leong-Hip Sing rivalry was leading to a deadly clash. The first indication came in September 1897, when a half dozen On Leong "soldiers"—as tong fighters were called—pounced on Mock Duck as he walked along Doyers Street. Several Hip Sings came to his aid and, in the melee, Mock Duck's left leg was gashed with a knife. Another man was cut on the shoulder. Mock Duck went to California to recuperate.[15]

THE FIRST TONG WAR

Mayor Strong's administration was inept. The reform experiment ended when Tammany candidate Robert Van Wyck was elected mayor in November 1897. The lid was soon off. An *Evening Post* reporter counted fifty fan-tan tables and eleven lottery rooms on Mott and Pell streets, estimating the net in protection money at thirty-five thousand a year.[16]

And now the war began. The On Leongs struck first. In August 1900 a Hip Sing soldier was killed in a rear tenement at 9 Pell Street. Police at the scene found five Hip Sings armed with three pistols, an assortment of knives, a pear-shaped piece of iron weighing several pounds suspended from a cord to be attached to a wrist, and an iron bludgeon eighteen inches long and weighing five pounds—the first time any such array of weapons was found among the Chinese.[17]

An On Leong, Goo Wing Chung, was tried for the murder but acquitted. Among those who provided him with an alibi was an On Leong named Ah Fee. In September about a dozen Hip Sings ambushed Ah Fee as he came out of a shop at 19 Pell. He turned to run and was shot in the back and killed. Stray shots slightly wounded an American woman and her child.[18]

Police arrested Sue Sing. The tong code guaranteed that if a soldier were arrested, the tong would hire a lawyer to try to free him. If convicted, his family would be cared for. If wounded, he would be treated by the best doctors available. If killed, his family would be indemnified. In this case, Sue Sing pleaded guilty and was sentenced to life in prison.[19]

The guilty plea was rare. If the Hip Sings thought the cards were stacked against them and were trying to save legal expenses, it would prove to be a bad precedent. A *Tribune* reporter noted: "Six murders have taken place in Chinatown in the last few years. In none of them has there been a conviction owing to the difficulty of getting evidence. In this particular case [Sue Sing] however, the D.A.'s office has been materially aided by Tom Lee, known as the 'good Chinaman,' a former deputy Sheriff. Lee belongs to the better element of the Chinese in the city, known as the Lung Gag Gong [cq] or Chinese Masons."[20]

The Lexow Committee hearings had made William Travers Jerome the most respected prosecutor in the city. When the hearings ended, he was appointed district attorney and thus was allied with Tammany. The hearings also made Frank Moss famous, but Moss retained his ties with Parkhurst's Society for the Prevention of Crime—usually shortened as the Parkhurst Society. Moss retained his ties with the Hip Sings.

District Attorney Jerome, representing "good Chinaman" Tom Lee, tried to use the Ah Fee murder as a weapon against the Hip Sings. A laundryman named Dong Sue was accused of complicity but, before he could be arrested, he fled to Boston, which, by then, had become a Hip Sing stronghold under the leadership of Warry Charles, who had left his family in New York to migrate, for safety, to Boston. Charles hired an expensive lawyer to fight the extradition, but failed. Dong Sue was extradited to New York. However, his trail ended in a hung jury and he was set free.[21]

(To digress: In 1904 Warren Charles, the son that Warry Charles left behind in New York, became the second Chinese American New York City policeman. His father, however, paid dearly for his life as a tong leader. In August 1907 the Hip Sings killed four On Leongs and wounded four others in what became known as the "Boston Massacre"—a blaze of guns on Oxford Place, in the center of the city's Chinatown. Three Hip Sings were convicted of murder, mainly on evidence supplied by the On Leongs. After long appeals, they were hanged in 1909. Warry Charles, as head of the Hip Sing Tong, was tried as an accessory before the fact and was also sentenced to hang, but this was commuted to life in prison. As for Patrolman Warren Charles, he married and had three children, and only once came in for newspaper attention. In July 1923 he saved two other patrolmen from being dragged down by a drowning man under the Brooklyn Bridge, for which he received a medal. He retired, at sixty-four, in 1941.)[22]

When Mock Duck returned to New York, he too was arrested in connection with the Ah Fee murder. His trial also ended in a hung jury, but he was sent to the Tombs without bail pending retrial.

In February 1902 Tom Lee marked his twenty-fifth year as de facto ruler of Chinatown with a huge New Year's dinner at On Leong headquarters at 14 Mott. The more than a hundred American guests included Police Commissioner Francis Vinton Greene (the office of police chief had previously been transmuted into commissioner) and two of his deputies, Judge Warren Foster of the Court of General Sessions, Justice Julius Mayer of Special Sessions, District Attorney Jerome and assorted assistants, "well rounded" aldermen, police captains, detectives, and sergeants.[23]

The next day Mock Duck, who had been held since the previous May, was again brought to trial. He had four lawyers, including Frank Moss, with Wong Get as an interpreter for the defense. Most of the Chinese called to the stand claimed they saw nothing. The jury failed to reach a verdict and the case was not retried.[24]

In 1902 George McClellan, the son of the Civil War general, was elected mayor on a Tammany ticket. He was strong enough in his own right to attempt to run a clean government. His most difficult appointment was that of police commissioner. He chose William McAdoo, a New Jersey state legislator who had served as Assistant Secretary of Navy under President Grover Cleveland and was then a practicing lawyer in New York.[25]

In July 1904, after the Hip Sings fed him tips on gambling houses run by the On Leongs, McAdoo tried to stage an end run around the Tammany-controlled Elizabeth Street precinct. He commandeered detectives and police from central headquarters, armed them with axes and crowbars, and sent them on simultaneous raids on Leong gambling rooms. At two of them, 18 Mott and 23 Pell, they had to smash their way through four sets of doors to reach the inner rooms and make arrests. As usual, those arrested were discharged at the Tombs police court.[26]

The following November, Mock Duck was ambushed in front of 13 Pell. A bullet was fired straight into his stomach but his life was saved when the bullet struck a large, silver half dollar he wore as a belt buckle. He suffered a serious contusion and spent two weeks in a hospital and then was taken to Hip Sing headquarters, now at 12 Bowery, to complete his recovery.[27]

At daybreak on November 23, On Leong bravados stole the crest and nameplate from outside Hip Sing headquarters. Two nights later, there was an exchange of more than thirty shots outside the building. No Chinese was hit but a stray bullet injured a pedestrian on the street and killed John Baldwin, who was standing in a saloon on the Bowery.[28]

An On Leong man was killed on the last day of January 1905. Another On Leong was shot and wounded toward the end of February.[29] In the middle of March, Mock Duck, who, after the crest was stolen from outside his headquarters had decided to complete his recuperation in California, returned to New York, bringing with him—or so the On Leong charged—four Hip Sing killers. A few nights later, shots were fired from an alley at Gin Gum, one of Tom Lee's principal lieutenants, as he walked along Mott Street.[30]

District Attorney Jerome was convinced that Mock Duck was behind the attack. Since he could not prove a connection, he had Mock Duck arrested again for complicity in the September 1900 murder of Ah Fee. Mock Duck was brought before Recorder John Goff. It was Goff who had hired Jerome and Moss as his chief assistants for the Lexow hearings. When Moss appeared for the defense of Mock Duck, all three Lexow Committee stalwarts reappeared for the first time in a single courtroom.

"This man is known to be a highbinder and a leading member of the Hip Sing Tong," Jerome told the court. "He went to San Francisco and returned quite recently in company of a band of friends just like himself for the avowed purpose of committing another murder. I don't care as long as members of that society stick to playing fan-tan, but when they take to murder then something must be done to stop their practices."

Frank Moss moved to have the charge dismissed on the grounds that Mock Duck had already been tried and acquitted twice in the Ah Fee case. He described Mock Duck as the most inoffensive Chinese in the city. Jerome admitted the charge was a slim basis for holding Mock Duck, but said he could not pick and choose his methods when he was given information that Mock Duck had returned to New York bent on murder.

"I might add," he said, "that until a certain society in this city began to monkey with Oriental affairs we heard of nothing worse than gambling in Chinatown but since then there have been plenty of shooting scrapes there."

"I regret," replied Moss, "that the district attorney has seen fit to inject into his argument veiled sarcasm against the Society for the Prevention of Crime and its counsel, this coming from a man who gained so much through its influences. His argument is not well taken."

"Well, if you will tell the truth about this matter..." Jerome began.

"Gentlemen, gentlemen," Goff interrupted.

"You might at least be respectful to me in court," Moss said to Jerome.

"Some people's characters don't entitle them to respect," Jerome drawled.

"I have a better character than you," Moss shouted.

"Well some people don't deserve politeness," Jerome replied.

Returning to the business at hand, Goff denied Moss's motion for dismissal. Bail for Mock Duck was fixed at one thousand dollars. The charge against him was later dismissed.[31]

Commissioner McAdoo tried again to control the Elizabeth Street station by promoting Detective Sergeant William Eggers—thirty-seven and a twelve-year veteran of the force—to the rank of captain. With a Hip Sing list of addresses fed to him by the Parkhurst Society, Eggers devised an elaborate plan to catch the Chinese in the act of gambling—thus collecting sufficient evidence for convictions. On a Saturday night in April, the day before Easter 1905, he led a procession of fourteen closed carriages crammed with police on a midnight raid of Mott Street. The police made straight for the selected buildings, running upstairs before the doors could be shut and bolted, and arrested almost two hundred Chinese.

By then, large open cars fitted with two rows of seats in the back were used for "Chinatown by Night" tourist tours. Several were in the area when the police stormed out of their carriages. Panic quickly subsided and the tourists sat back to enjoy the extra spectacle. The next day the prisoners were sorted out at Tombs police court. It was bedlam. Almost all were taken from known On Leong houses on Mott Street. Only two houses on Pell and one on Doyers were raided. Tom Lee was among those arrested. He was found to be carrying a revolver, for which he had a permit. He said he was a simple businessman, the owner of six laundries and four cigar stores. He was soon released. Commissioner McAdoo ordered "rubberneck" cars

145 GEORGE MCCLELLAN WAS ELECTED AS A TAMMANY MAYOR, PROMISING TO PUT THE LID ON GAMBLING AND VICE. FATHER KNICKERBOCKER ASKS, "TELL ME, IS THE LID ON"?

banned from Chinatown. Tourists would have to get out and walk and he hoped this would discourage them.[32]

On May 9, after the last prisoners were discharged, the *Evening Post* headlined the story, "That Chinatown Fiasco." The On Leongs got their revenge in the middle of May. Dong Fong, one of the signers of the Hip Sing charter of incorporation, was found guilty of wounding an On Leong soldier the previous February and was sentenced to Sing Sing for a term of up to five years. Tom Lee was in court to hear the sentence.

At the end of May, Eggers surrounded Chinatown with about seventy-five men, blocking all the streets. As squads rushed around smashing doors and windows and seizing what seemed to be gambling instruments, "Crowds of sightseers found much amusement in watching Chinese running over rooftops and climbing in and out of windows." It ended with the usual confusion at the police station and dismissal of all charges.[33]

During the sorting out of prisoners arrested in the Easter "Chinatown Fiasco," an interpreter named Jim Wang, supplied by the Parkhurst Society, was eager to help. He was identified as a "Chinese detective" and a lay reader at a Methodist Church. He had previously helped the police by identifying gambling rooms to be raided.

Here too the On Leongs got revenge. In June Wang was arrested for taking bribes to obtain the discharge of some of those arrested. An assistant district attorney said Wang had talked his way into the area where most of the prisoners were held prior to arraignment and promised to have them discharged for forty dollars apiece.[34]

On the night of August 6, 1905, a patrolman making his rounds noticed a number of Chinese entering a laundry on the south side of Chatham Square. This was unusual. It was in the Oak Street Precinct, across the wide square from Chinatown. The patrolman peeked through a curtain and saw a number of Chinese standing around a table throwing dice. Such an almost public display of gambling was also unusual. The patrolman called for aid and the Chinese were arrested. Soon Mock Duck appeared at the Oak Street station to put up bail for the arrested men. Was it a coincidence or a carefully contrived move to establish an alibi for Mock Duck? The truth was never established, but while Mock Duck was at the police station, establishing his alibi, his soldiers struck at On Leong men at the Doyers Street theater.

The Hip Sings were seated at the front and rear. A string of firecrackers was set off near the stage and as the audience rose in their seats to see what had happened, Hip Sing gunmen drew Colt revolvers and fired volleys of heavy bullets. Two On Leong men were killed on the spot, and two others later died of their wounds. The audience ran into the streets. Their screams were heard blocks away. Police reserves were shaken from their beds at the Elizabeth Street station, and reinforcements were called from all precincts below 14th Street. The first police who clubbed their way through the crowds found clouds of smoke, chairs and curtains riddled with bullets, the floor littered with hats, coats, shoes, and parcels of food, and terrified Chinese cowering under benches. More than a dozen men were arrested for the killings, but none was ever tried. When Mock Duck was picked up, his alibi was unshakable.

Chinatown was an ordinary New York slum, but after another string of shootings, in which three men were killed and seven wounded, newspapers invented dark alleys and concealed doors—an Oriental maze "honeycombed with underground tunnels and passageways through which tong killers slipped away."[35]

Police Commissioner William McAdoo resigned at the end of the year and Mayor McClellan replaced him with General Theodore Bingham.[36]

At the end of January 1906, Lee Toy set out for New Year calls. He had been Tom Lee's chief assistant and enforcer since the days when Huie Kin and his Christian stalwarts tried to rid Chinatown of crime in the mid-1880s. There had always been a truce during New Year celebrations and Lee Toy thought he could walk the streets with minimum security. He and his three bodyguards carried red packets of quarters to give to children. They walked down Pell, past the lanterns hanging like stage settings, the streamers, and the popping firecrackers, and turned into an alley between numbers 30 and 32. As they went up the stairs of a rear building, a half dozen Hip Sings followed and hid in stairways leading to basements. Others hid behind a swinging gate.

When Lee Toy and his companions came out, they were bracketed by bullets. They returned fire, driving the Hip Sings back into the street.

An On Leong man fell wounded. Three Hip Sings darted forward, placed their guns to his head and blew it to pieces. The police rushed to the scene and found another On Leong man dead in a doorway. Red packets of quarters had fallen from his pocket and were spread next to him, matching a pool of blood. A third On Leong lay moaning with bullets in both shoulders. Lee Toy, his left arm hanging useless and a Colt revolver clutched in his right hand, was running crookedly in an evasive path across Pell Street. He later died of his wounds.

About one hundred shots had been fired, smashing windows in nearby houses and burying themselves deep in brick and plaster. Pedestrians and tourists who had debarked from rubberneck wagons fled in terror or fell flat on the streets and sidewalks. A policeman was sent to question Mock Dock, only to find him in bed, dressed in his underclothes and smoking a cigarette. He said he had witnesses to prove he had been there all day.[37]

The police arrested four Hip Sings, including a waiter named Low Way, who went under the name of Louis or Lou Way. Four months later, he pleaded guilty to a lesser charge of assault and was sentenced to a maximum of nine-and-a-half years in prison.[38] Once again, the Hip Sings failed to do whatever was necessary to defend one of their soldiers—and for this they would pay a penalty many years later.

By now both sides were exhausted. A Chinese government official from Peking—F. F. Tong, who was studying commerce in the United States—arranged for Judge Warren Foster of the Court of General Sessions to work out a settlement in conjunction with the American lawyers of both tongs. A peace treaty was drawn up on February 2, 1906, in the judge's chambers at the Criminal Courts Building.

Neither Tom Lee nor Mock Duck was present. Judge Foster sat at the head of a horseshoe table flanked by F. F. Tong and Kit Fu Shan, the Chinese consul. A clerk began to read the treaty aloud: "Article One: that no Chinaman shall carry a revolver or other deadly weapon on his person or in the public thoroughfare under any circumstances."

"I object, if your honor please," interrupted On Leong Counsul Tom Dineen, known as the Demosthenes of Park Row for flowery speeches. "Many Chinese merchants need to carry revolvers and have police permits to do so."

"Very well," replied the judge. "I will amend Article One by adding the words, "unless having lawful authority to do so." There was no disagreement and the reading continued:

Article Two: That no tribute or tax shall be levied by either society or any member thereof, either directly or indirectly, upon any businessman, or upon any Chinaman on any pretext whatever, other than the ordinary dues which are paid it by members of these organizations.

Article Three: That other than the regular dues mentioned no members of either of the above societies shall pay any sum of money or other valuable gratuity to either of the above societies for a concession or privilege, favor, or business opportunity, either directly or indirectly.

The reading continued through the remaining five articles, which named a peace committee and swore both sides to end gambling and promote peace and prosperity.[39] As a peace treaty it failed. Although never saying so explicitly, it legitimized the division of Chinatown between the Hip Sings and On Leongs with the right to levy taxes and tribute on businesses and individuals, and to grant concessions and privileges within their domains: Mott Street for the On Leongs, Pell for the Hip Sings, with Doyers as neutral territory. A Hip Sing who strayed to Mott, or an On Leong who wandered to Pell, could be shot on sight.

There had been talk of a joint peace banquet, but the tongs celebrated apart. The On Leong banquet was subdued. Tom Lee remained in his uptown house. In contrast, more than three hundred Hip Sings gathered at a restaurant at 16 Pell, along with thirty or more officials of the Parkhurst Society and representatives from Frank Moss's law office. Waiters filled little gold-tipped cups of brandy and there were shouts of "Victory!, Victory!" as toasts were downed.[40]

The peace treaty notwithstanding, Manhattan Borough President John Ahern revived his predecessor's campaign to "wipe out a den of infamy and give a breathing space" by converting the Chinatown area into a public park.[41]

The only defenders of the Chinese to appear at a public hearing were the missionaries. A Mrs. Maxwell of the Morning Star Mission declared:

I have never been insulted by a Chinaman and I know many of them. It is not true that white women are locked up by the Chinese, as white women stay there voluntarily. I have three Chinatown Chinese who are now ready for baptism. The trouble is with the police. I have seen policemen talking with young girls, and the language they used was awful. I stand up for the Chinese.[42]

Few would agree. In his memoirs, former Police Commissioner William McAdoo wrote:

Chinatown is an ulcer-spot on the face of the city, which would be better off if the whole place could be levelled and rebuilt. [It] is inhabited largely by a lot of Chinese parasites who thrive and fatten on their unfortunate countrymen, a few degraded white women and degenerate white men, and some whites who trade on its vices. There is also a credulous army of tourists that throng in and out through narrow streets, buy joss-sticks at a dollar apiece in alleged joss-houses, eat weird dishes, and inhale strange smells. As the Chinese exclusion act is a bar to the importation of Chinese women, the so-called Chinese wives are probably, taken altogether, the most wretched, degraded, and utterly vile lot of white women and girls that could be found anywhere.[43]

Nevertheless, Ahern's proposal to wipe out Chinatown was shelved: If evicted, where would they go? When rumors spread that Chinese had bought property in the Bronx in anticipation of Chinatown's demolition, Julius Haas, a real-estate agent, announced: "I should strenuously oppose any project to foist the orgies of Chinatown upon the self-respecting people of the Bronx."[44]

THE FOUR BROTHERS WAR

Three years passed and it seemed that the peace would hold. Then, in July 1909, Elsie Sigel was murdered and Chinatown was turned inside out in the fruitless search for her killer. The excitement soon passed, and a month later, jazz pianos tinkled at the dine-and-dance chop suey restaurants lining both sides of Mott Street. At two o'clock of a Sunday morning, Chin Lem ran from an alley between numbers 17 and 19 Mott shouting for help and leaving bloody finger smears on the walls of shops as he steadied himself. A policeman ran to him and he cried, "I didn't do it."

The policeman ran into the alley and up the stairs to a third floor room where the door was ajar. On the floor, under glaring gas lamps and in a circle of blood, lay a woman in a yellow blouse, blue pantaloons, and sandals. There were slashes on her hands as if she had tried to grasp the weapon that killed her; a stiletto with an eight-inch blade and a bone handle now stuck into the floor.[45]

Her name was Bow Kum. She was twenty-one. Under questioning, Chin Lem, a professional gambler, claimed she was his wife, although he lived in an apartment across Mott Street. He said he went to his wife's room, saw her body on the floor, and tried to stop the flow of blood, thus explaining the bloody fingerprints down the hall and along the street. The On Leong arranged for Chin's bail and supplied information leading to the arrest for murder of Lau Tang and Lau Shong.[46]

The story of Bow Kum's short life was soon revealed. She was born in China, sold as a child by her parents, brought to the United States in about 1907, sold for two thousand dollars to Lau Tang in San Francisco and then "rescued" by Donaldina Cameron, a Scotswoman who spent much of her life trying to free tong slave girls. After being taught sewing and homemaking, Bow Kum was married to Chin Lem, who represented himself as a Christian farmer from New York looking for a bride. Apparently, Miss Cameron had no means to verify claims of Chinese from the East Coast.

The principal function of a woman such as Bow Kum was to ornament public functions. For instance, a newspaper description of an On Leong reception in early July noted a "row of silent, smiling, silken clad women" lining both sides of the room. Since this was only five weeks before her murder, Bow Kum was probably one of them.[47]

Lau Tang learned Bow Kum was in New York and came east and stayed with Lau Shong at a laundry in Brooklyn. He demanded that Chin Lem pay him three thousand dollars to keep Bow Kum and notices to that effect were posted in Chinatown.

In China, where might made right, it was imperative for small clans to unite against more numerous clans. Four surname clans—Lau (or Low), Quan, Cheung (or Chang), and Chew (or Chu)—had become the Four Brothers clan, one of the largest and most ancient of such amalgamations.

Tongs enrolled men of all surnames, while clans were formed of families of one surname or of traditional groupings. Clans tried to divorce themselves from the tongs of their members because of the domino effect: If one clan member helped another because of his tong activities, the entire clan might be drawn into the maelstrom. But, as what became known as the "Four Brothers War" demonstrated, it was difficult to maintain the distinction between clan and tong in American Chinatowns.

Chin Lem was a member of the On Leong Tong. Non-tong community leaders, trying to head off a war, persuaded On Leong and Four Brothers leaders to sign an agreement to keep the peace. But when a grand jury indicted both Laus for murder, mainly on the testimony of Gin Gum of the On Leongs, Four Brothers gangsters defied their clan elders. In September one

bravado was wounded as he daringly stood outside Gin Gum's store at 175 Worth Street. In early November two On Leongs, including one who had testified before the grand jury that indicted the Laus, were shot and wounded as they walked down the Bowery. The On Leong tong expelled fifty-four merchant-members who were Four Brothers, which meant if they had shops or other businesses on Mott Street (which Judge Foster's treaty had ceded to the On Leongs) they could be shot on sight. Well-to-do Four Brothers merchants, who lived in a new apartment house at 53 Bayard Street, went back and forth to their shops with bodyguards on both sides. So many merchants and others left for safety that Chinatown seemed to one reporter "like a deserted village."[48]

Single men from a clan or village lived in "company rooms" in ramshackle buildings with time-blackened windows, rudimentary lighting, and poor sanitation. The rear four-story building at 30½ Pell was used for Four Brothers company rooms. A dark and moldy inner courtyard, reached through a long, damp alley, was almost roofed over by the fire escapes of the front building. From there, shaky wooden stairs went up the front of the rear building, with doors leading directly into tiny rooms with wooden walls and ceilings so low a tall man had to bend over. A sign at the entrance to two rooms leading off the platform read, in Chinese, "Opium Sold Here." Low Jung and Low Fong, both about seventy years old, had lived there, surrounded by old kettles and pots, for forty years, selling the cheapest opium on the market: the reboiled scrapings from opium pipes. So many old men lived there it was known as the Old Men's Home.

Shortly after midnight at the end of December, four men ran down the alley, up the flight of stairs, pushed open the door, and sprayed the rooms with bullets. Low Jung was hit three times and almost cut in half. Low Fong was hit ten times. The force of the large bullets slammed his body back into a pile of coal under his bunk. Captain Galvin, still patrolling the streets, was there within minutes, but the killers had already escaped.[49]

The Four Brothers got revenge on the night of December 30 with the killing (as recorded earlier) of Dop Doy (Comedian) Hong at the Chinese theater.

The trial of the two Laus took place in the second week of January 1910. Frank Moss, now an assistant district attorney, was prosecutor. Guy Maine served as interpreter. Moss had gotten over his distaste for the On Leongs. With their help, he produced a witness who said he heard

146 Four Brothers tong soldiers outside their Pell Street headquarters.

the Laus threaten Chin Lem with death if the three thousand dollars was not paid. Another said he had looked through a partially closed blind and had seen the Laus in Bow Kum's room at about the time of the murder. A third said he had seen the same thing. The next two testified they had seen the Laus leave Bow Kum's room a short while later.

Defense witnesses swore Lau Tang was at the Doyers Street theater and Lau Shong at his laundry in Brooklyn at the time of Bow Kum's death. When called to the stand, both men said they never heard of either Bow Kum or Chin Lem. The trial lasted four days. The jury puzzled for five hours over the contradictory testimony and rendered a verdict of not guilty. Sam Lock, national president of the Four Brothers, had come to New York to supervise the defense. He had a victory banquet for one hundred guests. "Just a repast, a little repast," he said.[50]

When the war resumed a few weeks later, the first casualty was a Japanese walking along Doyers Street. He was mistaken for an On Leong and shot dead.[51]

After two more killings and two woundings[52] and months of secret negotiations, Chinese embassy and consulate officials persuaded Tom

Lee and Sam Lock to approve the draft of a truce treaty, but, at the last minute, Lock sent word he would not attend the signing on Mott Street, saying he feared treachery if he stepped onto On Leong territory.

"The Four Brothers are a bad lot," Tom Lee said during the wait for Sam Lock. "There may be more shooting. I don't know. Business is bad. There is no money in Chinatown. The whole situation has gone to the devil."

"Oh, you're getting old, Tom," said Captain "Big Bill" Hodgins, who had replaced Michael Galvin as head of the Elizabeth Street station. He had come to witness the signing. Lee just sat staring out the window, puffing on his cigar.[53]

In June Chew Hien of the Four Brothers was tried for the murder of an On Leong man two months earlier. Faced with contradictory testimony, the jury, like the one that heard the Bow Kum case, found the defendant not guilty.

A few weeks later, Chew was on picket duty outside the Chinese Delmonico's at 24 Pell Street as the Four Brothers gathered for their annual banquet. There were also policemen scattered along the street. On Leong soldiers ignored both and charged toward the restaurant. Chew saw them coming and emptied all chambers of his revolver before falling with a bullet in his thigh. Thirty shots were fired, shattering windows of two stores and pock-marking walls. Two men were killed. One was an On Leong attacker. The other was one of the most familiar and harmless men of Chinatown—Chun Mow— an old man who sold fruit and candy at a stand at the intersection of Mott and Pell.

The Transfiguration church was just south of the intersection. Spent bullets and chips of stone landed near an afternoon school class that was leaving the church. The pastor asked for a meeting with Mayor John Gaynor to plead for more police protection. He replied that he was too busy.[54]

In July Chu On was killed when he walked along Mott Street in defiance of the rule that the street was closed to a Four Brothers member. His assailant was chased, arrested, and brought to trial. Character witnesses insisted he could not have done such a thing and he was acquitted.[55]

Wealthy Four Brothers clansmen were eager for peace. One said his monthly trade had dropped to $2,600, compared to $4,500 a year earlier. They also complained that anyone named Lau, Chong, Kwan or Chu was dunned for as much as $50 a time to pay for lawyers and the cost of keeping twenty-five to thirty soldiers at clan headquarters.[56]

In October Mayor Gaynor appointed a new police commissioner—James Cropsey—who, in turn, appointed Clement Driscoll as his first deputy, with orders to end "fraudulent opium joints where tourists are taken to be shown a white woman rolling opium pills in company of a decrepit Chinese" and to shut down "chop suey restaurants where white girls are in company with Chinese residents of the neighborhood."

Driscoll's solution was to "segregate the white from the yellow population." Police went from building to building ordering non-Chinese to move. Within days, Driscoll said he was "satisfied that no white lived in the same tenement as Chinese." For his part, Commissioner Cropsey ordered sight-seeing auto companies to eliminate their "Chinatown by Night" tours. The decrees were so disastrous that some restaurants dismissed almost all their waiters.[57]

The war ended with a final fusillade that killed two brothers named Quan at their restaurant supply store at 31½ Pell. The assailants escaped. Newspapers were keeping score, like in a baseball game. They said these deaths brought the toll in New York to twelve.[58]

The Four Brothers were forced to admit they could not defend themselves even on Pell Street,

their home ground, and agreed to a peace treaty with a schedule of damages and reparations to be paid by each side. The Benevolent Association was decked with lanterns at the end of December and the large room on the fifth floor was ablaze with more lanterns and wreathed in the smoke of hundreds of incense sticks. Amid deep bows, Y. Y. Yung, the Chinese consul in New York, and Ou Shou-tchun, the ambassador from Washington, swept in dressed in their official robes. The peace treaty, on yellow paper six feet long, was signed, hands were shaken, and there was a wild burst of music from the orchestra almost hidden at the rear of the room while, on the street outside, firecrackers exploded and men cheered.

At On Leong headquarters, tall candles were lighted before Kwan Kung and billows of incense smoke clouded the air. There were two whole roasted pigs on the table before the image: an offering sent from the Four Brothers as a token of surrender.[59]

Each tong gave a feast. Joseph Singleton, whose Chinese name—Chew—made him a Four Brothers, presided at his clan's feast, but when reporters asked about tongs and traditions, Singleton talked of reform. He said two hundred Four Brothers had cue off their queues, fifty of them in the previous few days.[60]

Tong battles that started in one city invariably spread wide and far. This one had raged throughout the Midwest and East. The chairman and four secretaries of the commission that mediated an end to the struggle were members of the Chinese Students Club, located at Huie Kin's First Chinese Presbyterian Church on East 31st Street. Its first annual report in 1911 included a statement that fifty men were killed or wounded during the eighteen months of the senseless struggle.

For a few brief months, it appeared old hatreds and old ways would be forgotten: In October 1911 the Qing Dynasty was overthrown in the name of Sun Yat-sen, and China was declared a republic. A dozen boys with toy guns and wooden cartridges in belts slung over their shoulders marched through Mott, Pell, and Doyers streets to the cheers of their elders. That night more than a thousand Chinese gathered at the Rescue Society on Doyers Street to hear rousing speeches by leaders of the recently formed Young China Association.[61]

On January 1, when revolutionary leaders of the Provisional Government in Canton (Sun's faction) called for a two-million-dollar loan, Mock Duck and Wong Get walked the forbidden sidewalks of Mott Street to a building they never before had entered: the headquarters of the On Leong. Charles Quan of the Four Brothers also came. Tom Lee spoke of his rivals with almost fraternal affection as pledges were given for fifty-two thousand dollars. Wong Get told reporters, "We have buried the hatchet in the breast of the Manchu dynasty." To fill the pledges, a levy of five dollars was imposed on males over sixteen. Mock Duck and Wong Get each gave five hundred dollars. The Hip Sing Tong gave one thousand. The On Leongs gave two thousand in the name of the Chinese Merchants Association. Tom Lee had a personal reason for generosity. Five years earlier, his eldest son, Frank—who had been studying law at New York University—was sent by the Baptists to Canton for training as a missionary. Finding religion uncongenial, Frank Lee involved himself in underground plotting. When the revolution broke out, he was appointed Secretary of the Provisional Government.[62]

THE THIRD TONG WAR

But old ways and hatreds and the competition for gambling and prostitution domains were not easily ended. A new tong war began on January 12, less than a week after this patriotic conviviality. Muffled shots were heard from behind the whitewashed windows of a store at 21 Pell Street. Police ran to what was obviously a gambling room and found six Chinese standing silently beside the fan tan tables. There was a body under one of the tables. At the rear, in a small office, a man was standing calmly warming his hands over a stove. It was Mock Duck. "It's a very bad business," he said, shaking his head sadly.

The body was identified as that of Laing Yue, the national vice president of the Hip Sings. Mock Duck said another man, Hip Sing national president Chung Pun Sing, had been wounded and was taken to a hospital. Chung died a few days later. The fan-tan apparatus had been removed, but police found some lottery slips. For lack of any other excuse, Mock Duck was arrested for running a lottery.[63]

A few months earlier, a passage had been opened between Mott and Doyers streets. It was called an arcade but it had no shops. It was more like a tunnel with stairs going up and down at both ends and an "L"-shaped angle in the middle. The passage made it possible for someone to go from Doyers to Mott without trespassing on out-of-bounds Pell Street. One night, at the end of February, four Hip Sings slipped through the arcade and sidled along to 18 Mott. On the ground floor, masquerading as a fruit-and-

tobacco store, was a guardroom for the entrance to the Chinese Merchants Association, staffed by On Leong soldiers. The assault party rushed up the steps and sprayed the store with bullets, killing eighteen-year-old Lee Kay, who stood behind the counter. On Leong soldiers chased the invaders along Mott and into the arcade. Fifteen shots were fired, chipping brick from the sides and ceiling. A man named Sullivan, crouching under the steps, had his hat shot off. Eng Hing, a seventeen-year-old Hip Sing, was shot in his leg. He was arrested along with another Hip Sing named Lee Duck.

When the news traveled uptown, men in evening clothes and women in expensive dresses jumped into long touring cars to savor the excitement. Restaurants and even fruit and candy stores "did a land-office business while vast quantities of misinformation were given the visitors by Chinese waiters."[64]

In March an On Leong was killed and another wounded, and an Italian who lived on Mott Street was hit in the leg by a stray bullet. Then a Hip Sing gunman was shot and wounded in a Pell Street gambling room.[65]

Once again, Mock Duck was arrested, this time as an accessory after the fact in the killing of the two Hip Sings the previous January. This was later changed to a charge of running a lottery shop at 21 Pell Street, where the killings took place. The evidence was slim, but District Attorney Charles Whitman was determined to take him out of circulation. He succeeded. In June Mock Duck was convicted and sentenced to from one to two years in prison, the maximum possible.[66]

The killings went on. In early June, Yee Toy—a notorious Hip Sing killer known to his comrades as "Girl Face" because he was small and slender—was shot in the back and killed at tong headquarters by Cheung Hing, a former friend whose loyalty had been bought by the On Leong.[67]

The Hip Sings planned revenge. On June 23, the same day that a Hip Sing was killed in a Doyers Street basement, a package containing a bomb was left as an offering before the figure of Kwan Kung at On Leong headquarters at 18 Mott. It was set to explode at 10 P.M. on a Sunday when a general meeting was scheduled, but it went off an hour earlier, when the room was empty. The damage showed what might have happened: The image of Kwan Kung was shattered; metal fragments from the bomb were imbedded in the walls and ceiling and a hole two feet in diameter was blown through the floor, wrecking the room below. The bomb went off as Italians were walking in procession to

Transfiguration church carrying a statue of St. Gonzaga. A rumor spread that the Chinese had bombed the church, and police reserves were called from several precincts to restrain Italians who ran to the scene.[68]

In retaliation, a Hip Sing, who had been wounded in an attack a month earlier, and who had walked around with a gauze bandage covering his injury, was found dead in his Doyers Street room. He had been shot five more times.[69]

In October 1912 hundreds of Hip Sing members gathered outside the Criminal Courts building to await a grand jury's findings in the case of Eng Hing and Lee Duck, the two Hip Sings accused of killing Lee Kay the previous February. Word came that they had been indicted for murder in the first degree and the Hip Sings drifted the few blocks back to their headquarters. As they stood sullenly outside, someone began sneaking along Pell Street, hugging the wall to present less of a target.

His name was Lou Way. He had once been a Hip Sing soldier. In 1906, after the gun battle in which Lee Toy, Tom Lee's principal aide, was wounded, Lou pleaded guilty to a lesser charge and was sent to jail for a maximum of nine-and-a-half years. He was released in six-and-a-half years. The code of the tongs mandated that a tong must do everything to keep one of its soldiers out of jail. Lou Way felt the Hip Sings had abandoned him and spent those years in jail nursing his grievance and planning to get even.

As he sidled along the wall, a lookout drew his gun and fired one shot, whereupon every Hip Sing on the street drew guns and shot anything that moved.

Five men were killed in a hail of sixty bullets. Only one, the lookout, was a tong man. An Italian barber had just walked out of Pell Street, and stopped at the Bowery to look back when he heard the first shot, and was killed by a bullet in his head. A Chinese who heard shots and stepped onto the balcony of the Chinese Delmonico's was hit, fell back inside, and died. An Irishman walking in Pell Street was struck in the chest and died the next day in a hospital. A Jewish locksmith turning his wheel to make a key was struck in the head, staggered to Mott Street, and fell dead in the arms of a policeman. His assistant was grazed by a bullet across his scalp. Naughton's livery stable and funeral parlor on Mott Street, opposite the head of Pell, was riddled. A man sitting in the office was wounded in the leg, and a horse was killed. Every window on Pell Street was shattered.[70]

Tong leaders, alarmed at the repercussions from the killing of passersby, declared a cease-fire while the details for a peace treaty were worked out. With order restored, reform-minded Chinatown celebrated the American New Year on January 1, 1913, in streets decorated with the five-barred flag of the Republic of China.[71]

Three persons, arrested for the previous year's shootings, were brought to trial in February. The first was Cheung Hing, the Hip Sing who turned traitor for the On Leongs and shot Yee Toy in the back. The On Leongs managed his case so well that he was sentenced to only seven years in prison. The next two were Lee Duck and Eng Sing, the Hip Sings charged with killing Lee Kay, the teenaged guard at the entrance to the Merchant's Association. After their first trial ended with a hung jury, they were tried again and, in March, were found guilty and sentenced to die in the electric chair.[72]

Two months later a peace treaty was signed in Judge Foster's chambers. The most significant hidden clause ended the absolute division of Chinatown into Hip Sing and On Leong zones. Although each tong had the exclusive right to exact tolls from businessmen along their streets, tong members were free to walk where they chose. Guy Maine, who played a large role in the preliminary negotiations, was given a gold medal for his efforts.[73]

A month later—with two Hip Sings on Sing Sing's death row—the On Leong turned its Twenty-Fifth Annual Convention into a victory parade. More than eight hundred delegates came from branches across the country to march behind the 69th Regiment Band. The members wore white caps with a gilt star in front and carried small canes with the On Leong insignia at the tip. An open-deck Fifth Avenue bus packed with Chinese musicians followed the marchers. Then came twenty-five taxicabs, with Tom Lee and Guy Maine in the lead and merchants following behind. As the regimental band played "On the Trail of the Lonesome Pine" the procession wound through Mott, Bayard, and once-forbidden Pell Street and over to the East River to board a steamer for a picnic at Witzel's Grove.[74]

The final chapter of the 1912 tong war was written in 1915. The Hip Sings lavished money on detectives and lawyers to get evidence for a new trial, but all appeals were denied. On February 5, Lee Duck and Eng Hing were executed. Their bodies were brought to Chinatown, but the police, fearing trouble, insisted the funeral be held elsewhere. An Italian undertaker, C. Bacigalupo, arranged it at one of his branch offices on Spring Street. The funeral illustrated how strongly Hip Sing tong clung to the past. A coin was placed in the mouth of each man and a tightly corked

147 Tom Lee's funeral.

bottle with his name written on a paper inside was placed on his breast. A Taoist priest, dressed in dragon-embroidered robes glittering with threads of gold, chanted to the beat of a gong, the wail of a flute, and the weeping of four women. Sixteen Hip Sing soldiers lifted the coffins and carried them to waiting hearses. As the procession started, a man seated on one of the hearses scattered mock money. At Celestial Hill, roast pigs, nuts, chickens, eggs, rice cakes, and little cups of gin were placed on top of the graves, and the mourners bowed and left.[75]

The following April, when Gim Gum died, the On Leongs staged an elaborate modern funeral, conducted by the Reverend John Henry of the Church of All Nations, after which fifty carriages of flowers and another two hundred carriages of mourners followed the hearse to Cypress Hills Cemetery. Two wagons of Chinese musicians brought up the rear. The only bow to tradition was mock money tossed from the first carriage.[76]

The evolution of Chinatown since the revolution of 1911 was never more evident than at the funeral of the man who most typified the glory days—Tom Lee—who died in January 1918. Frank, his eldest son, was in China. His thoroughly Americanized youngest son, Tom Junior—who once tried out as a circus acrobat and was now an automobile salesman in Westchester—was there with his American wife and two plump children. Tom Lee had grown stout with a wisp of a beard and spent his final years sunning himself in front of the old ground floor command post at 18 Mott. As a man who loved flash and show, he would have appreciated a recognition that no other man of

150

Chinatown had received before him: five movie cameras to record his passing. If the filmmakers expected an oriental pageant, they were disappointed. A *Sun* reporter noted what was missing: "No perforated paper slips to distract devils, no roast pig, rice cakes, or other food, no packs of cards or cigarettes in the coffin, no incense burned in the room, no Buddhist priest, and no tom-toms."[77] There were only countless mourning cards from Chinese societies. An Episcopal minister presided. Sixty-one carriages followed a hearse ornamented with silver lamps, with an Italian band playing "Nearer My God to Thee." A *Reform News* reporter called it "A fine Republican funeral." The following April, Lee's body was returned to China.[78]

During World War I, and with a civil war raging in China, the tongs were quiet. In November 1920, as a fleet of tourist cars debarked three hundred men and women for a ten-minute glimpse of the Far East, a young Chinese ran through the crowd and into a Doyers Street poolroom. Three shots were fired, and the forty Chinese inside the room dropped their cues and ran out, along with the assailant. They were soon replaced by tourists demanding to see what they regarded as part of the show. In the chaos, the killer escaped. The murdered man was named Leong Yung. Reporters learned that he had been expelled from the Hip Sings as a police informant whose tips led to repeated raids on gambling houses. The reporters recognized the name. When Leong Yung was drafted, it was discovered he was an opium addict. He was treated and trained at Camp Upton, but the war ended a few days before his unit was to be shipped across the Atlantic. In reporting the shooting, the *Times* added: "The leaders of the Chinese Boy Scouts, a powerful organization in Chinatown, met last night and resolved that they would use all their power to prevent any clashing of the tongs."[79]

The post-war years were fat, and tong fighting seemed the last thing on anyone's mind. About five hundred Chinese-owned businesses flourished, as shops were busy morning and afternoon. Prosperity spilled across the river to Newark's Chinatown, known as Mulberry Arcade, between Mulberry and Lawrence streets, with a resident population in the early 1920s of more than three hundred, and with five clan meeting rooms, three restaurants, at least five gambling rooms, and two opium shops. On Sundays it attracted Chinese from as far away as Trenton.[80]

The Chinese Merchants Association—the peaceful disguise of the On Leongs—bought a four-story building at 41 Mott and remodeled it at a cost of three hundred thousand dollars with a red-tiled pagoda roof, restaurants on the first two floors, residential apartments on the next two, and a teak-lined reception hall on the top floor, whose principal ornament was a painting of Kwan Kung. The building was still under renovations during an eleven-day annual meeting in October 1921 that drew six thousand delegates from twenty cities in the East and Midwest.[81]

The ambiguity of the On Leongs—were they merchant pussy cats or snarling tong tigers—was, by chance, reflected at the entrance to the new building. The Triads used a picture of a tiger's head to warn against unauthorized entry. Stewart Culin had seen tiger's heads on boards outside the inner rooms of the Lun Gee Tong in the 1880s. In keeping with the practice, a picture of a tiger was painted on a board next to the door at 41 Mott, but the artist did not catch the spirit and it looked more like a laughing cat.[82]

The Hip Sings were rich too. Early in June 1924, they went on a steamboat excursion to Roton Point in Connecticut. No hard drinks were allowed, males were searched for arms, and mah jong was the most obvious pastime. Three hundred men were joined by one hundred women, including some wives and children, but most of the women were non-Chinese and single. A reporter mentioned "Chinatown lilies," some wearing sedate outfits such as "one might see on a debutante taking tea at the Ritz Carlton," while others sported sailor hats and "snappy knickers, polo vests or Deauville sweaters, and lots of chewing gum." He was especially struck by "a sweet young lassie with rouge and a very Callot Soeur tailored suit" and a male "collegiate oriental, with panama hat, green wasp-waisted golf coat, pink knickers, yellow socks, and green and white sport shoes, twirling a blue walking stick."[83]

THE FOURTH TONG WAR

The outward jollity was deceptive. A few years earlier, the Narcotics Squad raided Hip Sing headquarters at 16 Pell and found a cache of opium under the floorboards. They also found, behind a picture of Kwan Kung, two large-caliber revolvers, a Maxim silencer, four short swords (miscalled "hatchets" by reporters), a stiletto, and a thousand rounds of ammunition. Police called On Leong and Hip Sing leaders to headquarters and warned them to keep the peace. A few months later, two Chinese were questioned when they were seen unloading packages from a taxicab at a Chinese seaman's club on Bridge Street in Brooklyn. They were arrested when the packages were found to contain German revolvers and ammunition.[84]

Then, in January 1924, Chin Jack Lem and fourteen of his followers were expelled from the On Leongs in Cleveland after a dispute over real estate. Chin was indicted for extortion, but jumped bail and fled to Chicago, where he joined the Hip Sings, thus violating a clause of the 1913 peace treaty saying that neither tong would accept deserters from the other side. The police flooded Chinatown with uniformed patrols while plainclothesmen idled in restaurants and examined curio shop windows in excessive detail, trying—and failing—to look inconspicuous.

Still, a tense peace prevailed until the night of October 8. Detective Arthur Lavery was on Pell Street when a Chinese came by, pointed to another Chinese, whispered, "He got gun," and scurried away. Lavery ran toward the fingered man, later identified as Tom Fong of Hartford, and called for him to halt. Instead, Fong whirled and fired several shots, missing Lavery but wounding a fellow Hip Sing in the shoulder. Tong fighters were never known for marksmanship. Lavery returned fire and Fong crumpled to the sidewalk, mortally wounded.

Within twenty-four hours, three other Hip Sings were killed in New York, Schenectady, and Pittsburgh, the last being one of the fourteen who had been expelled with Chin Jack Lem from the On Leong. The other thirteen had fled to China.

A laundryman was shot and wounded in his shop in Brooklyn, and bulletin boards blossomed with brilliant red notices from merchants and clans saying they were not tong members and did not sympathize with either side. Police reinforcements from the Safe and Loft Squad, the Strong Arm Squad, the Radical Squad, and the Special Service Squad cordoned off Chinatown, searching all Chinese entering or leaving the area and ransacking tenements apartment by apartment. Few weapons were found.

Two more laundryman were killed in Brooklyn and Manhattan and two others in New Jersey. A fourth-floor apartment at 29 Allen Street was occupied by five Chinese, including Wo Tung and his brother. Wo Tung was an On Leong. He stayed indoors and wore a police whistle around his neck to call for help. On October 16, after his brother went to buy groceries, someone knocked at his door. Wo opened it and shrieked in terror. Three shots were fired and there was a faint sound as if Wo was trying to blow the whistle with his dying breath. Three more shots silenced him and there was the sound of footsteps running down the stairs. At the entrance, there were the excited words of the killer talking to two guards left at the street door, then silence as all three ran away. Only then did neighbors open their doors to call police.

Next, Jer Bong, the owner of a tea shop in Queens, was found dead with his head cut off. Hundreds of notices from clan and family association were posted on walls and doors: "We are Neutral," and "We Beg for Peace."[85]

At the end of October, police picked up seven emaciated men being helped out of taxis before 16 Pell. Two were so ill they had to be rushed to a hospital, where they died of malnutrition and beriberi. Survivors said they had been recruited by the Hip Sings in Hong Kong and packed into crates for the thirty-day journey to Brooklyn in the hold of a steamship. After two more killings in New York, a two-week truce agreement, written on red paper three feet long, was signed in New York.[86]

In November police acting on a tip staked out rail stations and followed a man to within two doors of Hip Sing headquarters at 16 Pell. He was none other than Chin Jack Lem, the source of all the trouble. He was extradited to Cleveland, where he was found guilty of extortion and sentenced to fifteen years in jail.[87]

With fifteen killed and about thirty injured throughout the East, including eight Hip Sings and one On Leong dead in New York, five leaders from each tong were escorted to police headquarters, where they agreed to extend the truce for another two weeks.[88]

A *Times* editorial expressed amazement: "That, to the uninitiated observers, amounts to a confession that the men making this promise were responsible for the murders already committed." Tong chieftains were called back to headquarters to hear a reading of the criminal code as it related to conspiracies to commit assault and murder.[89]

Christian leaders called a meeting at the Port Arthur. The Reverend Lee To was making an impassioned appeal and had gone on too long when someone in the audience called out, "Oh, do sit down, Reverend." Lee To paled, fell silent, and dropped to the floor. He was taken to his home at 52 Bayard Street and died of heart failure. He was sixty-one years old. Reporters recalled his early days when he stood on Chinatown street corners with a cornet player and soloist to persuade passersby to come to the Morning Star Mission.

When the truce expired on Thanksgiving Day, November 27, the killings resumed in New York, Connecticut, and North Carolina. Lee To's

148 Plainclothes detective and patrolman awaiting the worst.

stable. The old man who previously operated it was killed in June 1910 by a stray bullet during the Four Brothers War. The stand was taken over by Chin Song, who moved it to the East Side, less exposed to whatever fighting might erupt from Pell Street. By 1924 Chin Song was a Mott Street landmark.

Police were posted every twenty feet on a bleak December 14 when Chin closed his stand early because of lack of business. He packed a bag of fruit for his own use and walked to 39 Mott, passing through a narrow alley, across a dusk-darkened courtyard, and down a few steps to an areaway before his room in the basement of the rear house. Someone stepped from the shadows and sneaked behind him as Chin shifted his bag of fruit, fished out his keys and put one of them into the lock and turned it. With that, the stalker raised his gun to Chin's head, almost touching his gray hair, and pulled the trigger, blowing much of Chin's head off. The combination of the closeness of the gun to the head, the sunken areaway, and the inner court muffled the sound and the killer was able to saunter past the policemen on the street and fade into the night. The force of the falling body pushed open the door and the corpse lay with fruit scattered about until a friend stumbled on it in the dark a few hours later. His son said his father had lived in the United States for thirty years and never belonged to a tong.[92]

funeral was held the same day. Incongruously, amid the tong carnage, most stores closed their doors to honor this man of peace and members of both tongs attended services at the Morning Star Mission on Doyers Street. Still, such was the fear that few others ventured out on a cold and bleak afternoon to bid farewell to the man who spent his life, to his last breath, in the service of his community.[90]

Men from the Bomb Squad routinely swept Chinatown, even crawling through dank cellars, and restaurants piled chairs on tables, turning away the few customers who appeared. Cooks and waiters risked arrest for carrying arms, and yet they tucked guns under their aprons. A store that did business of four thousand dollars a day during the 1923 Christmas season was taking in less than two hundred. Street doors to tenements were locked and barricaded and rent collectors complained they could not communicate with residents. Building inspectors checking a complaint of unsanitary conditions in a building on Baxter Street had to force their way through five successive triple-locked doors in a fifteen-foot passageway.[91]

Neither age nor innocence was respected. The entire Chin clan had once been regarded as On Leong, as Chin Jack Lem was originally. In other cities, the Chins were divided, but in New York they were solidly On Leong and thus potential Hip Sing targets. For as long as anyone could remember, there had been a fruit stand at Pell and Mott streets. Originally it was on the west side of the street, just north of Naughton's livery

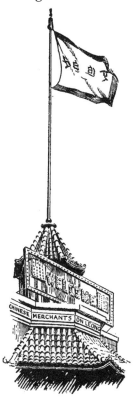

149 Truce flag on the On Leong building.

153

150 Mott Street with Port Arthur restaurant about 1925. The tower is on Transfiguration Church on the corner of Park Street. The pagoda-roofed building in the distance, with the flag pole, is the new Chinese Merchants Association/On Leong headquarters.

Early in January 1925, Chin Hing, a restaurant employee from Brooklyn, came to Chinatown to buy supplies and then went to a restaurant on Doyers Street, which was believed to be neutral territory. As he entered, there was a stirring among some customers. He stepped into a half-partitioned booth and several men followed. There were shots, but the sounds were obscured by the passing elevated train. When a waiter entered the booth, Chin Hing was found dead.[93]

A few days later, Wah S. Chan, a dentist whose name was actually Chin, was stabbed to death in his clinic at 22 Mott. Dr. Chan was the third generation of a Christian family. He graduated three years earlier from the Columbia University Dental School, was married to a non-Chinese woman, and lived in New Jersey, far from the intrigue of Chinatown. He was killed because of his name.[94]

A *Herald Tribune* reporter surveyed the economic damage: "Half a dozen restaurants and many more shops are closed and dusty....The lethargy of a siege broods over the district with police on fixed posts and clusters of plain-clothesmen acting as an army of occupation....One Chinese lad of eight plays tippy with an Italian lad in the center of Pell Street. Aside from that activity the thoroughfare might as well be given over to the owl and the bat."[95]

In March, after a Hip Sing restaurant owner was hacked to death in his home on Orchard Street and an On Leong baker was fatally shot at his home on Mulberry Street, intermediaries from California began secret negotiations. Then the consulate sponsored open negotiations at the Hotel Pennsylvania. On March 25, police escorted a Hip Sing delegation to 16 Mott, where On Leong leaders had already gathered, and a peace treaty was signed. The next day, Chinatown was decorated with banners, incense was burned, and there was a smell of roast pork as restaurants prepared for peace banquets.[96]

A *Times* editorial again complained of Chinese who "showed themselves to constitute an *imperium in imperio*, alien and isolated, possessing and exercising the power of life and death."[97]

Fifty-two tong men had been killed and more than two hundred wounded, over a period of eight months, in fighting that ranged as far west as St. Louis. Of these, sixteen were killed and four seriously wounded in New York.[98]

Only three of the shootings resulted in trials and convictions. Chin Sing, also known as Lu Chow, was sentenced to death for the decapitation of Jer Bong in his Queens restaurant on October 15. It was revealed at the trial that Lu had done it to collect a one-thousand-dollar reward posted for the slaying of any On Leong. Mock Yick Tong was sentenced to death for the murder of a laundryman in the Bronx on Thanksgiving Day. Lee Har was sentenced to twenty years as his accomplice. A fourth, Leung Fook, was sentenced to twenty years for critically wounding a laundryman in Brooklyn on November 28.[99]

The peace treaty contained a clause declaring an end to exclusive jurisdictions within cities throughout the East. Peace was proclaimed as "everlasting." Actually, it was more like a truce. In August, after two Hip Sings were shot and wounded in Boston (and a non-Chinese by-stander also wounded), three men walked into a basement at 15 Doyers, placed pistols against the stomach of Ho Kee, the cook, and almost cut him in half. In the next two days, five men were killed in Chicago, Pittsburgh, Baltimore, and Minneapolis, and one was wounded in St. Louis.[100]

When New York's District Attorney Joab Banton threatened tong leaders with arrest for conspiracy, they agreed to a two-week truce, but control had slipped from their hands. Sam Sing, a newly-arrived On Leong recruit from Chicago, was anxious to collect the thousand-dollar reward for the death of any rival. He was only nineteen and less than five feet tall. On September 2, he walked into a Hip Sing laundry on Albany Avenue in Brooklyn, pumped several bullets into its proprietor, walked out, and tossed the gun into the gutter. An off-duty policeman who happened to be passing scooped him up, holding him in the air until a patrolman arrived. The next day, an On Leong laundryman was killed and two of his sons were wounded in an attack on a laundry on East 31st Street in Manhattan.[101]

Banton again threatened serious action unless the fighting stopped. It didn't. A Hip Sing was killed in a Hester Street tenement and another was found dead, his head crushed by a blow from a hammer, in a boarding house on the Bowery.[102]

Now Banton arrested three On Leong officers, charging them with complicity in the latest murders. The *Times* was pleased: "It always has been humiliating when our police and prosecuting officials have been obliged to appeal for aid to the tong leaders—to treat them as if they were foreign sovereignties and to be more or less grateful when those leaders have consented to call their 'war' off."[103]

However, the three men were discharged by a judge who ruled there was no evidence implicating them.[104]

When it appeared that local officials lacked

powers both of persuasion and law, United States Attorney Emory Buckner assumed command. Federal immigration and narcotics agents threw a cordon around Chinatown and arrested sixty-eight men for questioning about their residence status, of whom forty-three were taken to Ellis Island for further examination.

Tong officials tried to placate Buckner. They had a meeting at the Chinese consulate, now at 13 Astor Place, at which they reaffirmed the March 25 peace treaty. It was too late. On the next two nights, more than one hundred federal agents and police swept through Chinatown, arresting men at random in homes, clubs, and restaurants and the two theaters. They "smashed windows, broke doors, and left the homes

151 THE FIGHTING IN CHINATOWN OCCASIONED A WEAK ATTEMPT AT HUMOR. A 1925 "TALK OF THE TOWN" NOTE IN *THE NEW YORKER:* "TIMES HAVE UNQUESTIONABLY CHANGED. THERE WAS A DAY WHEN PEOPLE OF ANY PRETENSE WHATEVER KEPT A LAUNDRESS. BUT IN THE LAST FEW WEEKS WE HAVE HEARD SEVERAL PEOPLE WITH IMPECCABLE POSITION STATING THAT THEY CAN'T GET THEIR DRESS SHIRTS WASHED, AND BLAMING THE TONG WAR."

opened and unguarded. When the Chinese returned from custody, they found their properties sacked."[105]

Another night of raids brought the number picked up to more than six hundred, of whom 193 were detained for further questioning. Still, the war went on. An On Leong was killed in a suburb of Philadelphia. When the news was telephoned to New York, a Hip Sing tailor was killed at Mott and Bayard streets.

Buckner doubled his forces and, in another dusk-to-dawn sweep, cleaned out several restaurants, dormitories, and clubs, smashing into locked pool rooms and tong headquarters. They again took away the audiences of both theaters, this time seizing the actors as well, still in their costumes. The number rounded up grew to more than twelve hundred. Even allowing for

152 A CHINESE CONTRIBUTED TO SENSATIONALISM. DRAWING FROM *TONG WAR,* A 1930 BOOK BY ENG YING GONG OF THE HIP SING AND JOURNALIST BRUCE GRANT. ALTHOUGH ENG WAS A HIP SING OFFICIAL IN NEW YORK, THE BOOK DEALS MAINLY WITH THE WEST, WITH VAGUE REFERENCES TO NEW YORK.

the fact that some were seized twice, this was a third or a half of the estimated two to three thousand permanent residents of the Chinatown area. After processing, 206 were held for deportation. Almost all were seamen who had been laid off in New York at the end of World War I and could not find berths to return home. Many of these stranded seamen, either unemployed or earning a pittance as waiters or laundry assistants, were eager to return home, but could not afford the fare.

The roundup finally brought peace to New York, but killings continued in other cities. When a Chinese was slain in Cleveland, on September twenty-first the director of public safety there took a lead from New York authorities. Police pulled laundrymen from behind their ironing tables, proprietors from their restaurants, and even students from night classes. The bullpen at police headquarters was crowded with prisoners, including several elderly men who had to stand all night. The Cleveland Bar Association demanded a halt and judges issued warrants of habeas corpus. Over the next few weeks, every one of those picked up was shown to be a citizen or a legal resident of the United States, and there was no evidence to link any of them to the September 21 murder.[106]

Newspapers in New York and other eastern cities had nothing but praise for Buckner and his imitations. The *Evening Post* editorialized: "Representatives of the groups of warring aliens, many of them having been smuggled into this country in violation of the Immigration Laws, solemnly met, declared a truce, and publicly sent out a dispatch advising their adherents throughout the United states to cease committing murder on the public highways. It is impossible to think of such a thing happening in London, Paris, Berlin, or Rome."[107]

But the *Nation* recalled that just one month earlier, America had joined other powers in sending a note to the government of China. It quoted one sentence: "The Government of the United States desires to impress upon the Chinese Government the necessity of giving concrete evidence of its ability and willingness to enforce respect for the safety of foreign lives and property and to suppress disorders and antiforeign agitations which embitter feeling." The *Nation* commented: "In light of our own inability to protect Chinese in the United States—or, worse still—of our official intention not to give them the equal protection of the laws, the wording of that note is either an insolent joke or mere hypocrisy."[108]

Prosecutors and juries continued to send a message to the tongs to keep the peace. A Hip Sing and an On Leong, originally accused of murder, pleaded guilty to lesser charges of murder in the second degree and were given mandatory sentences of from twenty years to life.[109]

The laundryman who was wounded on September 2 by Sam Sing—the small nineteen-year-old scooped up by the passing patrolman—survived for several months and was carried several times into court on a stretcher to testify. He later died, and Sam Sing was convicted of murder and executed in 1926.[110]

Although tong killings did not end, Buckner's roundups inspired tong leaders to squelch further hostility quickly. During three days in March 1927, eleven Hip Sings and On Leongs were killed and two wounded in Brooklyn; Newark; Manchester, Connecticut; Cambridge; Chicago; Cleveland; Pittsburgh; and just a few blocks from the White House in Washington. Tong leaders met at the Hotel Pennsylvania, after which

notices were posted reaffirming the peace treaty of March 1925.[111]

And justice continued firm. In November 1927 two On Leong tongmen, one from Newark and the other from New York, were hanged in Connecticut for the killing in Manchester.[112]

In October 1928, when six men were killed in Chicago, Philadelphia, Boston, and Washington, and two others in New York, a Hip Sing official in New York dismissed it all as a family quarrel over gambling.[113]

In August 1929 five men were killed and three wounded in several cities in the East, including two dead in New York. A Benevolent Association official—which, of course, was an association of merchants—complained that newspaper talk of a tong war was "extremely unfair and bad for business."[114]

In February 1930 a Hip Sing was shot dead at the Chinese Theater. The killing was ascribed to the desertion of thirty-nine On Leongs to the Hip Sings.[115]

A more serious clash began the following May. A quarrel involving $165,000 worth of smuggled opium led to fighting between the On Leong and the Tong On society, made up of Hakka seamen from the Pearl River estuary. The Hip Sings took advantage of the struggle to settle old scores by joining Tong On ranks.

The bill at the Chinese Theater was disrupted again on July 9 with the killing there of Hung Wah Hing, the head of the Tong On, the man accused of stealing the drug money. With his death, zeal for the struggle diminished, although fighting continued for the next few months. Total casualties were nine dead in New York, including a Chinese killed while playing at a miniature golf course in Brooklyn, and another nine in Newark and elsewhere.[116]

In April and May 1931 both tongs held their annual conventions in New York. The police, uneasy at such propinquity, quadrupled patrols along Mott and Pell streets. The Chinese Theater was jammed with out-of-town visitors. Detectives frisked two hundred men standing at the rear of the theater with their hands in their pockets and discovered four with loaded guns. But all went well and two thousand On Leongs and one thousand Hip Sings marched in separate processions.[117]

A sore point was a banner reading "27th Annual Convention On Leong Merchants Assn." stretching across Pell Street, where the Hip Sings had their headquarters. The Hip Sings insisted it be removed, but the On Leongs brandished a city permit and the banner remained. The man who represented the Hip Sings at the talks with city officials was its national president, who used the name Mock Si Wing—a dignified, courteous man of fifty-two who used a jaunty walking stick to compensate for a slight limp. A detective with a long memory told a reporter the man seemed to resemble someone from the tong wars before World War I, none other than Mock Duck, last heard of in 1912, when the district attorney, after many attempts, managed to convict him on the weak charge of running a lottery shop at the scene of the killing of two Hip Sing leaders. He was sentenced to one to two years in prison, the maximum possible. It now developed that Mock Duck had returned in 1914 to open a small gambling room. It was closed two years later by police using what was described as a "super dreadnought battering ram" to smash the icebox door. Mock Duck disappeared and there were some who later insisted he was dead and had been given a funeral with scores of carriages loaded with floral wreaths. A Hip Sing secretary confirmed that this, indeed, was Mock Duck, saying he lived such a secluded life in Mulberry Arcade in Newark that even Hip Sing officials had a hard time finding him.

153 Hip Sing convention in 1931.

As much as reporters claimed deep knowledge of all things Chinese, none knew that Mock Duck, under his real name of Mock Si Wing, had been elected national president of the Hip Sings in 1929, and that during the war between the On Leongs and Hakkas had directed Hip Sing affairs from a hideaway in Coney Island. He was reelected national president during the 1931 convention and then faded into obscurity.[118]

There were sporadic shootings, but nothing to revive talk of a tong war, until the summer of 1933, when a Hip Sing was killed in Boston and a middle-aged carpenter named Wing Gin was

154 MOCK DUCK WHEN HE RESURFACED IN 1931.

killed in New York. There were two other killings elsewhere and an On Leong man was stabbed in a Harlem chop suey restaurant. In August, after tong leaders were warned of mass deportations, On Leong and Hip Sing leaders promised "to maintain peace and quiet and to engage in no acts of lawlessness from this day on."[119]

Wing Gin, the carpenter, was the last tong war casualty in New York. He had few friends and no known enemies. A nominal On Leong, he was killed in retaliation for the killing of the Hip Sing man in Boston. By then, Naughton's funeral home had been demolished to make way for the Transfiguration church parochial school, and the Chinese antipathy to handling the dead had ended: Bert V. Eutemy had been licensed as the city's first Chinese undertaker. The name of his funeral home at 22 Mulberry Street could be translated "The Chinese Wish You Long and Happy Life Funeral Corporation." Wing Gin's body was sent to Eutemy's. A small hearse carried him to a grave in Mount Carmel Cemetery with a single carriage and a single mourner walking behind.[120]

By then there were more pressing things at hand—the depression at home and the Japanese invasion of China.

Americanization

In 1915 Lee Du, who was born and raised in San Francisco and later opened several successful restaurants in New York, formed the Chinese American Citizens Alliance. It had six hundred members when America entered World War I. At the age of thirty-five, Henry Chin signed up as a private and was killed in action on the Aisne in August 1918. Another member, Sing Kee Low, enlisted at nineteen. He was seriously gassed in the Argonne Forest, but continued to operate a message center for two days and was awarded the Croix de Guerre and the Distinguished Service Cross. He came home as color sergeant of the 77th Division. A third, Luke Chess, served in the Navy. After the war he was appointed to the New York Shipping Board.

Guy Maine, in his annual report for 1918, wrote that four members of his Chinese Guild saw military service, but did not name them. There were also a few draftees, while some of the elderly put on the uniform of the Home Defense League. Citizens and noncitizens alike subscribed to Liberty Loans, with the Chinese Merchants Association pledging fifty thousand dollars.[3]

Another landmark of Americanization was passed in December 1922, when Dr. Thoms awarded prizes at New York's first Chinese baby show—part of a bazaar held by the Chinese and American Women's Sewing Circle of the Doyers Street Morning Star Mission, with the proceeds to be used for the education of women in China. There were twenty-five babies from five months to five years of age.[4]

And yet reporters had another story about the Chinese as exotica. In March 1923 a boy was born to a Wong family at 13 Mott. A month later, on the night of the full moon, the family held the Feast of Head Shaving for "little slave girl," calling him that because demons would not consider such a child worth snatching away. Hundreds of hard-boiled eggs were dyed red. One was peeled and rubbed over the baby's shaved head. "Clean head, like clean egg. The

155 DOYERS STREET ON A SUNDAY IN 1899. ALMOST HALF THE MEN ARE WEARING AMERICAN CLOTHES AND HATS.

156 DOYERS STREET AS SEEN IN *HARPER'S WEEKLY* JUST THREE YEARS EARLIER. NO MATTER HOW MUCH THEY AMERICANIZED, THE CHINESE WERE PICTURED AS UNASSIMILABLE.

157 Sunday on Pell Street in 1899, looking east toward the Bowery "El." Doyers branches right. The building midway on the left, with the restaurant balcony, is probably Hip Sing Headquarters.

baby is safe now," Mr. Wong said.

Baskets of the remaining eggs were distributed to all who might be considered relatives, by birth, affection, or business ties. Small squares of red paper accompanying the baskets wished the receiver offspring as numerous as the eggs and invited him to a twelve-course Sunday dinner at the Port Arthur. The feast lasted until ten at night, with between-course speakers being certain that the child would be a great man like his father; that he would be a good boy and study hard and always obey his parents; that he would grow rich and

bring honor to his family; and that he would marry and have other fine babies so the great

159 Fearful grandmothers bundled children in layers of quilted coats, jackets, and shirts no matter what the temperature.

158 Baby show, with many categories to ensure all would be crowned.

161

and proud name of Wong would go on forever. When the last dishes were cleared away, a pyramid of eggs was placed in the center of each table and guests took one, leaving gifts in pieces of red paper—little rings, necklaces, gold and silver lockets, and pieces of jade inscribed "Long Life" on one side and "Riches" on the other.[5]

After the revolution in China, the Chinese school at Transfiguration church was moved to the first floor of the Benevolent Association, with students from China, who were then studying at Columbia and New York University, as teachers. There were about a hundred pupils, ranging from six to fifteen, for two evening classes six days a week: "Full of mad pranks, single, in twos and three, romping, skylarking, they run to school with satchel and coat....It is Mott Street's big hour, the hour at which Mott Street smiles."

Each carried a small, round can of black ink and a bamboo brush. Beginners put a printed character under a transparent leaf of their books and traced it, holding the brush stiffly between their fingers. Most girls wore their hair in a single braid down the back, with a bow at the top. One had her hair bobbed. Another wore a Dutch cut. Some wore sailor blouses, others wore blouses in subdued patterns. One small boy wore a checked suit with a Norfolk jacket. Another wore a sailor suit with a vivid tie.[6]

The *Times* reporter who wrote this description quoted the head teacher as saying it was important to study Chinese because "if they are to step into the places made for them in the Chinese world of trade and commerce they must be able to speak and write their language." This drew a testy *Times* editorial:

> If they think it is desirable that their children should gain something of their country's ancient scholarship, presumably they have good reasons for it. That they do think so merely evidences anew that they are unassimilable, for the learning of the Chinese characters by a child in America can mean only that some day that child is going back to China—that this is not "home" but merely a temporary abiding place, selected for reasons having nothing to do with American ideas and aspirations. And that is not a good thing for any strangers among us to emphasize.[7]

This was hypocrisy. If the Chinese tried to break out of their enclaves to apply for work like everyone else, they were beaten back. Two or three times a year, newspapers carried stories of Chinese discovered hiding in sacks or packing crates when ships or trains were unloaded.

Some were hauled out dead. In June 1923 Secretary of Labor James Davis warned: "Thirty thousand Chinese are waiting in Cuba today, watching for a chance to be smuggled into the United States. They are willing to pay $1,000 to $2,500 a head to anyone who will accommodate them."[8]

In fact, there were no thousands of Chinese waiting to enter because there was no work for so many. Those few who came, mainly by the "slot racket"—pretending to be sons of Chinese already here—were clan and kinsmen needed to maintain existing laundries or restaurants.

As evidence of the lack of work for strays and adventurers, there is the fate of seamen recruited in Canton and Hong Kong during World War I to replace drafted American merchant seamen, and then discharged in American ports when the war ended. Guy Maine, in his 1920 Chinese Guild report, estimated two thousand seamen were stranded in New York. In 1922 he wrote that fifteen hundred were still unemployed.

Once accidentally here, they faced the racist wall. State Senator Peter McGarry of Queens and Alderman Peter McGuiness of Greenpoint—two of the more flamboyant demagogues of the period—charged in 1922 that hundreds of Chinese had been imported to supply cheap labor to factories in their constituencies. "A white man hasn't got a chance when these Chinamen are brought in to work for practically nothing," McGuiness declared. Several raids were staged, and eventually 109 Chinese who were found to be employed in the back-breaking work of firemen and coal passers in factories were rounded up and deported. Almost all had papers identifying them as seamen.[9]

In April 1923 a company installing a sewer in Dover, New Jersey, advertised for job seekers in New York. An agency supplied fifty-five Chinese who, for their own safety, were kept on an isolated farm and trucked daily to the work site. They were paid forty-three cents an hour for ten hours a day, seven days a week. Local unions grumbled about "coolie" labor but, since no others could be found to replace them at the hard work, the men kept their jobs.[10]

In 1924 Congress extended ethnic exclusion to immigrants from southern and eastern Europe, reducing their immigration quota to almost nothing. Tucked in the act was another shackle on the Chinese: American-born Chinese were denied the right to marry Chinese-born women and bring their brides to the United States. The few defenders of the Chinese thought this was an oversight—that Congress could not have been so cruel as to deny native-born Americans the right to choose wives as they saw fit. They took the issue to a Congressional hearing and argued on the simple basis of citizenship-by-birth, but found themselves questioned about fraud and illegal immigration. Rationality and humanity failed.[11]

For an unemployed graduate of a New York school, there was always the possibility of emigrating to China, where educated men were in demand. But Chinese Americans knew little of Chinese culture. If what they saw in Chinatown was the Chinese world, they wanted nothing to do with it. They shared American aspirations.[12]

A few found work as clerks—always in back rooms—but the rest, even those with college degrees, could find jobs only in laundries or Chinese restaurants.[13]

It was easier for women, who were not considered competition for male jobs. When Alice Lee, born on Mott Street and educated at Washington Irving High School, was hired to be in charge of the lounge at the Hotel Claridge in 1915, she was the first Chinese woman to be employed in a New York hotel. Still, she was an exception. There was only one field where women were in demand outside Chinatown: If they wore Chinese dresses, they were hired to take tickets or sell cigarettes at movie houses showing the latest opium den thriller.[14]

Within Chinatown, a young woman could be her modern self. A writer who peeked into a Mott Street store saw "a very good looking Chinese flapper with a silky black mop of a bob and the latest in knee-topping skirts and straw-colored stockings. Her air is the air of a young person who serves haughtily on Fifth Avenue, but her manners are infinitely better. Probably she is a graduate of Vassar, Barnard, or even Radcliffe."[15]

The thirst for education among the Chinese outside their doors finally drew a response from the Transfiguration church. The mission started by a French priest in 1908 ended in 1919. A new mission began in 1923 and, a year later, the Reverend Charles Frigo, a Silesian, arrived from China. In the same year, the church built a parochial school at 29–31 Mott and bought 105 Park Street as a site for a convent for the Missionary Sisters of the Sacred Heart.[16] Six years later, a writer described the scene:

> At noon the yard is full of children and grave black-robed nuns looking after them. They are children of all complexions and all races, Italians, stray Nordics, even some Jews. And among them are many Chinese. Particularly well-dressed are these Chinese children, quite in the manner of Park Avenue children....On Sunday, when the Convent school does not keep, they play out in Mott Street and in Park Street around the corner. With their jet-black almond eyes set in smooth little ivory faces and wearing straight black bobs like a doll's, some of the little girls are indescribably lovely and lively. A few wear Chinese clothes but only a few....The boys are a sturdy lot dressed exactly like those who come out of the houses along the exclusive Block Beautiful in East 19th Street.[17]

The exoticism that drenched almost every newspaper story about the Chinese is obvious. The children were attending a school with the children of other immigrants. Their clothing proclaimed their parent's hope that the next generation would be part of the modern world. Still they were the "other," especially the girls. With the "little ivory faces" and black bobbed hair, they were "dolls."

During the day, Chinese children continued to attend P.S. 23 where, again, their modern clothing was noted: "Little Miss Chin Ling trots off to school in her Mary Jane slippers, socks, and straight, belted dress like a twin of Little Miss Park Avenue." By the mid-1930s, a third of P.S. 23 children were classified as Chinese although some of their mothers might have been American, Italian, German, or from some Caribbean Island.

In 1925 the Benevolent Association transferred its school to a derelict Public School at 64 Mott. Boys used the gym basketball court and other facilities and formed a Chinese Athletic Club. The auditorium was used for community meetings. For a while, the Chinese Chamber of Commerce sponsored a Chinese Boy Scout troop at P.S. 23. This was a rare instance of the Chinese sharing facilities with an American public institution. Even at the Methodist Church of all Nations, which was supposed to bring ethnic groups together, there were separate hours for Chinese children in the use of the gym and swimming pool.[19]

The church was a union of older churches left behind when their parishioners moved uptown. It was on 9 Second Avenue (now East Broadway), one block across the Bowery from Chinatown. By 1930, fifteen churches had been amalgamated into a church community center with twenty-one resident aides serving Italians, Russians, Ukrainians, Polish, Bulgarians, Czechs, Slovaks, Greeks, and Chinese.[20]

Because of their limited contacts, and because, with rare exceptions, their mothers could not speak English, most Chinese

American children grew up speaking barely adequate and heavily accented English plus "Chinglish"—a mixture of Toishanese, Cantonese, and American slang sufficient for life as a waiter in a chop suey restaurant or a clerk in a Chinese shop. On weekends, boys and girls gathered at the "Sugar Bowl" on Mott Street, eating hot dogs and that other famous American dish, chop suey. For any dance to be a success, notice had to be posted in the Sugar Bowl.

But no matter how American they thought of themselves, they were always reminded that others saw them as the "Other." When a Chinatown girl was elected president of P.S. 23's schoolwide Student Organization, a teacher was heard to say it was too bad the post "had to go to a foreigner." Another girl, Margaret Ling, recalled:

> I had to stand in front of a classroom while a teacher pointed out, on me, all the characteristics of a Chinese, since we were at that point studying about China. There were the slant, almond eyes, the black hair "coarse and straight, you notice, don't you class?" the nose that was practically no nose, the high cheek bones (which my fellow classmates wished to feel), and the general bland look....I felt there must be something wrong with my facial appearance to be so singled and pointed out at, and therefore when anyone looked at me, I immediately thought of my straight hair and non-existing nose.

She got over the incident and grew up thinking of herself as an American girl, only to have it come back when she arrived at college and was asked: "What part of China are you from?"[21]

Grace Wen recalled: "When I was young, before thirteen, I used to wish I had lighter hair and blue eyes." As an adult, she went to a convention and was asked "fifty times what part of China I came from, but an American girl, who was not born in the United States, was never asked what part of Europe she came from."[22]

The girls were members of a club whose leader, Florence Brugger, used her experience as the basis of her 1935 master's thesis. Brugger severely criticized Chinese missionary groups for keeping the Chinese in perpetual tutelage: "Chinatown seems to have been isolated from contacts with American social resources as though it was not on the Lower East Side of New York but on the foreign field."

She singled out Mary Banta's pioneer kindergarten on Doyers Street, which had an associate status, although separate, within the Church of All Nations. Brugger saw it as a primary example of missionary isolation of Chinese children, charging that Banta (thinly disguised as "Miss M") treated the Chinese as her own and never allowed them to take part in activities with other ethnic groups. Chinese mothers might object—privately—but it was not in their tradition to criticize openly a respected elder.[23]

In about 1935, when the Methodists withdrew from the Morning Star Mission, and it became the First Chinese Baptist Church, Mary Banta stayed on as a Baptist. When the True Light Chinese Lutheran Church was founded at 199 Canal Street in 1936, she associated her school with the Lutherans. She retired in 1954 at the age of eighty, having adopted and educated seven Chinese boys and girls, paying their way through college on her meager missionary stipend. At a testimonial dinner in 1955, she was honored as the "Mother of Chinatown."[24]

If newspaper reporters and all oth-

160 THEY THOUGHT OF THEMSELVES AS AMERICANS BUT THEY WERE SEEN AS THE "OTHER."

ers continued to see the Chinese as exotica, the Chinese brought it on themselves by flaunting their Otherness, making Mott, Pell, Doyers, and Bayard stand out as the most foreign enclave in a city where 85 percent of the population was foreign born or of foreign parentage. Vertical signs in black and red, painted fire escapes, narrow streets, and shops selling silks and mangled ducks baked in honey seemed the stuff of adventure. It was pure romance for a young man to take his girl to dine amid the carvings and embroideries of the Chinese Delmonico's on Pell Street, or dance with her among the red lacquer and gold filigree of the Port Arthur on Mott Street with an "orchestra" Victrola playing haunting songs.

The old Chinese New Year ceremonies were abandoned after the revolution in China as a sign of China's new modernity. But the On Leongs and Hip Sings revived them in 1928. Tong members disguised as prancing lions cavorted before shops, gobbling heads of lettuce with bills as high as twenty dollars attached. Drums,

cymbals, and firecrackers sounded and restaurants spread fifty-course dinners. A year later, Chiang Kai-shek's Nationalist government reissued the edict that the old-style New Year was not to be observed. Nevertheless, in February, the dust was knocked off the sixty-foot green-eyed lion (persistently miscalled a dragon) in a Doyers street warehouse, and the drums were tuned for the traditional celebrations. David Chow, the editor of New York's Nationalist *Mun Hey* [Public Sentiment] *Weekly* newspaper, hoped Americans would not get the wrong idea: "The old calendar was a relic of the imperialistic regime. It was abandoned...because new China desires to shake off whatever in the past had prevented its growth. The celebration of the New Year...is merely used as an occasion for fun-making. If the people of Chinatown pull a dragon through the streets and shoot off firecrackers it is not because they believe in dragons or are trying to frighten away devils."

When the Hip Sings showed their stuff, reporters were careful not to spoil a story with facts:

161 A VICTORY FOR TRADITION: THE REVIVED LION DANCE.

A long string, on the end a green leaf of lettuce to ward off evil spirits, hung yesterday from a fire escape of the Hip Sing headquarters in Pell Street. The secretary stood impassively on the fire escape weighting the string with oranges for good luck and knotting dollar bills in it at intervals of a foot or two as he lowered it toward the street....For almost an hour, the writhing continued, drums and cymbals sounded, and the dragon rolled glass eyes, fluttered cardboard lids, opened its two-foot mouth, bearded like a mandarin, and swallowed lettuce, oranges, and $30.

The On Leongs had a longer lion on Mott Street. Men with bright feathers on their legs to show they were fleet of foot snatched pale-lavender and pink gift envelopes from shop owners while athletes in black satin trousers with embroidered white stripes threw off their overcoats and went through the motions of t'ai chi ch'uan (then known as shadow boxing) amid the litter of firecrackers, cabbage leaves, and oranges. Three women proved equally adept. At nightfall the Chinese Merchants Association switched on an electric sign on their roof reading "Welcome." "This is like American boys playing firemen," scoffed David Chow.[25]

MEN WITHOUT FAMILIES

The 1930 Census counted 7,549 Chinese males and 865 Chinese females in New York City, nine males for every female. In Jersey City there were 129 males and 23 females and, in Newark, 622 males and 45 females. That the numbers were probably an undercount can be overlooked; the issue is sex disparity. A survey of New York City marriage registers for 1931–38 found 254 marriages in which at least one of the partners was Chinese. Slightly more than twenty-six percent were Chinese males with non-Chinese females.[26]

Ignoring statistical niceties, three out of four Chinese men in New York lived as bachelors, toiling almost all their daylight hours in steaming laundries or hot kitchens and sleeping either where they worked or in company rooms in ramshackle tenements. The widespread incidence of tuberculosis among them was traceable to these living conditions. The city's Tuberculosis Association reported in 1925 that Chinese were the greatest sufferers, with a mortality rate of 100 per 100,000 adult males, compared to 20 per 100,000 for adult, non-Chinese males.[27]

The Chinese paid about fifty dollars a month for three or four rooms with a single toilet and tub for bathing.[28] The rent was shared by as many as fifty men. An unemployed man could sleep on

162–64 PASSING TIME.

166

a cot for a dollar a month. Work and sleep occupied 90 percent of their time. They spent the remaining hours as lonely men do the world over:

in restaurants, pool-rooms, gambling dens, burlesque shows, movies, brothels, and dance halls. They pick up women where they can find them, and they find them most easily in the dime-a-dance palaces. Several of these cater exclusively to Oriental customers. The dime-a-dance girls know their Chinese and never miss a chance to turn a dishonest penny. For more than ten years one work-worn laundryman, now over fifty, has not missed the dance floor a single night except for sickness. He admitted he had "given away three laundries on account of his social life" in one dance hall with one taxi dancer, who flirts and lures, but keeps him at a safe distance.

One diversion was feasting. On any excuse—the birth of a child in China, the opening of a business, winning a lottery—a laundryman would invite a dozen friends to eat the best of foods and tell stories over toasts of fruit brandy. Family associations also arranged feasts on the last day of the traditional year, the spring and autumn festivals, the anniversary of the mythical clan founder, or whatever else might serve as an excuse.

Another was gambling. Fan-tan rooms—of which there were about fifty in Chinatown in the 1930s—were still controlled by tong gamblers. The tongs also controlled the lotteries. Unchanged from the first days of Tom Lee, whatever the tongs collected, the police got a share. There were occasional raids for show purposes, but hangers-on could be substituted—at a small fee—to fill the arrest quota, and the actual operators might resume a game as soon as the police left. Magistrates generally dismissed charges with small fines.

Most of the immigrants, especially the older ones, were apathetic about the world outside Chinatown, but gradually all were swept up in the thoughts of democracy and modernity awakened by the revolution in China.

When the modern American labor movement expanded during the depression, Chinese American restaurant workers joined Local One of a new Waiters Union. Then the union affiliated with the American Federation of Labor, and its Chinese members were transferred to other locals and promptly expelled. S. Gentili, the union organizer, admitted Chinese workers were "highly exploited," adding: "It's a shame the AFL does not take in Chinese and Negro workers."[29]

The difficulty faced in unionization was that the exploiters were fellow Chinese. Experience had taught the Chinese that they must show a united face to the outside world if they were to protect what little economic base they had managed to construct. The problem was: How to cut the ground from under their internal exploiters without pulling down the entire house.

Chinatown's entrenched establishment consisted of the Chinese Consolidated Benevolent Association and family surname and territorial associations. Most Chinese only knew the officers of the tiny family Fong where they gathered on a Sunday to gossip and gamble for small stakes. The leaders of community-wide organizations were a mystery.

Officers of the CCBA and larger clan organizations bought their posts and regarded them as the road to wealth and status, not an opportunity for public service. As Virginia Hyer observed in a Columbia University Ph. D. dissitation: "The Benevolent Association seems to be an office maintained for the benefit of its officers with a fund from which money has frequently been embezzled."[30]

The culprits were seldom punished lest they lose face. If someone complained, a "gentleman" might hint he would "show him some power." The most drastic action would be to report a man to immigration. Even if his internal passport was in order, he might be held in jail during an investigation and would need the help of the group's English secretary, and that would cost him money. A threat to report a man to federal, state, or local tax officials was equally terrifying: No Chinese paid taxes he thought he could evade. Similarly, a note to the building or fire department about possible violations could lead to complications and huge expenses. And there was always the ultimate threat—a visit by a tong thug.

As it had since its inception, the Benevolent Association's power lay in its "store foundation" (p'o Tai) records—careful descriptions and sketches of any store ever rented by a Chinese. It was these records that made the CCBA a government, with laundrymen as its obedient "citizens."[31]

In the 1930s there were still more than seven thousand laundries in the city, mostly two-men operations, although many smaller laundries were owned and run by a single man. It was a life of dull routine. A man might pick up an iron at 8 A.M. and stand at the ironing table until midnight, with a meal break of only half an hour. In a single-person laundry, a man spent eighty hours a week finishing five hundred shirts, along with other work. He devoted another forty hours

165 PURPORTED SKETCH OF LAUNDRYMEN IN SAN FRANCISCO IN 1870.

to sorting, marking, drying, starching, and taking care of customers. Most laundrymen cooked their meals in a kitchen in the rear of the store—two meals a day plus coffee twice a day, and went to sleep right after a late dinner without going out into the air.

After a fifteen-hour day, six days a week, they did not get out of bed until noon on Sundays, when they would go to a movie, visit friends in their Fong, gamble a bit, and maybe pool money for a nice dinner. They also had to shop for groceries and supplies for the following week. Until 1933 they saw themselves as too weak to resist the exactions of their misnamed Benevolent Association government. Then one man, energized by the revolution in China, inspired a small-scale revolt in New York, and the laundry-

men sought self-rule.

American-owned laundries attempted to drive the Chinese out of business by displaying placards in their windows that revived the canard of Chinese spitting on a shirt to dampen it. The Chinese consul general appealed to the police and succeeded in having most of the cartoons removed.[32]

The American owners then tried another tactic. A blatantly racist measure was proposed to the Board of Aldermen in 1933 to impose a twenty-five-dollar license fee and a thousand-dollar security bond on all laundries. American laundries could afford the fee. They operated with five or six employees and did bulk business, including wet wash. Chinese laundries, depending mainly on ironing shirts would have

168

difficulty raising that much cash.

There were three Chinese newspapers in the city. The largest was the *Chinese Journal*, a non-Chinese venture started in 1928 by the Barrow Mussey Company. Its circulation reached thousands. It was the only newspaper in Chinatown that made a profit. The other two were the *Chinese Nationalist Daily*, (previously known as the *Mun Hey Weekly*) the organ of the nationalist's Kuomingtang (KMT) and the *China Daily News*, which soon went out of business. A weekly—the *Chinese Vanguard*—was published by the Chinese Workers' Center, a thinly disguised Communist front.[33]

In 1932 Y. K. Chu, a journalist who once worked for the Nationalists in China, became editor of the *Chinese Journal*. In 1936 he published *Chinatown Inside Out* under the pseudonym Leong Gor Yun, to tell the story of the formation of the union and its later history.[34]

One of Chu's first acts as editor of the *Chinese Journal* was to publish the proposed ordinance in full, advising laundrymen to unite against it. Every day for three weeks he ran a double banner-headline:

166 IN THE EARLY 1930S, WITH ONLY THREE REGULARLY PUBLISHED NEWSPAPERS, THERE WAS NOT MUCH TO SELL AT A CHINATOWN STAND.

FELLOW COUNTRYMEN! STRUGGLE FOR YOUR EXISTENCE! YOU CAN'T LET YOUR LIFE-LINE BREAK DOWN!

A mass meeting of laundrymen was called at the auditorium of the Chinese School. The day before, Louis Wing, a wealthy laundry owner who had developed the most popular atomizer for dampening clothes, visited Chu to ask what could be done. Chu advised Wing to rally his friends and offered to act as their spokesman at the meeting. The first speaker was the Benevolent Association's English secretary, who hinted at the need to raise money, without saying exactly how it would be spent. Then Chu spoke, calling on laundrymen to form their own organization. The thought was so novel that, when a motion was made, but with only one seconder, to contribute two dollars to the Benevolent Association fund, it was passed by a voice vote.

The dispirited innovators went back to the office of the *Chinese Journal* and there were joined by George Lee, the seconder of the motion. He was persuaded to change his mind and signed his name to a statement that nullified the resolution. In a few hours, his statement was endorsed by more than a hundred laundrymen and was published the next day in the *Chinese Journal*, which was flooded with letters from laundrymen all over the East offering to support the movement. Louis Wing was a stalwart of the Democratic Party and knew how to arrange for police protection. He rented the basement of Transfiguration church for a mass meeting on April 23. The Benevolent Association, the tongs, and two leading territorial organizations muttered threats, but a show of police uniforms kept the peace as more than six hundred laundrymen voted unanimously to organize themselves to resist further exploitation.

Within days a planning committee was formed, an office was rented, a constitution drafted, and representatives were sent to Washington to apply for a charter (the organizers knew the establishment could block a charter in New York). On April 30, a membership meeting elected officers for what was now the Chinese Hand Laundry Association. Nothing like it had ever been seen before among Chinese in the United States. Its officers included college and high school graduates, men who had been schoolteachers and former minor military officers in China, and men representing twenty-two different family names, all Chinese political factions, and a dozen districts in Guangdong. Its first victory came in the middle of May, when the Alliance persuaded the Board of Aldermen to reduce the proposed license fee to ten dollars and the security bond to one hundred dollars.

A tong war broke out at this time, engaging the Benevolent Association, and giving the Alliance freedom to sign up more than two thousand members and divide the city into three hundred districts of about ten laundries each. For three dollars annual dues, laundrymen had an organization of their own, with an English secretary to handle what legal problems might arise. The Alliance became the largest and most independent Chinese organization in any American city. Its success was a setback for the Benevolent Association, which lost its ability to control the *p'o-Tai* registration for laundries and thus lost its hold on half the Chinese in New York and a major part of its revenues.[35]

When Franklin Roosevelt became president and sought a New Deal to be brought about by his National Recovery Act, the Alliance mustered more than five hundred laundrymen to march in a parade supporting the NRA. It was the first time any Chinese organization had participated in American domestic affairs and the first time Chinese had ever marched in a parade by the side of non-Chinese.

In 1933, its second year, the Alliance sent a delegation to a meeting of sixteen service trades at Carnegie Hall. There were ten different laundry organizations in New York, but a representative of the Alliance spoke for the entire trade—the first time a Chinese laundryman in New York spoke before an American audience in behalf of a partly American industry. The speaker was Louis Wing:

> We Chinese laundrymen are just as desirous and just as anxious to obtain higher living standards as any man on the face of this earth. Unhealthy living conditions and hard labor are just as disagreeable to us as to anybody else. Our laundrymen will support wholeheartedly any movement that has for its aim the bringing about of decent and human standards of life in industry and otherwise.

The Alliance set itself against what it perceived as the most flagrant failings of Chinese society in the United States. Its bylaws advocated democracy, austerity, and honesty, and forbade gambling, eating in the headquarters building, and observing the traditional New Year custom of sending gifts. Moreover, it was determined not to be drawn into the whirlpool of tong conflict:

> Members should be peaceful citizens. If individuals should commit a crime it is not the responsibility of the organization to protect such members. Members should not use the name of the organization to do anything illegal outside. Such actions are not the responsibility of the organization, but the organization has the right to punish such members.[36]

NATIONALIST AND ANTI-JAPANESE RALLIES

The struggle to form the Chinese Hand Laundry Alliance took place in the context of almost never-ending demonstrations and rallies against the Japanese aggression in China, with the subtext of the struggle for ascendancy between the Nationalists and Communists. There was an added subtext: the attempt by the American Communist Party to extend its influence. By rallying Chinese support for the anti-Japanese struggle, the Communists hoped not only to further the defeat of Chiang Kai-shek but also to strengthen their party and its program for revolutionary change in the United States.

Since Communist publications wholeheartedly supported the Alliance, the Benevolent Association attempted to use the club of anti-communism against Y. K. Chu. It accused him of being a secret member of the American Communist Party and the CHLA of being a Communist front. Chu denied the charge, and in April 1937 the New York State Supreme Court decided the accusations were groundless.[37]

Liberal, modernizing Chinese in New York did not need the American Communists to teach them the ways of modern democratic anti-imperialist struggle. They had their own teacher in Sun Yat-sen.

In 1914 the *Mun Hey Weekly* began publication at 16 Pell as the organ of the Chinese Nationalist League. In 1916 Ma Soo—who had been private secretary to Sun Yat-sen when Sun's government was suppressed by Yuan Shi-kai—came to New York and established a branch of the *Guomingtang* (KMT) or People's Party. During its early years the KMT attempted to mediate Chinatown affairs but it soon confined itself to matters affecting China.[38]

On October 10, 1920, almost two thousand persons, including six hundred Chinese, gathered at the Cathedral of St. John the Divine on Riverside Drive to commemorate the ninth anniversary of the Chinese republic. This was a significant gathering for the future of Chinese Americans. Those who attended formed the nucleus of a coalition of Wilsonian liberals who would confront Americans with the hypocrisy of preaching equality abroad while practicing racism at home.[39]

A year later, four thousand Chinese from New York and New Jersey gathered at City Hall Park to hear speakers call for diplomatic recognition of Sun's South China Republic, rather than Yuan Shi-kai's government in Peking. It was the largest mass meeting of Chinese on the eastern seaboard to that time.[40]

In 1927 the Nationalist/Communist split was echoed in New York when nine hundred Chinese gathered at the Chinese Theater to mark the second anniversary of Sun Yat-sen's death, with John Dewey of Columbia University as the principle speaker. The meeting was organized by the KMT. Most Chinese and Chinese Americans were Nationalists, although with little understanding of politics. A few were Communists, as a *Times* reporter noted:

> The little ring of Communists in the front seats of the theater, massed separately from the solid Chinese background extending up into the gallery, broke into its first outburst of applause when Dr. Dewey declared that Russia was aiding the Chinese Nationalist cause against other nations. They were silent when Dr. Dewey denied the Chinese movement was Communist.[41]

In May 1928 five thousand Chinese attended two KMT rallies to protest Japanese intervention in China. A few days later, fifty-six Chinatown organizations formed the Anti-Japan Association of Chinese Residents of New York and voted to raise a treasury of ten thousand dollars. After a

167 FOR THE FIRST TIME, PREVIOUSLY TIMID CHINESE AMERICANS WERE GALVANIZED TO TAKE PART IN PUBLIC DEMONSTRATIONS.

168 PARADE TO HONOR SOLDIERS.

169 WOMEN WHO HAD SELDOM STIRRED FROM THEIR HOUSES PUT ON UNIFORMS AS WAR WORKERS.

few more days, five thousand marched to City Hall Park to denounce the Japanese. The following month, two thousand gathered at the Chinese Theater to celebrate a victory of Chiang's forces in north China. Two months later, Communists, calling themselves the All-American Anti-Imperialist League, massed five hundred Chinese under a scorching sun at the corner of Mott and Pell for a two-hour lecture on correct political attitudes. On October 10, the seventeenth anniversary of the revolution, two thousand gathered at the Chinese Theater to hear a speech by Tom Lee's son, Dr. Frank Lee, who had became China's ambassador to Poland.[42]

In November 1931 the newly formed Chinese Patriotic Association announced it would raise two hundred thousand dollars to train pilots and ground crews from among the Chinese in the United States.[43]

The following February, four girls marched through the streets holding the corners of a Chinese flag as quarters, half dollars, and notes wrapped in red paper rained from windows to help the homeless of Shanghai. Posters demanded a boycott of Japanese goods "until

the third and fourth generation." At the end of March 1932, the Chinese Women's Patriotic League held an eight-day bazaar at the Chinese School to raise funds for the needy of Shanghai, selling Ming vases and old brocades donated by Chinese merchants. The following October 10th, while a young man whose father had a laundry on Madison Avenue flew overhead in a training plane, two thousand Chinese, including women and children, marched to City Hall to observe the twenty-first anniversary of the overthrow of the Manchus. They gathered before the steps, and Mayor Joseph McKee came out to greet them. They told him half of those present were American citizens and then they sang "America."[44]

In October 1937 a broad Communist-led coalition called the American League Against War and Fascism brought ten thousand people to Madison Square Garden to urge a boycott of Japanese goods. Speakers included Rabbi Stephen S. Wise, Bishop G. Bromley Oxnam, and Joseph Curran of the National Maritime Union. A year later, Chairman Martin Dies of the House Un-American Activities Committee charged that little of the money raised by such activities was

173

used for relief in China but, instead, was spent in the United States for Communist Party purposes under the guise of "peace education."[45]

Few Chinese understood political ideology. A simple longing for justice and freedom in China led students to skip meals and shine shoes, for women and girls to sell papers and flowers, for workers to give part of their daily wages, and for merchants to contribute a percentage of their profits. In April 1937 the Chinese School was jammed for a week of amateur opera productions, *t'ai chi ch'uan*, stick fencing, and other displays as part of a bazaar of the Chinese Women's Organization. The following October, the women led a parade through Chinatown to gather money for refugees. A month later, two thousand marched carrying a banner of dollar bills sewn in the shape of the Chinese characters for "Fight Against Japan to the Bitter End to Save China." In April 1939 Boy Scouts stood on street corners with little cans collecting money for quinine. In May twelve thousand Chinese from New York and other eastern cities marched through lower Manhattan and Chinatown on "National Humiliation Day," the twenty-fifth anniversary of Japan's Twenty-One Demands on China, while seven pilots from the training program flew overhead.[46]

When the Chinese took to the streets, they were no longer perceived as a menacing "Other." The wall around them began to crumble. Prohibition forced Bowery saloons out of business and Chinese merchants claimed the space. Then an opening to the north came in 1929 when Canal Street was widened, creating new shopspace. The depression forced building owners to be less selective and the Chinese moved in.

At the same time, there was a population explosion. An estimated quarter of the Chinese in the United States were unemployed by 1931, and there was a flight to the nearest Chinatowns to ask relatives for a roof and a bowl of rice.[47]

Moy Kee, a student at Columbia University, estimated that the Chinese population, including Newark, was thirteen thousand.[48]

Their arrival added to the demand for hulks of buildings that could house scores of men able to pay only a few dollars a month rent. Gradually, Chinatown took over the lower end of once solidly Italian Mulberry Street and spilled across the Bowery to the southern blocks of the Jewish ghetto on the Lower East Side.

Breaking out brought the first moves toward social integration. In 1934 the Chinese Community Committee was formed—completely separate from the Benevolent

170 FRONTISPIECE FROM CARL GLICK'S *SHAKE HANDS WITH THE DRAGON*, PUBLISHED IN 1941. THE TITLE IS A MISNOMER: THE CREATURE IS A FANCIFUL LION. THE LION DANCE, REVIVED IN 1928 OVER THE OBJECTION OF CHINA MAINLAND MODERNIZERS, HELPED TO FIX THE IMAGE OF CHINESE AMERICANS AS IMPERFECTLY ASSIMILATED EXOTICS.

174

Association—as part of the Lower East Side Association of Agencies, an umbrella organization through which City Hall maintained contact with community leaders. In June 1936 the Community Committee sponsored what was to become an annual baby parade and field day in Columbus Park between Mulberry and Baxter Streets. Nearly a thousand Chinese showed up, with Boy Scouts to lead the athletic events and one hundred and one infants and toddlers for the baby parade.

In times where all suffered, Chinese survival techniques once scorned by rope-skipping girls chanting "trying to make a dollar out of fifteen cents," were now seen as virtues. Surveying the show at Columbus Park, License Commissioner Paul Moss remarked: "There are no Chinese on relief in New York. They know how to take care of themselves and look after their relatives."[49]

Carl Glick, a young unemployed writer, was assigned by a federal "make-work" program to the Church of All Nations as a supervisor for the Chinese athletic program—a position of little responsibility that gave him a chance to meet the Chinese and spare hours necessary to write about them for *Colliers* magazine:

Old Charlie Sing, a laundryman standing in the window of his Kung Saw Fong, the family headquarters, beamed with pleasure as he saw the dragon come pirouetting up the street. It was the Year of the Monkey, Charlie had lost his laundry, had less than a dollar in his pocket, no job, no resources of his own. Yet Charlie wasn't troubled....When Home Relief started operating in 1931, there were no Chinese families sitting on the doorsteps asking for assistance. Didn't the Chinese need relief? Had those crazy Orientals who eat with chopsticks, dance a dragon in the street, and burn incense to their ancestors found a way of their own to sidestep the depression?[50]

According to Glick, the laundryman had contributed to his family name society and the society was bound to care for him. This was pure myth: exoticism in new dress. Assistance was the responsibility of immediate family members who would allow an elderly, unemployed relative to sort clothing, sweep floors, sleep on a cot, and wear abandoned clothes in a laundry or do similar work and eat leftover food in a restaurant. He got nothing from his clan and territorial associations. If the Chinese avoided city assistance, it was because they bore the psychological scars of rebuffs and insults from American officialdom and had learned that the only sure way to survive was by keeping a low profile.

The depression was harsh, yet during the long years of rallies to aid the government and people of China, more than two million dollars was raised from a people who barely had enough for themselves. Whether called modernization or Americanization, the effect was the same.

When registration for the draft began in October 1940, Sing Kee, who had won the Distinguished Service Cross in World War I for continuing to run his message center during a gas attack in the Argonne Forest, was named chairman of the Selective Service Board for Chinatown. (He joked that he won it for making the best chop suey in the AEF). Men were waiting at the doors when a draft office opened at P.S. 23. They poured in from New Jersey and farms on Long Island, knowing they would find interpreters in Chinatown. Men who looked like they could shoulder a gun were asked if they had registered. Soon New York's 165th Infantry Regiment, the old "Fighting Irish," had ten Chinese draftees.[51]

America entered the war and Chinese wore buttons with crossed Chinese and American flags so as not be mistaken for Japanese. Women previously seldom seen outside their homes or family shops went to work in factories as welders and carpenters, and men with degrees as chemists and engineers finally found their skills in demand. It was the first significant American utilization of Chinese labor since their expulsion from factories in California in the 1850s. Even the Navy, which previously segregated Chinese as messmen and stewards, sent recruiters looking for apprentice seamen.[52]

An estimated four thousand men of Chinese ancestry from the New York-New Jersey metropolitan area enlisted or were drafted. Benjamin Ralph Kimlau, whose parents lived at 28 Mulberry Street, was the first to become the pilot of a heavy bomber. The twenty-six-year-old lieutenant died with his crew when his B-24 was shot down on a mission from New Guinea. Part of Chatham Square was later renamed in his honor. He was one of about ninety men from New York City killed in the war.[53]

Among them were Lincoln and David, two sons of Ng Wing of 61 Chrystie Street. David was a twin to another brother, John. Lincoln was older and enlisted first. As soon as David and John became eighteen they went to the recruiting office once a week for more than four months, only to be rejected as underweight. They made it on their sixteenth try by drinking twelve bottles of milk in two hours and then rushing down to the recruiter's scale. After Lincoln and David were killed, John was sent home: the Ng's had done enough for their country.[54]

The boon of World War II for Chinese Americans was its glorification of "heroic" Chinese fighting an aggressor who had defeated the armies of Britain, France, and Holland. General Chennault and his Flying Tigers, "Vinegar Joe" Stillwell, and Madam Chiang Kai-shek, the Wellesley graduate who toured the United States, personified the link between China and America.

Sympathetic Americans realized there would never be a better time to seek repeal of the law that branded the Chinese unworthy of immigration and naturalization. They organized the Citizens Committee For The Repeal of Chinese Exclusion. One of its members was Carl Glick, whose 1941 *Shake Hands with the Dragon*, a collection of his romanticized magazine stories of Chinese life, became a best seller. Glick and others on the committee had strong links with America's political and journalistic establishment, and soon magazines and newspapers were explaining the evils of exclusion and how the

171 A CHINATOWN MAN AS AN AIR RAID WARDEN. BY 1943, IN *THREE TIMES I BOW*, GLICK HAD CHANGED HIS APPROACH. HE PICTURED THE CHINESE AS FULLY AMERICANIZED, DOING THEIR UTMOST TO HELP THE WAR EFFORT.

laws gave credence to Japanese propaganda. Public and radio debates were arranged and letters written to newspapers. Republican Congressman Walter Judd of Minnesota, a former missionary in China, was consulted before the committee was formed and piloted the legislation through the currents of America's racist phobias. During the hearings, Congressman Leonard Allen of Louisiana repeatedly asked witnesses for their views on "social equality among races." Witnesses were coached to present repeal as a means to counter Japanese propaganda. President Roosevelt sent a message to Congress asking that it "correct an injustice to our friends." Congressional approval was swift and, on December 17, 1943, Roosevelt signed the repeal of exclusion laws that had been in force for sixty-one years.

It was a victory not of principle but of narrow self-interest. An attempt to broaden the action to end similar restrictions on other Asians was smothered because it would have meant extending equality to the Japanese, who were the enemy. An attempt to grant citizenship to the Chinese wives of Chinese Americans was scotched for tactical reasons: It was feared opponents would cite this as an attempt to open the floodgates of Oriental immigration.[55]

The war ended and Chinese Americans staged their own victory parade up Fifth Avenue, past a reviewing stand at the New York Public Library on 42nd Street, and on to Central Park. It took three hours, with more than twelve thousand in the line of march plus a company of acrobats on stilts and seven of the never-to-be-omitted lion dancers.[56]

Exclusion had ended but racism was still strong. Chinese American soldiers who had lived and fought with other soldiers, and Chinese American workers who had been accepted as equals in factories and shipyards were again second only to blacks, with few job openings except in laundries and restaurants.

Exoticism also remained. Hucksters on Times Square corners sold $2.30 tours of Chinatown, including a visit to what was now called the Mott Tai Temple in the dark room behind the "World's Smallest Post Office." As they left their bus, the guide warned, "Please stick together until we reach the Mott Tai Temple. If you hear shooting, I'll be four blocks away."[57]

But mind-sets were changing. In 1943 representatives of the American Legion had been among those who testified before Congress against repeal of Chinese exclusion. In April 1946 three hundred Chinese Americans paraded through Chinatown to dedicate the first Chinese

American Legion post in the East to the memory of Lt. Benjamin Kimlau.[58]

The formal end to exclusion did not bring a significant change in immigration, since the Chinese came under existing quota regulations and were assigned the lowest possible number—105 a year. The most meaningful event was the War Brides Act of August 1946, which swept through Congress as part of a unanimous consent act to reward veterans. One of its clauses repealed the 1924 restriction on the immigration of Chinese wives of American-born Chinese.

Brides were sought through relatives and by the exchange of photographs. In the next few years, four thousand women were brought to New York and Chinese names replaced those of Italians and Jews on letterboxes in dingy tenements in Little Italy and the Lower East Side.[59]

In dress and thought, the brides were more modern than the tradition-bound families of their husbands. They wore the increasingly skimpy dresses of the period, shopped in supermarkets, and, at classes run by Maryknoll sisters at Transfiguration church, they brushed up on the English they had already learned in Canton and Hong Kong. They were appalled at the squalid housing their husbands and in-laws had accepted without complaint. Two out of three buildings had toilets in the hall and almost all needed repair. The brides covered the walls of fourth-floor walk-ups with light-colored paint and hung bright curtains on the inadequate front and rear windows.[60]

Ending unequal restrictions on immigration and breaking barriers to equal employment and housing were battles still to be fought, but the brides were pointing to the future. One hundred and fifty years after Chinese seamen were first noted as "common dock loafers," they were creating New York's first fully-rounded Chinese American society.

172 Post-war women, as seen by a 1949 British visitor.

12 Postscript

A Golden Age Club was started in May 1951 on the third floor of 24 Pell. The Chinese Community Club donated the rooms and the city's Welfare Department and the voluntary Community Service Society provided staff and other assistance. The CSS was amazed at the club's acceptance. By 1962 it had a membership of well over a thousand and daily attendance of 150. They were survivors of the period of lonely men, with 44 percent living on fewer than fifty dollars a month and 88 percent on one hundred dollrs or less. Until enactment of federal assistance, they could not afford medical care of any sort. Stuart Cattell, a CSS official, commented: "The experience of the Golden Age Club, plus the acute health needs of older men in Chinatown, throws grave doubts on views of those who claim that family associations are able to take care of members and outside help is not needed."[1]

Postwar newspapers were filled with stories of youth gangs but also ran articles like, "Why Chinese Kids Don't Go Bad," comparing the

173 THE MUCH-PRAISED POSTWAR YOUTH AS SEEN BY THE SAME ARTIST.

increase in juvenile delinquency in New York with its absence in Chinatown. Chinatown was "a refreshing little oasis where juvenile delinquency is unknown." Writers suggested that the explanation could be found in the Chinese thirst for education. In P.S. 23, where 85 percent of the enrollment was of Chinese ancestry, it was said to be difficult to make children stay home even when they were sick.[2]

The writers glossed over the obvious: there were few juveniles to be delinquent. That ended in 1962 when a presidential order designed to relieve crowded conditions in Hong Kong brought five thousand sponsored immigrants to New York. A greater surge came after 1965, when the Naturalization and Immigration Act raised the immigration ceiling to twenty thousand for each independent country, with entry favoring those with relatives in the United States.

A flow of capital preceded that of people. Rich Hong Kong and Taiwan families were eager to transfer resources from the shadow of mainland China. In 1925 only thirteen buildings in the core three streets of Chinatown were owned by Chinese. By 1940, when the boundaries of Chinatown had tripled, the number of Chinese-owned properties had grown to twenty-eight. By 1945 forty-five properties were registered in Chinese names. In the middle 1950s Chinese were buying properties at an average of one parcel every two months.

Another index was the opening of restaurants. By 1966 there were thirteen hundred Chinese restaurants in New York City, with so many crammed into a nine-block stretch of Second Avenue that newspapers wondered if the Chinese might outnumber French and Italian restaurants.[3]

The new capitalists brought with them the oppressive working conditions of Hong Kong and Taiwan. New arrivals stepped off planes already in debt for their passage money and other arrangements and had to find work fast. Men accepted $150 for a sixty-to-seventy-five-hour week. Women were crammed into dozens of sweatshops with a single, often nonfunctioning, toilet in the hall. The owners kept two sets of books and forced the women to sign receipts for a weekly wage of sixty dollars but paid them only thirty. As bad as it was, it was better than the twenty-cents-an-hour pay in Hong Kong.[4]

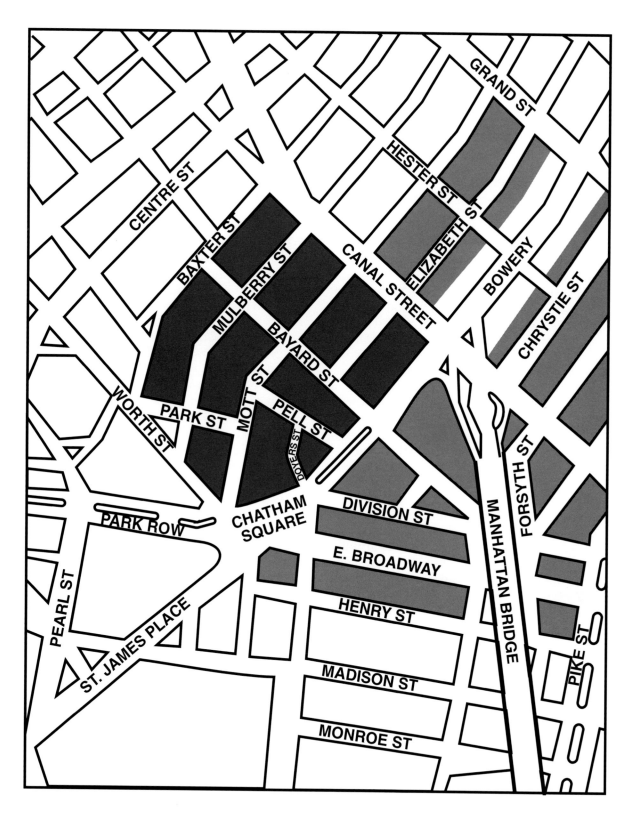

CHINATOWN ABOUT 1965. THE CORE AREA HAS BEEN SOLIDLY OCCUPIED. CHINESE STORES HAVE EXPANDED NORTH OF CANAL STREET ALONG ELIZABETH STREET. THE MOVEMENT WEST INTO LITTLE ITALY WAS FIERCELY RESISTED BY THE ITALIAN RESTAURANT OWNERS ALONG MULBERRY AND MOTT STREETS. THE MOVEMENT EAST INTO THE SLUM STREETS UNDER THE MANHATTAN BRIDGE MET NO RESISTANCE. THIS AREA AND BEYOND HAS LONG SINCE BECOME SOLIDLY CHINESE AMERICAN.

179

As many as six hundred thousand Asians settled in New York from 1965 to 1985. Most of those who came from Taiwan avoided Chinatown altogether and settled in Queens and Brooklyn in an agglomeration that included Koreans, Hispanics, Indians, Pakistanis, and almost every other nationality.[5] Now that the walls were down, second- or third-generation Chinese also moved to the outer boroughs and suburbs, where they developed their own community centers, Chinese language schools, women's committees, and other social support groups.

Those left in lower Manhattan consisted mainly of the elderly from earlier waves of immigrants and new immigrants who spoke little English and had little choice but to work at low wages in dead-end jobs in the unstable restaurant and garment trades. Chinatown became the most densely populated neighborhood in New York. Ten adults and children lived in two or three rooms with only a kitchen laundry-sink for bathing and a toilet in the hall. Their rents were kept low by city controls, but they had to pay several thousand dollars in key money.

New capital from Taiwan and Hong Kong, combined with the easily-cowed non-English-speaking arrivals, laid the basis for—in Peter Kwong's phrase—a "dynamic growth of industries and commerce." More than two thousand restaurants in Chinatown and the greater metropolitan region are supplied by a network of wholesalers dealing in everything from sacks of rice to used kitchen equipment. Chinese entrepreneurs also rescued New York's garment industry just as it was losing out to low-price factories in the South and overseas. This "new" Chinatown is also the center of an extensive white-collar service industry of banks, insurance companies, newspaper publishers, and real estate brokers. Especially on weekends, it draws thousands of Chinese and other Asians looking for bargains or ethnic specialties in food, clothing, household goods, and luxuries, with a dozen Chinese movie houses as an added attraction.[6]

Growing social and political awareness were evident. In 1978 twenty thousand Chinatown residents demonstrated against police brutality. In 1980 there was a successful three-month strike against the area's largest Chinese restaurant. In 1982, when Chinatown factory owners refused to raise the minimum wage, twenty thousand women garment workers demonstrated to support their new union contract. By 1989 80 percent of the twenty-two thousand garment workers in Manhattan were Chinese Americans and, with the exception of a few hideaway shops, they were all represented by Local 23–25 of the International Ladies Garment Workers.[7]

What is not new about the "new" Chinatown is the extortion of gangs. New arrivals in the 1960s included teenagers from the mean streets of Kowloon sporting trademark duck-tailed haircuts and black leather jackets, while their girls, in heavy makeup and mid-thigh skirts, affected bored indifference. They called themselves White Eagles, Black Eagles, Kwan Ying, Hong Kong Refugees, Oriental Sisters, and International Brothers. Newspapers and magazines now wrote of the "darker shades of Chinatown life than the conventional wisdom is prepared to admit." Headlines proclaimed: "New York's Other Mafia, Young Warriors Fight For Their Place in Chinatown," and "New Kind of Tong, the Youth Gang."[8]

The postwar gangs were the creation, under different names, of the traditional tongs although some, recruited from the non-Guangdong areas of China and the Chinese diaspora, such as Viet Nam, were largely autonomous. All efforts by city, state, and federal authorities to eliminate them proved fruitless. As late as June 1995, federal prosecutors announced the indictment of leaders of "fraternal and businesss organizations"—also identified as tongs—that "had carved up Chinatown into distinct criminal districts." On Leong, Hip Sing, and Tong On leaders were said to have "control of violent street gangs" that "extorted money from virtually every business in Chinatown."[9]

Chinatown, with its gangs and crowded schools, its businessmen in suits and merchants hawking live fish at a curbside, its height-of-fashion young women and mothers with string shopping bags, its clogged, narrow, and dirty streets, its many languages and dialects and noisy streets with huge red signs, is not merely an enclave; it is an economically viable, largely autonomous city within a city. It will not disappear. The Chinese have developed community centers, schools, and social institutions to protect a way of life they find psychologically, culturally, and economically rewarding.

Notes
Abbreviations

NEWSPAPERS AND MAGAZINES

AM	*American Mercury*	NC	Newark *Call*
BE	*Blackwood's Edinburgh Magazine*	NM	*New Metropolitan*
BJ	*Brother Jonathan*	NR	*Niles Weekly Register* (Baltimore)
BT	Boston *Evening Transcript*	NYM	*New York* (magazine)
C	*Colliers*	NYr	*The New Yorker*
CA	New York *Commercial Advertiser*	P	New York *Post*
CE	*Courier and Enquirer*	PG	*Police Gazette*
Ch	Chambers *Edinburgh Journal*	PL	*Puck's Library*
ChA	*Chinese Annual* (organ of N. Y. Chinese Students Club)	PN	Philadelphia *News*
		Pu	*Puck*
Cr	*Coronet*	RD	*Readers Digest*
DA	Newark *Daily Advertiser*	RR	*American Review of Reviews*
DE	Brooklyn *Daily Eagle*	S	New York *Sun*
DG	New York *Daily Graphic*	SEP	*Saturday Evening Post*
DN	New York *Daily News*	SG	New York *Sun and Globe*
DT	New York *Daily Tribune*	Sr	New York *Star*
EE	New York *Evening Express*	SRG	*Survey Graphic*
EP	New York *Evening Post*	St	New York *Standard*
G	New York *Globe*	SW	New York *Semi Weekly Courier and Enquirer*
H	New York *Herald*		
HM	*Harper's Monthly*	T	New York *Times*
HT	New York *Herald Tribune*	Te	New York *Telegram*
HW	*Harper's Weekly*	Tl	New York *Telegraph*
IA	*Illustrated American*	Tr	New York *Tribune*
L	*Life*	VV	*Village Voice*
LI	*Leslie's Illustrated*	W	New York *World*
LD	*Literary Digest*	WH	*Weekly Herald*
Lk	*Look*	WJT	New York *World Journal Tribune*
MC	*Morning Courier and New York Enquirer*	WSJ	*Wall Street Journal*
		WTS	New York *World Telegram Sun*
N	*The Nation*	YN	*Yankee Notions*

CHURCH AND MISSIONARY JOURNALS

AD	*Christian Advocate*	MS	Missionary Society of the Methodist Episcopal Church, annual reports
An	*Chinese Annual*		
BM	New York City Baptist Mission society, annual reports	MT	New York City Mission and Tract Society, annual reports
CG	St. Bartholomew's Episcopal Church yearbooks	MW	*Missionary Review of the World*
CJ	*The Church Journal*	PB	*Parish Bulletins* (also *Catholic News*), Transfiguration church
EN	*Encyclopedia of the Presbyterian Church of the U.S.A.* (1884)	SM	*The Spirit of Missions*, Board of Missions of the Protestant Episcopal Church in the USA
FM	New York Foreigners' Mission, annual reports		
IN	*The Independent* (New York)		
MR	*Monthly Record*, Five Points House of Industry		

1 WAIFS AND STRAYS
1. Wilson, 1902, 1:303, 304.
2. Porter, 1931:142–49.
3. LaFargue, 1940:133.
4. T, Nov. 10, 12; NR, Nov. 1, 29; S, Nov. 9.
5. Odell, 1927, 4:42, 43, 106, 107, 177; 5:398.
6. July 13.
7. H, July 15; Chapin, 1934:3–12.
8. MC, July 12, 13.
9. H, July 24, 26, 28, 31, Aug. 2–7, 9, 10, 12–14, 16–21, 25–30.
10. Odell, 1927, 5:370.
11. EE, Sept. 6; H, Aug. 31, Sept. 1, 2, 4.
12. Chapin, 1934; Ch, July 15.
13. Peters, 1850; WH, Jan. 13, 20; Tchen, 1996.
14. Odell, 1927, 5:577.
15. MC, April 10, 1850.
16. DT, April 11; BE, July, 1852:105.
17. Bryan, 1927, 1:401.
18. 1920:129.
19. EP, Jan. 31; CE, Feb. 7.
20. Rodecape, 1944:101–03.
21. H, June 29; EP, June 29.
22. EP, May 24.
23. May 24.
24. H, June 29.
25. EP, July 2; H, July 4.
26. H, July 16, 27.
27. EP, July 12, 16, Aug. 17.
28. EP, Sept. 3, 1853; SW, April 17, 1856.
29. H, Oct. 11.
30. Except where noted, this and future references to Syle's mission are drawn from SM, Aug, 1854:323–28.
31. Ladies of the Mission, 1854:31–93.
32. IN, July 6; CJ, Aug. 24
33. April, 1854.
34. May 19, 1855.
35. May 1855.
36. CA, April 16, 1856; SW, April 17, 1856.
37. Sketches of Old New York:12.
38. Tchen, 1990.
39. April 19, 1856.
40. April 22.
41. SM, 1854:323–28.
42. W, Oct. 22, 1876; Tr, Oct. 23, 1876; Wylie, 1967:55.
43. Culin, 1887A:5.
44. T, Dec. 26, 1856.
45. March, 1858.
46. Feb. 6.
47. T, June 20, 1859.
48. LI, March, 19, April 23; H, March 9, 10; Tr, March 9, April 12; T, March 9, April 12; S, March 9; BJ, March 19, April 16; PG, May 14.
49. June 28.
50. BJ, July 2, Nov. 19, 1859; March 3, 1860; LI, Nov. 19, 1859; Beck, 1898:9.
51. T, Sept. 30, 1871, Oct. 21, 23, 25, 1876; Tr, Sept. 30, 1871; Oct. 21, 23, 25, 1876; W, Oct. 21, 22, 1876; H, Oct. 22, 29, 1876.
52. Beck, 1898:10, 11, 260

2 HERVEY'S HEATHENS
1. McClellan, 1971:45.
2. McClellan, 1971; Saxton, 1971.
3. Nov. 11, 1899.
4. Elsen, 1964.
5. Miller, 1969:29.
6. 1859, 2:98, 99.
7. T, Aug. 11, 1878; S, Aug. 11; H, Aug. 11, 13, 14, 1878.
8. Tr, Aug. 17, Sept. 28, 1904.
9. S, Nov. 29.
10. H, July 16.
11. HW, Sept. 19, 1868.
12. EE, July 15, 1863; T, Nov. 22, 1865, Oct. 6, 1869; H, Nov. 22, 1865, Oct. 6, 7, 1869; Tr, Jan. 4, Oct. 6–8, 1869; S, Oct. 6–8, 1869.
13. Dec. 26, 1869.
14. Tr, Oct. 5, 1869.
15. Feb. 21, 1869.
16. Tr, Jan. 4.
17. Jan. 22, 1870.
18. MR, April/May, 1870.
19. Saxton, 1971:103, citing Oakland *Daily Transcript* (Henry George's newspaper), Nov. 20, 1869.
20. T, Oct. 12, 1869.
21. H, June 16, 17, 19, 24, 26, 27; Shanks, 1871:495–97; Rudolph, 1947:2–28.
22. 1990:226, 227.
23. Tr, July 1; T, July 1; St, July 1, 8, 13, 14.
24. LI, June 4; St, June 27.
25. Wylie, 1967:265; T, July 7; H, July 7; St, July 7.
26. DA, Sept. 22, 24, 28; Sr, Sept. 22, 24.
27. Sept. 22.
28. Tr, Oct. 1.
29. Oct. 8, 1870.
30. H, Feb. 19; LI, March 11.
31. Miller, 1969:135–37.
32. DA, Sept. 24, 1870; St, Sept. 28, 1870.
33. Sr, Sept. 29; W, Sept. 29; DA, Sept. 29.
34. DA, Oct. 8, 10, 21, Nov. 22, 29, 1870, May 15, June 7, Aug. 30, Sept. 2, Dec. 23, 27, 1872.
35. Nov. 13.
36. Feb. 18, 1871.
37. Dec. 21.
38. DA, Feb. 6, 8, 1875; Tr, Feb. 6, 1875; H,

Feb. 7, 1875; LI, Feb. 12, 1876; T, June 10, 1876; S, Jan 28, 1879.
39. W, Feb. 15, 1877.
40. Culin, 1895:166, 167; Tr, Sept. 15, 1895.
41. S, Feb. 17.
42. Culin, 1895:167, 68; Tr, Sept. 15, 1895.
43. DA, Feb. 20, 1882; Tr, Feb. 19, 1883.
44. DA, Jan. 26, 28, 1884; NC, Oct. 9, 1932.

3 STEREOTYPING

1. O'Connor, 1966:119–23; Fenn, 1933:45; Keim, 1941:441, 449.
2. Odell, 1927, 6:328, 586.
3. Hyde, 1955.
4. Aug. 1.
5. Hyde, 1955:362.
6. Aug. 23.
7. T, Sept. 17.
8. Hyde, 1955:363, 364.
9. Dec. 26, 1873.
10. March 18.
11. T, Feb. 16, 1874; S, Feb. 16, 1874; Tr, Feb. 16, 1874.
12. Oct. 8, 1870.
13. T, Jan. 29, Feb. 17, 25; Tr, Jan. 29, Feb. 17; S, Jan. 29, Feb. 2; W, Jan. 29–31, Feb. 1–4, 25.
14. Jan. 29.
15. W, Feb. 2.
16. W, Feb. 3.
17. T, Aug. 11; H, Aug, 11, 13, 14; S, Aug. 11.

4 HYSTERIA AND EXCLUSION

1. PB (undated); Dolan, 1975:47–51; Ulmann, 1901:264; Franklin, 1928:149–58.
2. June 29.
3. Congressional Record, 45th Congress, 3rd session, Vol. 18, Feb. 3–24, 1879.
4. March 5, 1880.
5. H, March 3–7; T, March 4; Sr, March 5.
6. Tr, March 4; T, March 6.
7. H, Aug. 11.
8. S, April 28, 1883, Jan. 11, 1918; Tr, June 21, 1885, Sept. 28, 1904, Jan. 11, 1918; T, Aug. 17, 1904, Jan. 11, 1918; H, April 25, 1883, Jan. 22, 1918; EP, Jan. 22, 1918.
9. DG, March 26, 28; S, March 27.
10. H, Feb. 5, 1879; W, Feb. 28, 1880; T, April 27, 1880.
11. S, Jan. 31, 1881.
12. Davis, 1971:39, 40; Lyman, 1977:79–82.
13. Culin, 1887:2.
14. March 22.
15. March 7, 1880.
16. H, March 3.
17. T, May 6, 7; W, May 2; EP, May 10.

18. April 25, 1883.
19. S, May 13, 1883; Tr, May 13, 1883.
20. S, May 11, 1883; H, May 11, 1883; Tr, May 11, 1883.
21. Tr, May 12, 1883.
22. T, July 11; Tr, July 11; H, July 11; LI, July, 27.
23. H, Nov. 28, 30; S, Nov. 29.
24. Tr, Sept. 10, 1884, HT, Aug. 9, 1941.
25. W, March 23; Tr, March 24.
26. Baldwin, 1890.
27. T, March 18.
28. Tr, March 11; Konvitz, 1946.

5 WONG CHIN FOO

1. Feb. 5, 1883.
2. Oct. 4, 1873.
3. Aug. 17, 1874.
4. April 29, 1877.
5. Barker, 1933, 1:149, 150; Williams, 1946:121.
6. T, April 30, 1877; W, April 30, 1877.
7. May 8, 1877.
8. May 26, 1877.
9. PL, Jan. 1, 1888.
10. T, July 16, 19, 21, 1883; Tr, July 20, 23, 1883.
11. Aug. 1, 1883.
12. Tr, July 15, 1884.
13. Pu, April 22, 1885; T, Aug. 10, 1883, March 4, 1885; Tr, Oct. 14, 1883, March 4, 1885.
14. Aug. 1887; Tr, July 31, Aug. 11, 16, 1887.
15. Sept. 1887, T, July 3, 7, 1887; Tr, July 4, 1887.
16. T, May 8, July 22, Aug. 10, 1892; Tr, May 15, 1892.
17. T, Aug. 21, Sept. 11, 14, 23, 1892; Tr, Sept. 23, 1892; DE, Dec. 20, 1892.
18. T, Jan. 26, 1892.
19. DE, May 6, 1893; Tr, May 7, 1893; T, May 11, 1893.
20. Konvitz, 1946:47–55.
21. Glick and Hong, 1947:105; Sharman, 1965:4–44, 61–63.
22. Tr, Aug. 2, 1894.
23. DE, Dec. 6, 30, 1896.
24. T, Nov. 24, 1897; Tr, Nov. 24, 1897; DE, Nov. 24, 1897.

6 CHINATOWN AND ITS ENVIRONS IN THE 1880S

1. T, Sept. 15, 16; Tr, Sept. 16.
2. T, April 2.
3. T, April 7, 12; Tr, April 8; S, April 28.
4. T, April 24–26, May 3, 17; 8, April 24, 26, May 3, 4; Tr, April 25, 26, May 3, 8; H, April 25, May 3; Asbury, 1928:174–202.
5. Tr, May 17, 22; T, May 19, 22; S, May 17; H, May 22.

6. T, March 6, 1880; Tr, Oct. 18, 1885.
7. T, Dec. 8, 1884; Culin, 1891:1–5.
8. Culin, 1887A:8; 1891:5.
9. T, Dec. 8, 1884.
10. Jan, 21, 1884.
11. H, March 3, 1885.
12. Culin, 1891:7–11; Beck, 1898:102–104.
13. Culin, 1894:250–52; Beck, 1898:105, 106.
14. 1887:423, 424.
15. Tr, July 24, 1882.
16. HW, Dec. 1, 1888; Culin, 1887A:20, 21; 1890A:194.
17. Tr, June 21, 1885; Wong, 1888.
18. April 24, 1885.
19. Wong, 1888.
20. *See* Sui, 1987, a study of Chicago laundrymen. Since the pattern was inflexible over time and place, much of it is applicable to New York.
21. T, Dec. S.
22. Tr, May 29, June 23, 1883, July 24, 1884; S, May 29, June 23 1883; Culin, 1891:347–52.
23. T, May 28, 1890; Beck, 1898:3.08–116, Huie, 1932:107.
24. W, July 12; H, July 12.
25. Wong, 1888.
26. Tr, June 21, 1885.
27. Wong, 1888.
28. July 17.
29. Wong, 1888; HW, March 10, 1888.
30. HW, Dec. 15, 1888.
31. T, Nov. 25, 26.
32. Tr, July 10, 14; T, July 10, 14.
33. T, April 2; Culin, 1887A:20; 1890A:195.
34. LI, Oct. 11, 1884; T, Sept. 28, 1890.
35. LaFargue, 1942.
36. T, May 23, 1883; Tsai, 1983:70, 71.
37. T, Sept. 2, 1881; Jan. 9, 24, March 11, 1882; LaFargue 1942,
38. June 2, 1883.
39. T, Aug. 30, 1883; Jan. 8, 9, 1884; Tr, Jan. 28, 1884.
40. July 20.
41. Armentrout-Ma, 1983:113.
42. Tr, Dec. 7; T, Dec. 7.
43. Dec. 28.
44. T, April 17, 1887; June 18, 1888; March 20, 1890; Culin 1887A:9, 10; 1890A:192, 193; 1891:347–52; Beck, 1898:13, 20.
45. Lee, 1960:147–61.
46. Leong/Chu, 1936:64, 65.
47. Sept. 13.
48. IEP, Sept. 24; Tr, Sept. 13, Oct. 7–9.
49. T, July 23, 24; Tr, 24.
50. T, Dec. 26, 1883; McAleavy, 1968.
51. W, Oct. 22; S, Oct. 28, 30; T, Oct. 30; Tr, Oct. 30.

7 THE SIX CHINESE THEATERS IN NEW YORK

1. Tr, June 24, 25, 3,889.
2. HW, June 29, 1889.
3. June 25, 1889.
4. Tr, July 1, 1889.
5. T, March 26, 27, 1893; Tr, April 11, 1893.
6. Tr, July 22, 30, 1895.
7. T, June 21, March 20, 21, 1896; Tr, Jan. 20, 1896; DE, May 28, 3.896.
8. Tr, Aug. 31, 1896.
9. Tr, May 2, 8, 1897; T, May 8, 1897.
10. Tr, March 8, 1896.
11. Tr, July 29, 1900.
12. Except as otherwise noted, the history of the theater is drawn from Townsend, 1900; Tyrrell, 1903; H, April 19, 1903, and a magazine article by Will Irwin in T, April 10, 1921.
13. Beck, 1898:77–79.
14. Moss, 1897, 2:410–13.
15. T, Aug. 7, 8, 1905; Tr, Aug. 7, 8, 1905; EP, Aug. 7, 8, 1905.
16. T, Dec. 30, 31, 1909; EP, Dec. 30, 1909. Asbury, 1928:310–12, repeats an erroneous story that the killer was lowered by a boatswain's chair from the roof.
17. T, Feb. 20, March 6, 1910, March 30, 1924, April 24, 1927; EP, April 23, 1910; Asbury, 1928:309; Tsu, 1910:28.
18. T, July 21, Aug. 18, 1924.
19. T, Jan. 15, 1925,
20. T, May 15, 1927; Graham, 1927;179, 180.
21. Brock and Golinkin, 1929:165.
22. T, Sept. 15, 1925; N, Oct. 14, 1925.
23. HT, Sept. 19, 1925.
24. W, June 6, 1929.
25. HT, Feb. 11, 1930.
26. T, Feb. 15, 1942; NYR, April 11, 1942; C, Nov. 15, 1947; L, May 1, 1950.

8 THE BIRTH OF THE RESTAURANT AND TOURIST INDUSTRY

1. Clark, 1905;5; Forman, 1898.
2. Nov. 29.
3. Kane, 1882.
4. Mayer, 1958:417, 418.
5. Jan. 9.
6. T, May 25.
7. Sept. 12, 1896.
8. T, Aug. 12, 23, 29–31, Sept. 2–4; Tr, Aug. 24–26, 29–31, Sept. 1–5, 7; DE, Aug. 31.

9. EP, Sept. 12, 1896, Jan. 14, 1899.
10. IA, Sept. 4, 1897; EP, Sept. 30, 1902.
11. Tr, Nov. 28, 1897, March 5, 1899.
12. EP, Dec. 29, 1900.
13. Tr, July 20, 1900; EP, Dec. 29, 1900.
14. Tr, July 21, 1900; EP, March 5, 1899, Dec. 29, 1900.
15. Beck, 1898:64; EP, Dec. 29, 1900.
16. EP, March 23, 1901.
17. EP, Dec. 29, 1900.
18. Feb. 3, 1901.
19. T, Nov. 15.
20. NM, July 1903.
21. T, March 23.
22. T, May 18, 1895; EP, Dec. 29, 1900; HW, Sept. 7, 1905; Beck 1898:28, 29.
23. T, Oct. 1.
24. Moravsky, 1922.
25. Sept. 7, 1924.
26. Dec. 19, 1923.
27. HT, July 19.
28. LD, Nov. 1, 1921; MW, July 1924.
29. HT, Feb. 18, 1931; Brugger, 1935:13; AM, Feb. 1953; NYR, Aug. 2, 1947.
30. Irwin, 1926;89.
31. Chen, 1941:107.
32. Brock and Golinkin, 1929:159; Walker, 1933:78.
33. March 2, 1930.
34. Chu, 1939:35.

9 THE SUNDAY SCHOOL MOVEMENT
1. Rosenberg, 1971.
2. EP, May 27.
3. H, Feb. 23; DG, Feb. 23, 25.
4. T, Feb. 27; Tr, Feb. 27.
5. T, April 25, May 5.
6. May 12.
7. S, May 13; T, May 28.
8. May 14.
9. HW, July 19, 1879; DG, April 10, 1880; MS, Jan. 1882.
10. H, Feb. 10.
11. S, Feb. 10.
12. Feb. 1.
13. T, March 6, April 18, 1882; Tr, May 7, April 18, 1882; April 10, 17, 1883; H, May 14, 1883; notes scattered through MS and MT annual reports.
14. July 30, 1883.
15. Tr, June 10, 12.
16. June 23.
17. T, March 16; Tr, March 16.
18. Condit, 1900:157.
19. Huie, 1932:3, 24, 25, 37, 46–53.

20. T, March 14.
21. Tr, March 21.
22. T, Sept. 19, 21; Tr, Sept. 19, 21.
23. T, Oct. 24.
24. Dec. 13–15, 28, 30.
25. T, Dec. 29, 30, 1891, Jan. 8, 29, 1892; DE, Jan. 6, Feb. 2, 3, 5, 1892.
26. T, May 14, 20; Tr, May 14.
27. DE, May 20, 21.
28. T, Nov. 12, 1904.
29. DE, June 18.
30. Details of the murder and search are drawn from: T, June, 30, July 1–7, 14, 17, 24, Aug. 3, 1B, Sept. 10; Tr, June, 1930, July 4, 5, 7, 8, 12, 13, 17; EP, June 22–25; Radin, 1962:139–43.
31. T, May 7; Tr, May 7; H, May 7.
32. Tr, June 8–10; T, June 8–10, 26.
33. T, Nov. 6, 1893; DE, May 6, 1895.
34. Tr, Oct. S.
35. Unless otherwise noted, references to the Guild are drawn from year books of St. Bartholomew's Church.
36. Beck, 1898:266.
37. Tr, Nov. 19, 1887; T, Nov. 19, 1887.
38. T, Dec. 19, 1890.
39. T, July 31.
40. Tr, July 10, 11.
41. T, Aug. 15.
42. DE, Nov. 21.
43. T, July 31; Tr, July 31.
44. DE, March 7; Tr, Sept. 27.
45. Tr, March 17.
46. Oct. 6, 1901; Armentrout Ma (1990:50, 58) notes a congratulatory telegram from Singapore in the Summer of 1900 on the formation of a New York branch, but this appears to be an error in communications with Singapore.
47. Tr, Nov. 19, 1902; T, Feb. 18, 1903; Van Norden, 1918:33; Armentrout Ma (1990:91) ascribes the formation of the New York branch to Hsu Chin, an aide to K'ang Yuwei, but again Chinese sources appear faulty.
48. Tr, May 24, 1903.
49. T, Feb. 18.
50. Tr, May 24, Nov. 21; CG, 1903.
51. T, 13, 14, 1903; Tr, Jan. 10, 1902; May 14, 24, 1903.
52. Van Norden, 1918:55; Huie 1932:100.
53. Tr, June 26.
54. EP, Feb. 9, 18; Tr, Feb. 24.
55. Tr, June 15, 30, July 1, Nov. 1, 2, 21, Dec. 5, 12, 1901, March 12, 1902; Gompers and

Gutstadt, 1908.
56. EP, Aug. 23.
57. T, Dec. 20, 1903; May 8, 1904; Tr, Feb. 22, March 10, 1904.
58. Glick and Hong, 1947:66.
59. Tr, June 23, 27–29, July 2; T, June 26, 28, 29; EP, Tune 20.
60. Tr, Sept. 13, 1906.
61. Armentrout Ma, 1990:95.
62. Huie, 1932:67–70.
63. T, Nov. 17; EP, Nov. 13, 18.
64. T, May 21, 1896; Clark, 1905:27.
65. Beck, 1898:244.
66. Huie, 1932:57–67.
67. T, Dec. 30, 1901; Dec. 28, 1902; Tr, Dec. 30, 1902; Jan. 15, 1902.
68. T, March 17, 19; EP, March 18; Harlow, 1931:508.
69. T, March 4, 1901; PB, 1902–1903:16, 17, PB, 1908–1909:23, 24; Burgess, 1909:33–39.
70. EP, July 15, 193,0; ChA:1.
71. T, July 16.
72. EP, Oct. 7, 1911; Burgess, 1909:33, 34; Van Norden, 1918 has scattered references.
73. BM, Nov. 11, 1913:9, 10; Van Norden, 1918:54; Palmer 1934:169.
74. Huie, 1932:79, 81, 92.
75. EP, March 30, April 3, Oct. 7; T, April 4, 9.
76. Van Norden, 1918:34, 95.
77. T, Oct. 14, 15, 1911, EP, Oct. 14, 1911; W, Jan. 28, 1912; Armentrout Ma, 1983:141, 142.

10 THE WARS OF THE TONGS
1. Rose, 1992:332, 333.
2. Ibid., 333.
3. Werner, 1957; T, Nov. 17, 1935.
4. Tr, April 17, 1893; April 10, 11, 17, Aug. 7, 8, Oct. 4, 1895; July 11, 12, 1896; Moss 1897, 3:121–134; Beck, 1898:250–260.
5. Lexow, 1895:2, Proceedings from June 5 to June 29, 1894:162ff.
6. 1890:42.
7. T, July 25–29, Aug. 1, 2, Sept. 3, 10, 30; Tr, July 25–29, Aug. 1–4, 16, 19, 31, Sept. 3, 10, 30, Oct. 3, 4, 7.
8. T, Sept. 8, Oct. 12, 14, 20, 30, 1893; Tr, Oct. 12, 29, 1893; DE, June 18, 1894.
9. Tr, Aug. 4.
10. Lexow, 1895:2, Proceedings from June 5 to June 29, 1894:224ff.
11. Tr, April 5, May 14, 1895.
12. T, Nov. 8.
13. Tr, Sept. 10, Nov. 23, 29, 1896; Feb. 13, Sept. 4, 1897; T, Aug. 21, Sept. 10, 1897; DE, Feb. 12, 1897; EV, Aug. 20, 1897.

14. 1936:359.
15. DE, Sept. 26.
16. April 28, 1900,
17. T, Aug. 13, 14; Tr, Aug. 13, 14.
18. Tr, Sept. 22.
19. Tr, April 16, 1901; DE, April 15, 1901.
20. April 21.
21. Tr, July 11, 1903.
22. BT, Aug. 3, 5, 19, 1907, March 9, 1908, July 3, 12, Oct. 12, 1909; T, Aug. 3, 5, 19, 1907, Oct. 12, Nov. 6, 1909, April 17, 1910, July 15, 1923; HT, June 22, 1941.
23. Tr, Feb. 18; EP, Feb. 18.
24. T, Feb. 19, 22.
25. Syrett, 1956.
26. Tr, July 22, 23.
27. T, Nov. 3, 4.
28. T, Nov. 26, 27.
31. Tr, Feb. 1, 3; T, Feb. 25.
30. T, March 19, 21; H, March 20; Tr, March 22.
31. Tr, March 23; T, March 23, 28.
32. Tr, April 24, 25, 27; T, April 24–28.
33. T, May 31; Tr, May 31.
34. EP, June 22; T, April 27.
35. Tr, Aug. 12, 13, 21, 22, Sept. 19, Oct. 18; T, Aug. 21, Oct. 18, 19.
36. Tr, Dec. 31, 1905; W, Jan. 24, 1906.
37. T, Jan. 25; Tr, Jan. 25; W, Jan. 25; EP, Jan. 24, 25.
38. EP, May 28, 29.
39. EP, Jan. 26; Tr, Jan. 31, Feb. 3, 7, 13; T, Feb. 3, 7; W, Feb. 3.
40. Tr, Feb. 12, 13; T, Feb. 12, 13; W, Feb. 12.
41. Tr, March 6; W, March 6.
42. EP, March 20.
43. 1906:170.
44. Tr, July 25.
45. T, Aug 16, 17; Tr, Aug. 16; W, Aug. 16.
46. Tr, Aug. 25, 1909.
47. Tr, July 6.
48. Tr, Sept. 13, Nov. 6, EP, Nov. 6, 24; T, Nov. 6, 7; H, Nov. 16, W, Nov. 6, 17; S, Nov. 25; Eng and Grant, 1930:183.
49. T, Dec. 28, 29, EP, Dec. 28; Tr, Dec. 29,, S, Dec. 29.
50. T, Jan. 5–8, 11; W, Jan. 6, B.
51. Tr, Jan. 24.
52. T, April 13.
53. T, April 12, 14, 15, 17, 19, 23; EP, April 16, 22; Tr, April 22, 23, 25.
54. T, June 27, 28; W, June 27, 28; H, June 28; EP, June 27; Tr, June 28, July 28.
55. EP, July 16; W, July 17.
56. Tr, July 28.
57. T, Oct. 24–27.

58. T, Dec. 5; EP, Dec. 5.
59. T, Dec. 30; Tr, Dec 30.
60. T, Jan. 3, 1911; Van Norden, 1918:77, 91, 92.
61. T, Oct. 23.
62. Tr, Dec. 13, 1911; W, Jan. 28, 1912.
63. T, Jan. 6, 7; H, Jan. 6, 7; EP, Jan. 6.
64. T, Feb. 28; W, Feb. 28; Tr, Feb. 28.
65. Tr, March 13, 18; S, April 1.
66. T, April 13, June 8, 1912; Tr, June 7, 8, 1912, March 1, 1913; S, April 12, 1912.
67. T, June 18; Eng and Grant, 1930:203–10.
68. T, June 24; Tr, June 24.
69. Tr, July 15.
70. T, Oct. 15, 16; W, Oct, 15, 16; H, Oct. 15.
71. T, Jan. 2; H, Jan. 2.
72. T, Feb. 8; Tr, Feb, 8; S, Feb. 8.
73. T, May 22, 29, 31; EP, May 22; H, May 23; Tr, May 29; CG, 1914.
74. EP, June 17, 19; T, June 18.
75. T, Nov. 27, Dec. 5, 13, 1913, Oct. 6, 7, 29, Nov. 1, 1914, Feb. 5, 1915; Tr, Nov. 27, 1913, Feb. 6, 8, 1915.
76. T, April 24, 25; Tr, April 25.
77. Jan. 15.
78. T, Jan. 11, 15; H, Jan. 11, 15; Tr, Jan. 11, 15; SP, Jan. 11; S, Jan. 11, April 4.
79. Nov. 22.
80. Chih, 1924:7, 19–22; T, April 12, 1926.
81. T, Nov. 21, 1920; Oct. 1, 2, 1921; Tr, Oct. 2, 1921.
82. T, Nov. 21, 1920; Oct. 1, 2, 1921; Tr, Oct. 2, 1921.
83. SG, June 2.
84. T, Dec. 2, 1922, July 17, 1923.
85. T, Oct. 9–15, 17–21, 24, 26; HT, Oct. 10–13, 15, 17, 18, 26; DE, Oct. 19.
86. T, Oct. 27, 30, 31; HT, Oct. 27, 31.
87. T, Nov. 10, 1924; HT, Nov. 10, 1924, Feb. 19, 1925.
88. HT, Nov. 9, 12; W, Nov. 9; T, Nov. 13, 14.
89. T, Nov. 11, 20.
90. HT, Nov. 24, 27, 28; T, Nov. 27, 28.
91. T, Nov. 27–30, Dec. 1–5, 8, 9, 11–14; HT, Nov. 27–30, Dec. 12; W, Dec. 1, 2.
92. T, Dec. 15: HT, Dec. 15.
93. T, Jan. 5; HT, Jan. 5.
94. T, Jan. 5, 8; HT, Jan. 5, 8.
95. Feb. 27.
96. HT, March 3, 24, 26–28; T, March 25, 26.
97. March 27.
98. T, Aug. 30.
99. T, Nov. 11, Dec. 2, 4, 24, 25, 27, 30, 33, 1924, Jan. 6, 8, 1925; HT, Dec. 2, 1924, Jan. 10, Feb. 5, 1925.
100. T, Aug. 26, 27; HT, Aug. 26.
101. T, Aug. 27–29, Sept. 1, 3–5, HT, Aug. 27, Sept, 3–5.
102. T, Sept. 9, 10.
103. Sept. 10.
104. T, Sept. 9–11; HT, Sept. 10, 11.
105. Chen, 1941:178.
106. T, Sept. 11–13, 15–20, 24–27; HT, Sept. 12–16, 19, 20, 22, 25, Oct. 18; W, Sept. 26; LD, Oct. 3, 1925:14, 15.
107. LD, Oct. 3, 1925:14.
108. Oct. 14.
109. T, Oct. 1; HT, Oct. 1.
110. T, July 20.
111. T, March 25–27, 29; HT, 25, 26, 28.
112. T, Nov. 8.
113. T, Oct. 15, 16, 18, 19; HT, Oct. 15, 16, 19, 26; TI, Oct. 17, 18.
114. T, Aug. 5–7, 13; HT, Aug. 6, 11; W, Aug. 7, 11.
115. T, Feb. 11; HT, Feb. 11.
116. T, May 3, 4, 15, June, 6–9, July 10, 31, Aug. 1, 8, 16–20, 29, 30, Sept. 2, 3, 12; HT, May 3, June 6–9, July 10, 13, 31, Aug. 1, 5, 9, 15, 17–20, 27, 30, Sept. 2–4, 12; S, June 26, July 31, Aug. 15, 19; W, June 7, 10, Aug. 1, 19.
117. HT, April 25, 28.
118. HT, July 29, 1931; T, Feb. 29, 1932; S, May 18, 1933; NYR, Dec. 30, 1933.
119. T, July 23, 29, 30, Aug. 1, 2, 4, 18; HT, July 23, 29–31, Aug. 19.
120. HT, Jan. 5, 1930; T, Aug. 1, 1933.

11 AMERICANIZATION

1. 1990:36, 37.
2. Ibid., 52, 53.
3. T, June 6, 11, 1917, April 26, Oct. 20, 1919, Sept. 4, 1921; Van Norden, 1918:48.
4. T, Dec. 6.
5. T, April 1.
6. T, May 29.
7. May 30, 1922.
8. T, Feb. 28, 1913, Nov, 28, 1918, June 6, 1920, Aug. 14, 15, 21, 1921, March 30, June 17, 1923.
9. T, July 30, Aug. 4, 12, 13, 1922, June 8, 1923.
10. T, June 8.
11. Bari, 1927; Chan, 1991.
12. Chen, 1941:100, 161.
13. Brugger, 1935:82; Leong/Chu, 1936:162, 164.
14. T, Oct. 17, 1915; Brugger, 1935:82.
15. Brock and Golinkin, 1929:159.
16. PB:1923, 1924.
17. Brock and Golinkin, 1929:183.
18. T, March 30, 1924.
19. Brugger, 1935:83.
20. HT, May 3, 1930.

21. Brugger, 1935:181–91.
22. Ibid., 129–31.
23. Ibid., 68–74.
24. NT, Sept. 11, 1949, WTS, May 7, 1954; T, May 10, 1954, May 24, 1955; Berger, 1960:83, 84.
25. T, Jan. 23, 24, 1928; Feb. 11, 1929; HT, Feb. 9, 11, 1929.
26. Palmer, 1934:177; Schwartz, 1951:562–64.
27. T, Feb. 16.
28. Unless otherwise noted, references to living conditions and community organization in the 1930s, and details of the formation and later history of the CHLA, are drawn from Leong/Chu, 1936.
29. Chu, 1939:43.
30. 1954:17.
31. Hyer, 1954:122–29.
32. T, Dec. 20, 1931; March 21, 1932.
33. Sayford, 1938:28, 29.
34. Kwong, 1987:100.
35. Heyer, 1954;133.
36. Heyer, 1954:89–92.
37. Yu, 1992:67–70.
38. Van Norden, 1918:71; LD, Nov. 1, 1919; EP, Aug. 9, 1920; T, Aug. 15, 1922.
39. T, Oct. 11.
40. T, Sept. 17.
41. March 14.
42. T, May 14, 21, 29, July 11, Aug. 6, Oct. 11.
43. T, Nov. 13, 14, 22.
44. T, Feb. 3, March 28, Oct. 11; Tr, Oct. 11.
45. T, Feb. 23, 1935, July 7, Sept. 19, 1936, Sept. 17, Oct. 2, 28, Dec. 12, 1937, June 9, Nov. 23, 24, 1938; HT, Dec. 11, 1938; Kwong, 1979.
46. T, April 11, Sept. 6, Oct. 11, Nov. 8, 12, 1937, April 23, May 10, July 8, Dec. 3, 17, 1938, Feb. 12, July 8, 1939; HT, Nov. 1, 1937, April 14, May 10, 13, 1938, July 8, Aug. 21, 1939, April 1, 1940, May 26, July 8, 1941; Hsiong, 1939:50.
47. Chen, 1941:107.
48. HT, June 9.
49. T, June 17, 21.
50. June 19, 1937.
51. HT, Oct 17. 1940, Feb. 10, 1941.
52. HT, Dec. 20, 1941, May 29, 1942; Lee, 1942.
53. HT, July 25, 1944; T, June 8, 1959.
54. HT, March 11, 1945.
55. Riggs, 1950.
56. T, Sept. 19, 1945.
57. NYR, May 4, 1946.
58. T, April 29, 1945.
59. T, Aug. 22, 31, 1947, Dec. 24, 1948; HT, Jan. 31, 1965.
60. HT, May, 25, 1950; T, May 25, 1950.

12 POSTSCRIPT
1. 1962:1, 48, 57.
2. DN, April 1, 1955; P, July 11, 1955; SEP, April 30, 1955; C, Dec. 1955; T, Oct. 6, 1957; L, April 29, 1958; RD, Feb. 1959.
3. T, Feb. 28, 1965; WTS, April 15, 1965; HT, Feb. 27, 1966.
4. HT, Jan. 31, 1965; T, July 11, Nov. 1, 1965; WST, Sept. 13, 1966; WJT, Dec. 1, 1966; DN, Nov. 18, 1966, March 17, 1968.
5. Chen, 1992.
6. Kwong, 1987.
7. DN, Dec. 20, 1979; T, Dec. 3, 1989.
8. HT, Jan. 31, 1965, T, July 11, Nov. 1, 1965, June 29, 1968; WSJ, Sept. 13, 1966; WJT, Dec. 1, 1966; DN, Nov. 18, 1966, March 17, 1968; NYM, June 11, 1973; VV, Jan. 31, 1977.
9. T, Feb. 2, 1995.

Literature Cited

Armentrout Ma, Eve. *Revolutionaries, Monarchists, and Chinatowns: Chinese Politics in the Americas and the 1911 Revolution.* Honolulu: University of Hawaii Press, 1990.
_____. "Urban Chinese at the Sinitic Frontier: Social Organizations in United States' Chinatowns, 1849–1898." *Modern Asian Studies* 17 (Jan.1983): 107–35.
Asbury, Herbert. *The Gangs of New York.* New York: Garden City Publishing, 1928.
Baldwin, Esther. *Must the Chinese Go?* New York: H. B. Elkins, 1890. (Third revised edition of 1881 pamphlet).
Bari, Valeska. "Citizens who may not have wives." *The Woman Citizen* 12 (Dec.1927): 20–21.
Barker, A. Trevor, ed. *The Complete Works of H. P. Blavatsky, I:1874–1879.* London: Rider, 1933.
Beck, Louis. *New York's Chinatown.* New York: Bohemia Publishing, 1898.
Berger, Meyer. *Meyer Berger's New York.* New York: Random House, 1960.

Bernstein, Iver. *The New York City Draft Riots: Their Significance for American Society and Politics in the Age of the Civil War.* New York: Oxford University Press, 1990.

Brock, H. I. and J. W. Golinkin. *New York Is Like This.* New York: Dodd, Mead, 1929.

Brugger, Florence. *The Chinese American Girl: A study in Cultural Conflicts.* Master's thesis, New York University, 1935.

Bryan, George, ed. *Struggles and Triumphs, Or The Life of P. T. Barnum.* New York: Alfred Knopf, 1927.

Burgess, John Stewart. *A Study of the Characteristics of the Cantonese Merchants in Chinatown.* Master's thesis, Columbia University, 1909.

Cattell, Stuart. *Health, Welfare and Social Organization in Chinatown, New York.* New York: Community Service Society, 1962.

Chan, Sucheng, ed. *Entry Denied: Exclusion and the Chinese Community in America 1822–1943.* Philadelphia: Temple University Press, 1991.

Chapin, Howard. "The Chinese Junk Ke Ying at Providence." *Rhode Island Historical Society Collections* 27 (Jan. 1934).

Chen, Hsiang-shui. *Chinatown No More: Taiwan Immigrants in Contemporary New York.* Ithaca: Cornell University Press, 1992.

Chen, Julia I. Hsuan. *The Chinese Community in New York 1920–1940.* Ph.D. diss., American University, Washington D.C, 1941.

Chih Meng. *The Chinese of Newark, New Jersey: A Social Survey.* Master's thesis, Columbia University, 1924.

Chu, Louis. *The Chinese Restaurants in New York City.* Master's thesis, New York University, 1939.

Clark, Helen. *Report of the New York Foreigner's Mission.* Privately printed, 1905.

_____. *The Lady of the Lily Feet.* Philadelphia: The Griffith and Rowland Press, 1900.

_____. 1896. "The Chinese of New York Contrasted with their Foreign Neighbors. *The Century* 53 (Nov. 1986): 104–13.

Condit, Ira M. *The Chinaman as we see him and fifty years of work for him.* Chicago: Fleming Revell, 1900.

Culin, Steward. "Divination and Fortune-Telling Among the Chinese in America." *Overland* 25 (Feb.1895): 165–73.

_____. *"Tsz Fa,'* or 'Word Blossoming." Overland 24 (Sept.1894): 249–54.

_____. "The Gambling Games of the Chinese in America." *University of Pennsylvania, Series in Philology, Literature and Archeology* 4. 1891.

_____. "Chinese Secret Societies in the United States." *Journal of American Folklore* (Feb.–March 1890): 39–43.

_____. "Customs of the Chinese in America." *Journal of American Folklore.* (July–Sept. 1890A): 191–200.

_____. "The *I'Hing* or Patriotic Rising," A Secret Society among the Chinese in America." *Proceedings of the Numismatic and Antiquarian Society of Philadelphia for the years 1887–89.* (Nov. 3 1887): 51–57.

_____. *The Religious Ceremonies of the Chinese in the Eastern Cities of the United States.* Privately printed, 1887A.

Davis, Fei-Ling. *Primitive Revolutionaries of China: A study of secret societies of the late nineteenth century.* London: Routledge & Kegan Paul, 1971.

Dolan, Jay. *The Immigrant Church: New York's Irish and German Catholics 1815–1865.* Baltimore: The John Hopkins Press, 1975.

Elson, Ruth Miller. *Guardians of Tradition: Schoolbooks of the Nineteenth Century.* Lincoln: University of Nebraska Press, 1964.

Eng Ying Gong and Bruce Grant. *Tong War!* New York: Nicholas L. Brown, 1930.

Fenn, William Purviance. *Ah Sin and His Brethren In American Literature.* Peking: California College in China, 1933.

Forman, Allan. "Celestial Gotham." *The Arena* 7 (April, 1898): 620–28.

Franklin, Allan. *The Trail of the Tiger: Tammany 1789–1928.* New York, privately printed, 1928.

Gellner, Earnest. *Postmodernism, Reason and Religion.* London: Routledge, 1992.

Giddens, Anthony. *The Consequences of Modernity.* Stanford: Stanford University Press, 1990.

Glick, Carl and Hong Sheng-Hwa. *Swords of Silence: Chinese Secret Societies—Past and Present.* New York: Whittlesey House, 1947.

Glick Carl. *Three Times I Bow*. New York: McGraw Hill, 1943.

_____. *Shake Hands with the Dragon*. New York: Whittlesey House, 1941.

Gompers, Samuel and Herman Gutstadt. *Meat vs Rice: American Manhood Against Asiatic Collieism, Which Shall Survive?* San Francisco: American Federation of Labor, reprint of Senate Document 137, 1902, with introduction and appendices by Asiatic Exclusion League, 1908.

Graham, Stephen. *New York Nights*. New York: George H. Doran, 1927.

Harlow, Alvin. *Old Bowery Days*. New York: D. Appleton, 1931.

Havens, Catherine Elizabeth. *Diary of a Little Girl in Old New York*. New York: Henry Collins Brown, 1920.

Heyer, Virginia. *Patterns of Social Organization in New York's Chinatown*. Ph.D. diss., Columbia University, 1954.

Hsiong, George. *Chinatown and the Mother Country*. New York: New China, 1939.

Huie Kin. *Reminiscences*. Peiping: San Yu Press, 1932.

Hughes, Rupert. *The Real New York*. New York: The Smart Set Publishing, 1904

Hyde, Stuart. "The Chinese Stereotype in American Melodrama." *California Historical Society Quarterly* 34 (Dec. 1955): 357–65.

Irwin, Will. *Highlights of Manhattan*. New York: D. Appleton-Century, 1937.

Kane, H. H. *The Chinese Opium Pipe as a Therapeutic Agent*. New York: Putnam, 1882.

Keim, Margaret Laton. "The Chinese as Portrayed in the Works of Bret Harte." *Sociology and Social Research* 25 (May–June, 1941): 441–56.

Kingston, Maxine Hong. *The Woman Warrior*. New York: Knopf, 1976.

Kohler, Max. *Immigration and Aliens in the United States*. New York: Bloch Publishing, 1936.

Konvitz, Milton. *The Alien and the Asiatic in American Law*. Ithaca: Cornell University Press, 1946.

Kwong, Peter. *The New Chinatown*. New York: Hill and Wang, 1987.

_____. *Chinatown, N.Y. Labor and Politics 1930–1950*. New York: Monthly Review Press, 1979.

Ladies of the Mission. *The Old Brewery and the New Mission House at the Five Points*. New York: Stringer & Townsend, 1854.

LaFargue, Thomas. *China's First Hundred*. Pullman: State College of Washington, 1942.

_____. "Some Early Chinese Visitors to the United States." *T'ien Hsia Monthly* 2 (Oct.–Nov. 1940).

Lee, Rose Hum. *The Chinese in the United States*. Hong Kong: University of Hong Kong Press, 1962.

_____. 1942. "Chinese in the United States Today." *Survey Graphic* 31 (Oct. 1942):42.

Leong, Gor Yun (pseud. for Y.K. Chu). *Chinatown Inside Out*. New York: Barrows Mussey, 1936.

Lexow Committee. *Report and Proceedings of the Senate Committee Appointed to Investigate and Police Department of the City of New York: Transmitted to the Legislature January 18, 1895*. New York: Albany, 1895.

Lyman, Stanford. *The Asian in North America*. Santa Barbara: ABC-Clio, 1977.

McAdoo, William. *Guarding a Great City*. New York: Harper Brothers, 1906.

McAleavy, Henry. *Black Flags in Vietnam*. New York: Macmillan, 1968.

McClellan, Robert. *The Heathen Chinee: A Study of American Attitudes Toward China 1890–1905*. Columbus: Ohio State University Press, 1971.

Mayer, Grace. *Once Upon A City*. New York: Macmillan, 1958.

Miller, Stuart Creighton. *The Unwelcome Immigrant*. Berkeley: University of California Press, 1969.

Moravsky, Maria. 1922. "Those Wicked Chinamen." *The Outlook* 131 (July 1922): 485.

Moss, Frank. *The American Metropolis*. New York: Peter Fenelon Collier, 1897.

O'Connor, Richard. *Bret Harte: A Biography*. New York: Little Brown, 1966.

Odell, George. *Annals of the New York Stage*. New York: Columbia University Press, 1927.

Palmer, Albert. *Orientals in American Life*. New York: Friendship Press, 1934.

Peters, John. *Miscellaneous remarks upon the government, history, religion, agriculture, trades, manners and customs of the Chinese as illustrated by the Chinese Collections, 539 Broadway*. New York: Redfield Printer, 1850.

Porter, Kenneth Wiggins. *John Jacob Astor: Business Man*. Cambridge: Harvard University Press, 1931.

Radin Edward. *It's Times to Tell*. New York, William Morrow, 1962.

Riggs, Fred. *Pressures on Congress: A Study of the Repeal of Chinese Exclusion*. Westport, Conn.: Greenwood Press, 1950.

Rodecape, Lois. "Celestial Drama in the Golden Hills: The Chinese Theater in California 1849–1869." *California Historical Society Quarterly* 23 (June 1944): 97–116.

Rose, Peter. *Sons of the Gods, Children of Earth: Ideology and Literary Form in Ancient Greece*. Ithaca: Cornell University Press, 1992.

Rosenberg, Carroll. *Religion and the Rise of the American City*. Ithaca: Cornell University Press, 1971.

Rudolph, Frederick. "Chinamen in Yankeedom: Anti-unionism in Massachusetts in 1870." *American Historical Review* 53 (Oct.–July 1947–48).

Sayford, Irving. "Front Page News in Chinatown." *Travel* 70 (April 1938): 28, 29.

Saxton, Alexander. *The Indispensable Enemy*. Berkeley: University of California Press, 1971.

Scharf, J. Thomas. "The Farce of the Chinese Exclusion Laws." *The North American Review* 166 (Jan. 1898): 88–97.

Schwartz, Shepherd. "Mate Selection Among New York City's Chinese Males." *American Journal of Sociology* 56 (May 1951): 562–68.

Shanks, William. "Chinese Skilled Labor." *The Century* (1871): 2: 494–99.

Sharman, Lyon. *Sun Yat-sen, His Life and its Meaning*. Hamden, Conn.: Archon Books, 1965.

Siu, Paul. *The Chinese Laundryman: A Study in Social Isolation*. New York: New York University Press, 1987.

Sketches of New York. A bound, unpaged collection of newspaper and magazine clippings in the local history room of the New York Public Library.

Syrett, Harold. *The Gentleman and the Tiger: The Autobiography of George B. McClellan, Jr.* New York: J. B. Lippincott, 1965.

Tchen, John Kuo Wei. "Staging Orientalism and Occidentalism: Chang and Eng Bunker and Phineas T. Barnum." In *Chinese America: History and Perspectives, 1996*. Chinese Historical Society of America (1996):93–131.

———. "New York's First Chinatown." *Seaport* (Summer 1990):18–24.

Townsend, Edward. "The Foreign State in New York: The Chinese Theater." *Bookman* 12 (Sept.1900): 39–42.

Tsai, Shih-Shan Henry. *China and the Overseas Chinese in the United States 1868–1911*. Fayetteville: University of Arkansas Press, 1983.

Tsu, Andrew Yu-Yue. *The Use of Leisure Times Among the Chinese Immigrants of New York City*. Master's thesis, Columbia University, 1910.

Tyrrell, Henry. 1903. "The Theater of New York's Chinatown." *The Theater Magazine* 3 (July 1903): 170–72.

Ulmann, Albert. *A Landmark History of New York*. New York: D. Appleton, 1901.

Van Norden, Warner. *Who's Who of the Chinese in New York*. New York: privately printed, 1918.

Van Dyke, John. *The New New York*. New York: Macmillan, 1909.

Walker, Stanley. *The Night Club Era*. New York: Frederick Stokes, 1933.

Walling, George. *Recollections of a New York Chief of Police*. New York: Caxton Book Concern, 1887.

Werner, M. R. *It Happened in New York*. New York: Coward-McCann, 1957.

Williams, Gertrude Marvin. *Priestess of the Occult: Madame Blavatsky*. New York: A. A. Knopf, 1946.

Williams, Jesse Lynch. *New York Sketches*. New York: Scribners, 1902.

Williams, Samuel Wells. *The Middle Kingdom*. New York: John Wiley, reprint of 1849 edition, 1859.

Wong Chin Foo. "The Chinese in New York." *Cosmopolitan* 5 (Aug. 1888): 297–311.

Wylie, Alexander. *Memorials of Protestant Missionaries to the Chinese*. Taipei: Che'eng-Wen Publishing, 1867 (reprinted 1967).

Yu, Renqui. *To Save China, To Save Ourselves*. Philadelphia: Temple University Press, 1992.

Zeisloft, E. Idell. *The New Metropolis*. New York: D. Appleton, 1899.

List and Source of Illustrations

(Unless otherwise identified, illustrations are from books and magazines in the New York Public Library.)

Index

Acong, John (a/k/a Akkomb/Acomb), 11, 17, 37-38, 40, 48

Actors, stranded. See *Tong Hook Tong* Company

"Ah Sin," 33

Ah Woh, John, 17, 48

Ahern, Manhattan Borough President John, 144

All-American Anti-Imperialist League, 173

Allen, Rep. Leonard (D-LA), 176

American Federation of Labor, 130; Chinese Waiters Union expelled from, 167

American League Against War and Fascism, 173

American Legion, 176-77

American Museum, 1, 3

Americanization, 111, 159-77

Anti-coolie clubs, 22, 41

Anti-Japan Association of Chinese Residents of New York, 171

Appo, George Washington (a/k/a George Leonard), 11, 15-16, 136-38

Appo, Quimpo, 11, 14-15, 137

Arthur, President Chester, 48

Assing, John (a/k/a Ah Ting/Ah Sing), 21, 36, 38, 40, 48

Assing, William, 48

Astor, John Jacob, 1

Asylum/Hospital for the Criminally Insane, 15, 137-38

Baby parade/show, 159, 161, 174

Bacigalupo, C., 149

Baldwin, Rev. and Mrs. Stephen Livingston, 27, 48-49, 59

Banta, Mary, 133; criticized, 164-65; honored as "Mother of Chinatown," 164

Banton, District Attorney Joab, 155

Baptiste, James, 19, 42, 45, 61, 86

Baptist(s), 35, 114, 117-18, 132-33, 148, 164; Bible Teachers Training School, 133

Barbers, 76-77

Barnard College, 130, 163

Barnum, Phineas T., 2-3, 5, 88

Barry, Rev. James, 47

Bassett, Richard, 116

Beach, George, 5-6

Bencher, William C., 123

Belleville, NJ, 26-27, 29-32, 38

Bernstein, Iver, 24

Bingham, Police Commissioner Theodore, 143

Black Flag rebellion, 85

Blacks: welcomed in Chinese restaurants, 105,

Blackwell's Island, 7, 15

Blavatsky, Helena Petrovna, 54

Board of Aldermen, 168-69

Boardinghouses, 8, 10-12, 19-20, 36, 38

Bow Kum, 144-46

Bowery Mission, 123

Boxer Rebellion, 127, 130

Brooklyn Chinese Sunday School, 113

Brown, C. S., 113-14

Brugger, Florence, 164-65

Buckner, United States Attorney Emory, 155-58

Buddha (image), 110

Burlingame, Sen. Anson, 18-19

Burlingame Treaty, 18, 48

Calvary Chapel, 123

Cameron, Donaldina, 145

Campbell, Bartley, 35

Candy seller, 18

Canton Christian College, 129

Carnegie Hall, 170

Carto, Augusta, 114, 117-18

Casebolt, George, 32

Castle Garden, 2, 6, 26

Cathedral of St. John the Divine, 170

Cattell, Stuart, 178

Cemetery of the Evergreens, 77, 80, 86, 123

Central Congregational Church (Brooklyn), 97, 132

Central Pacific Railroad, 42

Cepirio, François, 56

Ceremonies, 13-14, 29, 32-34, 39-41, 70; "Feast of Head Shaving," 161-62; sacrifice to invisible spirits of location, 11-12

Chan Kew, 97, 132

Chang, Mary, 20

Chang Yu Sing as "Chinese Giant," 33

Chant, John, 130

Charles, Warren (policeman), 139

Chee Kung Tong, 121

Cheng Tsao-ju (Minister to Washington), 82

Chess, Luke, 159

Chiang Kai-shek, 165, 170, 173

Children: clothing 103-4, 161; postwar delinquency, 178

Children's Court, 127

Chin, Henry, 159

Chin Jack Lem, 152-53

Chin Lem, 144-46

Mow, Fung Y., 132
Moy, Afong, 1, 3
Moy, Dr. Jin Fuey, 114, 124-26, 132
Moy Jin Kee, 113-14, 122, 132
Moy Kee, 174

Nast, Thomas, 27-28, 30, 48, 50-51
National Recovery Act (NRA), 170
Naturalization and Immigration Act (1965), 178
Naughton, James, 85, 104, 123, 149, 153, 159
New Canton Theater, 93
New York Bay Cemetary, 38
New York University, 134, 148, 162
Ng, Lincoln and David, 175-76
Ng Que, 109-10
Niblo's Garden, 1, 5
North Adams, MA, 23-24, 26
Northall, W. K., 2

Old Brewery, 7-8
"On a Chinaman in Broadway" (poem), 9
On Leong Tong, 136; 25th annual convention, 149; ambiguity of parallel relations with Chinese Merchants Association, 151. *See also* Tong wars, Triads, Lun Gee Tong
Open Door Treaty, 16
Opium selling/smoking, 11, 14, 26, 36-37, 40, 46-47, 61, 65, 68, 75-76, 82, 87, 137, 145, 152, 157; as "American disease," 96; faked pictures, 107; smoking staged for tourists, 147
Opium War, 11
Oriental Club, 121
Oriental Restaurant, 105
Ou Shou-tchun, 147
Ou-yang Ming, 80
Oxnam, Bishop G. Bromley, 173

Pacific Mail Steamship Company, 25, 42, 122
Palmer, Marie Antoinette, 4
Parkhurst, Reverend Charles, 136-37
Parsloe, Charles, 34
Parsons, S. L., 114
Passaic Steam Laundry, 26-27, 29-32
Pease, Rev. Louis, 8, 19, 112
Pennington Seminary, 124
People's Theater (Chinese), 95
Peters, John R., 3
Pindar, 135
Police, 108; guides for newspaper reporters, 18-19, 46, 107; bribery, 61-62, 65-66, 138-39, 167; special units, 151-53; as cat's paw to enforce tong rulers, 124-25. *See also* Elizabeth Street Station
Poolon Kongsi, 36-37, 46

Port Arthur restaurant, 120, 133, 152, 154, 162, 165
Post office, "World's Smallest," 110, 176
Poy Yee, 110
Presbyterian(s), 25, 112 116, 122, 132, 134, 136, 145
Price, Edmund, 43, 45, 138
Potestant Episcopal Board of Missions, 23
Public School 23, 133, 163-64, 175, 178
Punqua Wingchong, 1
Pwan-ye-koo, 3-4

Qing (Dynasty), 80, 82, 129, 135; Chinatown celebration of overthrow, 147
Quinby, Harriet, 105
Quinn, David, 122
Quong Yuen Shing, 128-29

Radcliffe College, 163
Railsback, Lycurgus, 19, 134
Rallies and marches: against Japanese invasion of China, 170-73; insupport of NRA, 170; postwar demonstrations against police brutality/for better working conditions, 180; World War II victory parade, 176
Reid, George Washington, 113-14, 124
Rescue Society on Doyers Street (Chinatown Midnight Mission), 93, 107, 109, 134-35, 147
Restaurants/cabarets, 71-75; Americanization, 97-99, 101, 105-6; effects of Depression/Prohibition/Repeal, 110-12; postwar expansion, 178, 180; menus and prices, 102, 111; furniture, 102-3, 105
Restaurants: Chinese Delmonico's, 97, 129-30, 146, 165; Fulton Royal, 112; Mandarin Tea Garden, 134; Oriental, 105; Port Arthur, 120, 133, 152, 162, 165; Sugar Bowl, 164; Young's 112
Riis, Jacob, 109
Roosevelt, President Franklin D., 170, 176
Roosevelt, President Theodore, 16, 130
Russell, Horace, 61

Sabbath closing laws, 88, 90
St. Andrew's Church, 120
St. Bartholomew's Episcopal Church, 123, 126
St. Crispins, order of, 23
St. George's Episcopal Church, 8
St. Gonzoga (image), 149
St. John's Guild, 112
St. Patrick's Cathedral (Prince Street), 46
St. Vincent's hospital, 122
Sam Hop Hui (Triads), 46
Sam Lock, 146
Sampson, Calvin, 23-24, 26

About the Author

I began my journalism career in 1942 as a copy boy with the New York *Daily News*. In 1946 I joined CBS Radio as a news writer. From 1953 to 1961 I was a foreign correspondent for CBS radio and television, with other free-lance magazine writing, in India and Southeast Asia, including Vietnam and Laos. During the next two years I had additional assignments in Africa and Latin America. By then, my wife and children had enough of life overseas. We settled in New York and I became a news writer and producer of television documentaries for CBS and later NBC. Among other programs, I was associate producer for *A Tour of the White House with Mrs. John F. Kennedy.*

In 1985 I took early retirement from NBC and became a special correspondent for the *New York Times* in Afghanistan. I then wrote *Among the Afghans*, which was published by Duke University in 1987. After extended journeys to India, I wrote *Averting the Apocalypse: Social Movements in India Today*, published by Duke University in 1990. With further research, I was the lead writer of *Democracy in India: A Hollow Shell*, published by The American University Press in 1994.

When I resettled in New York after years as a foreign correspondent, I could see the city with the eyes of a newcomer. An all-too-obvious social ill was homeless men made dysfunctional by drugs and alcohol. I asked myself the question that would be obvious to any foreign correspondent: not why were they there, but what was being done to help them. Research led me to Jerry McAuley who, in 1862, while a prisoner in Sing Sing, had a vision of God and went on, in 1871, to found the world's first religious mission specifically to feed, clothe and, if possible, help to rebuild the lives of those whom others considered beyond redemption. In 1967 I wrote *Jerry McAuley and His Mission*, published by Loizeaux Brothers, Neptune, New Jersey. A revised edition was published in 1990.

Part of my research into the life and times of Jerry McAuley was done at the New York Public Library's microfilm library, then on West 43rd Street in Manhattan. In grinding through scratched and blurred newspaper pages, I kept seeing long articles on the Chinese in New York. It was obvious that Chinatown was rapidly expanding: streets that had been almost solidly Italian were festooned with signs in Chinese. But I could not find a single book on the beginnings of Chinese life in New York and only stray references in journals or magazines.

Over several years I spent much of my free time (I often worked evenings or nights and had my days free) in the microfilm library transcribing every article I could find concerning the Chinese, mainly from the *New York Times*, but in a dozen other newspapers as well. I further searched through what were then walls of card-file drawers in the New York Public Library for every mention of the Chinese in New York in books or magazines or in long-forgotten scholarly studies and dissertations. In all, I amassed eight, single-spaced typed volumes containing more than three thousand newspaper articles and reports. It took another three years to digest, condense and arrange the material into its final form.

NOTE

The material gathered during the research for *Alas! What Brought Thee Hither? The Chinese in New York 1800–1950*, consisting of eight volumes of extracts from newspapers, magazines, scholarly dissertations, and church records, have been deposited with the Oriental Division of the New York Public Library.